Penguin Education

The Politics of Physical Resources

Edited by Peter J. Smith

The Politics of
Physical Resources

0338(42)Smi

Edited by Peter J. Smith
at The Open University

Penguin Education
in association with The Open University Press

Penguin Education
Penguin Books Ltd,
Harmondsworth, Middlesex, England
Penguin Books Inc.,
7110 Ambassador Road, Baltimore, Maryland 21207, U.S.A.
Penguin Books Australia Ltd,
Ringwood, Victoria, Australia
Penguin Books Canada Ltd,
41 Steelcase Road West, Markham, Ontario, Canada
Penguin Books (N.Z.) Ltd,
182–190 Wairau Road, Auckland 10, New Zealand

First published 1975
Reprinted 1975

Made and printed in Great Britain by
Hazell Watson & Viney Ltd, Aylesbury, Bucks
Set in Monotype Times

Contents

44
57
31
68
31

Maps

Preface

Although a great deal has been said and written in recent years about the scientific, social, political, economic and environmental problems associated with the exploitation of the Earth's physical resources, much of it has been general and even vague in character. To a large extent it is inevitable that this should have been so. Widespread concern over the possibility of severe resource shortages in industrial societies in the relatively near future is a recent development; and the early life of any newly espoused issue is bound to be characterized by broad thinking rather than detailed studies. More importantly, perhaps, resource problems are essentially concerned with the future; they relate to periods for which reliable information is difficult, and in the last analysis impossible, to obtain. Conclusions must therefore be based largely on prediction and speculation, however much that fact may be concealed by the sophistication and intelligence of the analyses concerned. Confronted with argument and discussion of the *Limits to Growth** variety, the average person could be forgiven for supposing that the whole resource debate is simply a philosophical, or perhaps even an ideological, exercise, with little direct relevance to day-to-day living. It is true, of course, that the political manipulation of oil supplies has given a little insight into the harsh realities of the resource situation – but at the same time, and for the time being, life goes on more or less as before, albeit accompanied by increasing resource-related inflation.

By contrast, the one aspect of resource exploitation which really brings the matter close to home – and that in a most literal way – has received comparatively little attention, at least outside the relatively ephemeral world of journalism. This is the conflict which arises when the 'need' (however defined) for more resources impinges on the less material aspirations which have come to be known collectively as the 'quality of life' – when the need for more iron ore and copper means destroying parts of Oxfordshire and the Snowdonia National Park, when the need for more water means flooding a valley in Upper Teesdale, when the need for more oil and aluminium means industrializing Anglesey, and when the need for brick means polluting Bedfordshire. These particular examples are discussed in this book – but there are many more, and they all raise rather similar issues. As Roy Gregory has put it in his book, *The Price of Amenity*:

Motorways and airports, power stations and overhead transmission lines,

* A Report for the Club of Romes Project on the Predicament of Mankind, by Dennis Meadows, 2 vols., Earth Island, 1972.

mineral workings and reservoirs, gasholders and natural gas terminals, New Towns and housing estates, factories and oil refineries, all invade the countryside and change the face of cities and towns. Necessary and desirable they may be; but, as often as not, these developments interfere with the amenities of the locality chosen for the project. Indeed, their impact is frequently felt far beyond the particular patch or strip of land on which they are situated. They may spoil the natural beauty of the countryside and coastline, ruin the appearance of part of a town, destroy buildings of historic and architectural value, or wipe out precious reserves of wild life. In their wider effects, they may create noise and disturbance, or pollute the atmosphere, rivers and lakes.

Conflicts of this sort are far from new, of course, and any planner reading this book may smile wryly at the thought that a group of academic scientists has only just discovered them. Nevertheless, I think a case can be made for suggesting that the traditional development–amenity conflict is about to take on a new dimension in the light of the problem of resource shortages, whether those shortages arise from arbitrary political action or from genuine natural limitations. A small, highly industrialized, but far from self-sufficient island such as Britain is extremely vulnerable to outside pressures on resources and will naturally begin to look more closely at its own resource potential if it comes to feel that its standard of living, and possibly even its existence as an industrial nation, is threatened. But the exploitation of Britain's own resources poses an additional dilemma not usually present in developments such as motorways, airports, power stations and reservoirs. The latter are more or less permanent features and must be balanced against the permanent destruction of the corresponding amenity. But in the case of exploiting mineral resources, it is a matter of balancing a permanent destruction of amenity against a short-term material gain. As Graham Searle points out in Chapter 3 of this book, the copper in the Capel Hermon area of Wales would satisfy current world demand for only four weeks. Are we to destroy part of the Snowdonia National Park for that?

It is clearly important for everyone in this overcrowded island that this and similar issues be discussed at length. The case histories in this book were written primarily for students of the Open University's course on the Earth's physical resources, but in view of my previous remarks I hope they will receive a far wider readership. The approaches of the various chapters differ quite widely, partly because the subjects differ but largely because the authors are drawn from quite different spheres; and no attempt has been made to impose a common style. Roy Gregory is an academic (politics), and the two chapters from his pioneering book *The Price of Amenity* reflect the disinterested approach one would expect from studies supported financially by the Social Science Research Council; Graham Searle was formerly the Director of the British arm of Friends of the Earth and personally played a central role in the fight against the Rio Tinto-Zinc Company in Snowdonia; Jeremy Bugler is a journalist who has investigated the activities of the London Brick Company partly in the course of his work and partly for the purpose of writing a book (see the NOTE ON FURTHER READING); and Richard West and Paul Foot are also journalists who wrote their pieces originally to draw attention to particular activities of companies involved in the growing industrialization of Anglesey. The opening chapter, which sets the legal and quasi-legal scene for the case histories that follow, was ably written at very short notice indeed by Robin Grove-White of the Council for the Protection of Rural England. I am grateful to all the contributors for putting their expertise at the service of our students, who, as a result, will be better able to understand the hard political and social decisions which have to be made in relation to the exploitation of physical resources at the local level.

In the context of the Open University, this book will be used as basic material for decision-making exercises by the students; and in order not to pre-empt this activity, I am afraid that I must resist a natural inclination to draw conclusions and make recommendations on the basis of the case histories themselves. Nevertheless, I think it is worth making one general point. During the preparation of this book it has become quite obvious to me that far too little has been published in detail on the local activities of physical resource-based companies, and so far too few people are aware of the processes by which their heritage is being eroded. To say as much is not to prejudge the question of whether such erosion is, or is not, desirable or necessary but only to point out that, in the absence of information and discussion, choices rightfully those of the community are likely to be influenced and biased by the more limited interests of commerce. I hope that this book will go some way towards enabling more informed choices to be made in future conflicts, not only by itself but also by encouraging others to undertake more detailed investigations of how, and by whom, resource-related decisions are made.

April 1974   PETER J. SMITH

Note on units

Generally, SI units are used throughout this book. Distances are thus given as km or m, as appropriate (except that in a few instances very short lengths are expressed in cm), areas are given as m^2 and volumes are given as m^3. However, large masses (for example, of minerals) are usually given as tonnes (t), where 1 tonne = 1000 kg. Masses expressed in terms of (long) tons in previous versions of material in this book have been converted to tonnes without numerical change; in other words, the conversion factor of 1·016 (1 long ton = 1016 kg = 1·016 tonne) has been ignored. Imperial units in original quotations have not been removed but are followed by metric equivalents in square brackets. Finally, those who feel more at home with land areas expressed in acres rather than m^2 may like to know that 1 acre = 4047 m^2 to the nearest whole number.

1 The Framework of Law: Some Observations

Robin Grove-White

Every serious clash between amenity and development involves the law. The procedures by which the conflict is regulated are set down in law; the bodies involved in the clash have certain rights and duties in law; and the developer, if he is allowed to proceed, will be regulated in his activities by law.

Furthermore, every serious clash between amenity and development involves politics. The arguments advanced by either side are arguments about priorities, about what Roy Gregory (in *The Price of Amenity*) has called the 'allocation of values – and of costs'; and that fact alone makes them political. The final decision for or against a proposal will be taken on the basis of a value judgement by one or more politicians, generally by the application of policy to the facts of a particular case. In exceptional cases of the kind this book describes, a proposal may raise issues of wide public importance which put it dramatically in the public, and thus the political, domain. At such times the behaviour of the participants in the controversy will be influenced by the need to be politically effective, for the Ministers[1] with ultimate powers to say yes or no to most developments are responsible to Parliament. A dispute will arise when people feel that a particular site is unsuitable for a proposed development and do all they can to prevent it. This happened in the cases of the Shell Anglesey terminal (Chapter 6), Oxfordshire ironstone (Chapter 2), RTZ in Snowdonia (Chapter 3), RTZ in Anglesey (Chapter 6), and the Cow Green reservoir (Chapter 5) in the present book. In each case the developer argued that he had, in effect, no alternative but to use the chosen site; the facts of economic geography – even sheer physical facts about the location of mineral ores – made it necessary. His opponents – local and national amenity societies, naturalists and, in some cases, local authorities – demurred. Arguments were publicly deployed on both sides, and a Minister or Parliament made a final decision in favour of one side or the other.

Finally, every serious clash between amenity and development involves the public interest. But how well-represented can that interest be in these clashes between such pairs of frankly biased opponents? The function of a public inquiry or private bill committee is to provide the data on which a Minister or Parliament can base an informed decision. A Minister will have his government department to advise him on the broader aspects, and Parliament will have 635 MPs who can contribute. In theory, the decision will be taken on a basis which includes all possible factors. In fact, as will emerge from the case histories, both public local inquiry and private bill committee systems are vulnerable to criticism.

But there is one certain way in which the public interest is represented in conflicts of the kind this book describes. The articulation of considered opinions is a good in itself. Provided all voices are heard, the disciplined clash of views and ideas is the very stuff of democracy ; it is also, as John Stuart Mill noted, the surest support for democracy. So if democracy is in the public interest, disputes about value judgements in planning also tend to be in the public interest – however tiresome they may seem in particular cases to particular people. An important theme in recent academic discussion of democratic institutions and attitudes has been the feeling of 'alienation' of individuals from those who govern them – the 'them–us' syndrome. But public arguments over planning issues in which the conflicts are sharpened under the discipline of public inquiry procedures engage the attention of communities and individuals and bring them into the political process.

The paragraphs that follow consider two matters : firstly, the framework of law – that amalgam of statutory rights, duties, powers and procedures within which development may be allowed to take place. And secondly, the ways in which the advocates and opponents of particular schemes tend to behave within this framework – their political behaviour, in fact.

Private bills and public statutes

In five out of the six cases with which this book deals, the essence of the conflict was simple. One side sought to do something to a rural area which the other side disliked.

Until little more than a century ago, the rules governing developments in rural areas were simple : a landowner could build what he liked on his own land, unless there was some very specific legal provision – a restrictive covenant, say – to the contrary. Anyone (be he government body, private or commercial developer) who wished to build on or work land not his by right would, in default of agreement with the landowner be obliged to ask for powers from Parliament to do so by means of a private Act of Parliament. The eighteenth and nineteenth century history of Parliament shows hundreds of private Acts each year, granting powers to a variety of bodies for the enclosure of common land, or the acquisition and use of land for canals or railways. The private Act is still a feature of our system of government, and in two of the cases in the book (the Shell Anglesey Terminal[2] and the Cow Green reservoir) this very procedure was used, to obtain powers necessary to proceed with the schemes.

A private bill is distinct from a public (that is, government) bill, and also from a private member's bill. For as the name suggests, it seeks to confer an interest or benefit on a particular person or body of persons, rather than on the public in general. The promoter of a private bill may be a statutory or public authority seeking particular powers in furtherance of its duties, a private interest – such as the shareholders of a company – or indeed anyone wishing to ask Parliament to give powers which the promoter does not normally possess under the general law of the land. However, because of its limited scope a private bill is likely to receive detailed scrutiny by Parliament only if outsiders object to it by means of a parliamentary petition, on the ground that enactment of the bill would be detrimental to their interests. Determined opposition to a bill by stubborn petitioners can lead to difficult hurdles for promoters, particularly if a hard core of MPs support and endorse the formers' objections; the Anglesey Marine Terminal Bill, for example, was the subject of no less than seven Parliamentary debates and three extended committee hearings during its passage through Parliament in 1971-2.

The relatively hazardous and expensive nature of such a manner of proceeding – so much at the mercy of unpredictable political attitudes and events – makes it unlikely that any body would resort to private bill procedure if alternative means of acquiring the necessary powers were available. Certainly only the direst necessity led the promoters of the two bills described in Chapters 5 and 6 to have recourse to Parliament. In the Anglesey terminal case, the formal promoters were the Anglesey Council, who sought powers to make themselves the harbour authority at Amlwch, to extend the jurisdiction of the harbour authority two miles out to sea (in order to encompass all the works of which the terminal was to be composed), and to enable the terminal facilities to be constructed in the sea and at Amlwch. It still remained for Shell themselves to seek planning permission under the Town and Country Planning Acts (described below) for the diversion of a public footpath, as well as to obtain authority under the Pipelines Act 1962 to lay pipelines along the North Wales coast to their refinery at Stanlow.

The Tees Valley and Cleveland Water Bill, on the other hand, was thought necessary by the promoters (the Tees Valley and Cleveland Water Board) if they were to avoid highly complicated alternative procedures under the Water Act 1945, the Land Acquisition (Authorization Procedure) Act 1946, and the Commons Act 1899. Rather than face three distinct sets of procedure – and at least three separate public inquiries – the promoters took the calculated risk of asking Parliament for omnibus powers by means of a private bill which could override all the other enactments.

In 1846, at the height of the railway boom, more than 600 private bills were lodged in a single parliamentary session (in 1973, the equivalent figure was 28). Fortunately for potential promoters, it is now only in cases of a highly unusual character that it is necessary to go directly to Parliament. Over the last 130 years, by a succession of statutes, Parliament has delegated more and more of its powers to regulate developments affecting the environment to Ministers and lesser public authorities. As new needs have arisen for controls over new forms of development – nuclear power stations and motorways are two recent examples – Parliament has legislated accordingly. Moreover, the physical pressures and demands of an increasingly complicated society and the problems caused by Britain's rapid population growth (10·9 million :1801; 54·1 million :1971) have led to a generally enlarged system of public controls and intrusions by the executive and administrative arms of government. Private bill procedure is now almost the only aspect of the law bearing on the environment to have remained essentially unchanged since the mid nineteenth century.

The legal framework is now complex. The types of development having an impact on the environment are extremely varied, and the rules surrounding them are legion. Almost any development in the UK now needs authorization, unless it is specifically exempted by law. For most classes of development, authorization comes from a Minister or local authority. Many public utility developments by statutory undertakers – for instance motorways, electricity power stations or reservoirs – are authorized under procedures set down in Acts which relate only to that form of development. In the cases cited, these include the Highways Act 1959, the Electric Lighting Act 1909 and the Water Act 1945, respectively. In each case development may involve the compulsory purchase of land. Such a non-voluntary transfer of private rights could formally have only been authorized by Parliament and so would have necessitated a private bill by the undertaker. But Parliament has instead delegated the power to a Minister to permit the acquisition and subsequent development.

Parliament has retained more influence over some types of undertaking than over others. Proposals by the Central Electricity Generating Board (CEGB) to construct electricity power stations, whether nuclear, oil or coal powered, require the consent of the Minister responsible for energy. The Electric Lighting Act 1909 and the Electricity Act 1957 give him a number of responsibilities – notably, for the review of particular applications by the CEGB to construct power stations, for considering objections to these applications, and for allowing the applications on such conditions as he sees fit, or rejecting them. The Minister has an absolute discretion, and so Parliament has no opportunity to review particular power station consents. But the situation is different with water undertakings such as reservoirs. In the most straightforward cases of reservoir construction, under the Water Act 1945 and the Water Resources Act 1963 (though not in fact in the Cow Green case, with which Chapter 5 deals), the Minister has been delegated the power to consider and hear objections to particular proposals before he makes an Order to allow a reservoir to be constructed. However, no doubt because reservoirs have historically been regarded as more intrusive and irrevocable developments than power stations, Parliament has retained an additional safeguard against the Minister's exercise of his powers. In certain special cases, where objections to a reservoir proposal continue unabated after the Minister has drawn up his final Order, the objector may appeal to Parliament, and his objection will be heard by means of 'Special Parliamentary Precedure'. This enables a joint committee of members of both Houses of Parliament to sit in judgement on the conflict of interest between the promoters of the reservoir and objectors to the Order, and may result finally in the Order not being made. This difference between the statutes governing reservoir proposals and power station proposals suggests that Parliament's restraints on the use of delegated powers will vary according to political judgements made at the time of different enactments. Parliament appears to have felt it less likely that individual rights – or indeed the public interests – could be damaged by electricity supply facilities than by water undertakings. Such a conclusion raises interesting questions of public priorities, particularly in the light of possible safety problems arising from the country's growing commitment to nuclear energy.

Town and country planning

Most proposals for development – including most of those dealt with in this book – fall under the framework of rules, rights, duties and powers for 'development control' defined by the Town and Country Planning Act. Town and country planning in the UK derives historically from the grim circumstances of cities which proliferated haphazardly in the industrial revolution of the early nineteenth century. The absence of minimal standards of hygiene or sanitation, or of any legal restraints on the rights of a landowner to build as many or as dangerous houses as he liked on his own land created an intolerable situation in which Parliament was compelled to intervene. The stream of Public Health Acts between 1848 and 1875 imposed requirements for adequate sanitation and reduced housing densities, very gradually creating a climate in which more extensive controls became acceptable to public opinion. In 1890 local authorities were first given powers to remove slums and build new housing, and in 1909 the Housing, Town Planning, Etc. Act was passed, which recognized, albeit mildly, that 'amenity' and 'the laying out and use of any neighbouring land' were factors to be considered in preparing planning 'schemes' for land which was about to be developed. A succession of Town and

Country Planning Acts (notably in 1932, 1947, 1962, 1968 and 1971) have progressively expanded the scope of the powers exercised by the Minister (now the Secretary of State for the Environment) and by local planning authorities (generally county councils and district councils). The latter now have extensive planning responsibilities under the Minister's guidance and control. The powers and duties of these authorities cover the two main facets of town and country planning. On the one hand, they define and describe the context within which particular developments may take place. On the other, they decide whether to allow particular proposals to be accommodated within this planning context, by awarding planning permission.

The complexity of modern industrial society has made a necessity of positive forward planning; and the Town and Country Planning Acts have increasingly reflected this. Perhaps the most illuminating example of the nature of recent social change as it has affected planning is to be found in a comparison of certain provisions in the 1947 and 1971 Town and Country Planning Acts. The differences between the Development Plan provisions in the 1947 Act and the Structure and Local Plan provisions in the 1971 Act are particularly striking.

A Development Plan under the 1947 Act consisted primarily of a written statement and a map of a county, showing by means of markings the actual or potential uses for all units of land for the next twenty years. Following an extensive public inquiry into all objections to the proposals, the final plan would be formally submitted for approval by the Minister. From that point on, any application for planning permission within the county would be considered in the light of the plan (and other 'material' factors). But by stages it became apparent that Development Plans were inflexible and tended to become quickly out of date. They could not take account quickly of changes in economic, demographic and social trends; and they were particularly ill-suited to cope with the massive social and physical consequences of the growth in private mobility since the war.

The new Structure Plan system outlined in the 1971 Act seeks to improve the position. Like Development Plans, Structure Plans are generally to be put together by county planning authorities. But where the old plans discussed only land uses, Structure Plans are to contain strategic policies for a wide range of social questions such as employment, recreation, population and transport over the next 20 to 30 years, as well as policies for more traditional planning matters. Rather than being drawn on a map, a Structure Plan will consist of a written policy statement with accompanying diagrams; the Minister's approval will thus be required only for matters of broad strategic importance. The more prosaic business of day-to-day development control will be spelt out in detail in Local Plans, which will not usually need his approval. The new system is designed to enable planning authorities to make a more positive and active contribution to the quality of their environment than was possible under the largely static provisions of the 1947 Act. At the time of writing (April 1974), the very first Structure Plans are awaiting the Minister's final approval.

In preparing a Structure Plan, a planning authority is obliged to undertake a number of 'surveys' of particular topics of importance to the county – green belt, housing and recreation might be examples. Certain counties are already using this opportunity to develop a long-term perspective on the rate and manner of exploitation of mineral resources within their boundaries. Somerset County Council have completed an impressive virtually national study of limestone resources and the limestone industry – a subject close to the county's concerns, as a trip round the Mendip Hills will confirm. Other authorities – Denbighshire and West Riding, for instance – have embarked on similar exercises. In such studies brute necessity has pitched Structure Plan teams into consideration of problems which may not have been systematically analysed before. However, so far only a minority of planning authorities have taken the view that the rate of working of mineral resources must be actively *limited* by the planning authority for reasons external to, and not sympathetically regarded by the extractive industries themselves. Inevitably, most counties feel obliged to accept market demand forecasts from the industry, and their prime concern is therefore to ensure that the rate of extraction entailed by the forecast volume of demand will not be achieved at the expense of other interests (such as water, recreation, agriculture, etc.) for which a planning authority is also responsible. Even so, the new Structure Plans provide opportunities to planning authorities for the first time for strategic thinking about physical resources within their boundaries.

The Development Plan or Structure/Local Plan sets the context in which all particular proposals for development are considered by the local planning authority or, more rarely, the Minister. The developer must seek planning permission within this context. In principle the procedure for obtaining planning permission for an open-pit copper mine is no different from that required for an application to build an extension to a bungalow. The law is broadly the same for each. A planning application in detail or in outline must be lodged with the responsible authority. In certain circumstances it may then be advertised locally – the copper mine proposal would certainly have to be advertised, as mineral workings are statutory 'Bad Neighbours'.[3] People or bodies with objections to the application would then send comments to the planning authority or, where the application involved a 'substantial departure' from the Development Plan, to the Minister. With the majority of applications, the process ends when the planning authority considers the application and allows it or rejects it. If it is allowed, the mine or bungalow extension goes ahead, perhaps subject to appropriate conditions. However, if objections sent to the Minister suggest to him that the application embodies a controversial proposal, whether or not it is consistent with the Development Plan, he may announce his intention to hold a public local inquiry. Similarly, if the local planning authority rejects the application, and the applicant appeals – as is his right – over the authority's head to the Minister, this will frequently lead the Minister to order an inquiry to be held. In either case the stated purpose of the inquiry will be to provide the Minister with the information he needs in order to arrive at a decision on the merits of the application.

Later in this chapter, some aspects of the politics and procedure of public inquiries are discussed; for the present it is enough to note that an inquiry is held locally, and is conducted by an Inspector appointed by the Minister to supervise, record and evaluate the proceedings. The Inspector records his findings and recommendations in a report to the Minister – though in relatively minor cases he (the Inspector) may also arrive at a decision on behalf of the Minister. In major cases, the report forms the basis for the Minister's decision, though he is in no sense bound to follow his Inspector's advice, and in fact his decision may reflect government policies which were not raised at the inquiry. The only appeal against the Minister's decision is to the High Court on a point of law. Apart from this the Minister's decision is final.

On what basis will planning permission be awarded or refused ? Section 29(1) of the Town and Country Planning Act 1971 requires a planning authority to reach its decision 'having regard to the provisions of the development plan, so far as material to the application, and to any other material consideration'. Similarly, the Minister, when dealing with a 'called-in' application or an appeal, will consider the information in his Inspector's report and other factors which seem to him 'material'.

The Development Plan (or Structure/Local Plan) will represent the approved planning strategy for the county. The other 'material' considerations may include matters of government policy or political priority, or their equivalents at local government level. National and regional social and economic policies usually reach the local planning authority by means of departmental circulars and notes. In the development control field, departments of central government tend not to *tell* local planning authorities what to do ; rather they indicate government policies and leave the planning authorities to interpret them. The fact that a developer can appeal to the Minister if his application is rejected tends to guarantee a broad consistency in planning policies throughout the land. Policies on matters such as green belt, transport and roads, housing and employment will all weigh with planning authorities and Ministers in determining planning applications.

There are a number of additional statutory facts which are also material to decisions on planning applications, as they define other interests which may be important. For instance, there are in England and Wales a number of areas designated under the National Parks and Access to the Country-side Act 1949 as National Parks, Areas of Outstanding Natural Beauty (AsONB), Nature Reserves, and Sites of Special Scientific Interest (SSSIs). In 1973, there were, respectively, 10, 33, 137 and 3165 in each category. Proposals for development in such areas will encounter special problems. The Act in each case imposes special obligations on Ministers and local planning authorities, and names the National Parks Commission (since 1968, the Countryside Commission) and the Nature Conservancy (since 1973, the Nature Conservancy Council) as the bodies responsible for identifying areas suitable for designation and for doing their best to ensure that the logic of designation in each case is sustained. Local authorities are also empowered to designate local Nature Reserves in certain circumstances.

The purposes of Britain's National Parks are clearly described in the 1949 Act. The Parks are extensive tracts of land in which natural beauty and potential for enjoyment by the public are to be enhanced by 'necessary measures'. These measures are now the responsibility of national park authorities assisted by the Countryside Commission. The Commission has powers to advise, instruct and make grants to authorities within National Parks where appropriate. The designation does not grant the public un-restricted access to land within the Parks, nor does it in any way alter the ownership of land. It is a strong indication of planning priorities within the designated area rather than a hard-and-fast barrier to development. And it is a sad fact of life that often those beautiful and remote areas[4] which qualify for designation are the very areas where unemployment rates are highest and industrial developments incompatible with natural beauty may be given rousing local support. The conflicts which can arise in such a situation are graphically illustrated in the RTZ Snowdonia case. Had RTZ decided in 1972 to apply for planning permission for a fully-fledged copper mine within Snowdonia National Park, the conflicts between employment needs and National Park designation could have involved the Minister in an agonizing decision.

Strong presumptions in favour of the protection of natural beauty are also intended to apply in Areas of Outstanding Natural Beauty. The Countryside Commission has responsibility for advising and consulting with local authorities and for designating AsONB. Once an order is made, the AsONB will be shown on the county Development Plan.

Part 3 of the 1949 Act provides for the designation of land which is of particular importance 'to the flora and fauna of Great Britain and the physical conditions in which they live' for the purpose of study or conservation. These areas are Nature Reserves, and the Nature Conservancy Council acts as their overseer. In certain senses Nature Reserves may have stronger protection from unsuitable development than National Parks or AsONB – land may be compulsorily acquired in the absence of agreement by a landowner, and the Reserves are actively *managed*. Again, however, designation constitutes no absolute barrier to development. The title, Site of Special Scientific Interest, reflects a lesser degree of importance than Nature Reserve, though such designations are again the responsibility of the Nature Conservancy Council. The local planning authority is simply informed of the designation and notes the fact on its Development Plan. The authority is then under a statutory obligation to inform the Nature Conservancy Council about proposed development on the Site. Nature Reserves and SSSIs played an important part in the Cow Green reservoir controversy, and some idea of the weight that attaches to designation can be gained from that case. All four types of designation will usually have an important bearing on the determination of planning applications which might affect them.

So too will the view of the bodies with responsibility for enforcing the law controlling pollution of water and air. Until the passing of the Water Act 1973, responsibility for controlling the content of all discharges into watercourses rested with the 29 River Authorities. From 1 April 1974, this duty has been vested in the 10 new Regional Water Authorities. Responsibility for the control of air pollution is divided between the Public Health Inspectorates and the more specialized Alkali and Clean Air Inspectorates. The former enforce the Clean Air Acts (1958 and 1968) on behalf of their local authorities, a task which may involve the control of smoke, grit, dust and fumes from familiar industrial and domestic processes as well as the creation of 'smoke control areas' in which smoke emissions are not allowed. Their concerns are largely outside the scope of this study.

The Alkali and Clean Air Inspectorate, on the other hand – a body with a history dating back to 1863 – specializes in the control of emissions to the atmosphere of sixty of the most intractable industrial processes. Under the Alkali Etc. Works Act 1906, the Inspectorate is required to ensure that the 'best practicable means' are used to control possible air pollution. For reasons of administrative policy, however, emission standards agreed between the Inspectorate and a factory cannot be made the subject of a *condition* in a planning consent. For while the Inspectorate, like the planning Inspectorate, is responsible to the Secretary of State for the

Environment, it operates independently of planning procedures under the Town and Country Planning Act 1971 and establishes its own agreements with factories. The judgement of the Inspectorate on the capacity of a new factory to minimize pollution will be an important factor for the planning authority or Minister to consider in determining a planning application. The problems arising from the Inspectorate's relative autonomy are illustrated in the cases of the RTZ Anglesey smelter and London Brick (Chapter 4).

In granting planning permission, the local planning authority or Minister may attach conditions to the consent. Normally these relate to matters such as hours of working, noise restrictions, constraints on the use of certain roads, and so on. But there is a limit to what an authority may seek to achieve by imposing conditions. It would not, for instance, be proper for a planning authority to allow the construction of a house on the condition that the developer also built a free block of council flats nearby – for such a condition would not 'fairly and reasonably relate to the permitted development' (in the words of Lord Denning in a 1958 judgement on the point). The Ministry has suggested, in a Circular to local authorities, that a planning condition should be necessary, enforceable, precise, reasonable and relevant both to planning generally and to the development to be permitted. A condition which does not conform to these criteria may be struck out on appeal to the Minister, or indeed on appeal to the Courts.

The problems which can arise from an ambiguously worded condition are graphically illustrated in the case of London Brick ; the company has argued that the condition requiring them to restore land from which they have extracted clay allows them to do so only when they can make a profit from restoration. The planning authority interprets the condition differently. The explanation may be that the condition imposed was imprecise and unenforceable. The problem of restoration is difficult, and various solutions – such as Performance Bonds or Trusts – have been suggested. But London Brick's contention that the best solution lies in the natural operation of market forces has many supporters. Indeed, in recent years, sand and gravel operators have had spectacular success in using worked-out gravel pits to satisfy an apparently limitless demand for water recreation facilities and refuse tips. But such solutions would hardly be appetizing to a local authority in a remote National Park confronted with a possible openpit copper mine. Tighter legal requirements will surely become steadily more necessary.

Procedure and politics

Almost every controversial planning proposal is the subject of a public local inquiry or parliamentary hearing. As has already been seen, the majority of public local inquiries arise in one of two ways: a planning applicant appeals to the Minister (under Sec. 36 of the Town and Country Planning Act 1971) against the decision of a local planning authority to refuse him planning permission, and the Minister orders an inquiry to hear the cases for and against the proposal – alternatively, some major project is proposed, and the Minister orders an inquiry under the relevant Act to consider objections to it. This can happen with called-in planning applications (under Sec. 35 of the Town and Country Planning Act 1971), as well as motorways, reservoirs, power station proposals and many other kinds of project. Several of the inquiries in this book arose in this way, including those into the land aspects of Shell's Anglesey terminal, the Oxfordshire ironstone proposals, and the two RTZ ventures. In Parliament on the other hand, a private (opposed) bill committee hearing is held automatically if a petition is lodged against a bill by parties who claim their interests would be adversely affected.

In many respects, public inquiries and private bill committee hearings follow similar patterns; this is hardly surprising as the one is a descendant of the other. Participants tend to approach either form of hearing with much the same considerations in mind, as will be seen. However, there are differences which can best be brought out by considering each separately.

A public inquiry under the 1971 Act takes place locally in the vicinity of the site for the proposed development, under the aegis of an Inspector who acts on behalf of the Minister. In this way it is possible for local people to contribute their views at minimal expense. The scope of the inquiry is defined in advance in a letter from the Minister to the planning authority. The letter is available to all participants in the inquiry and lists the matters on which the Minister feels he needs information. In complex cases, such as those dealt with in this book, both the developer and the principal objectors may be represented by Counsel with experience of planning law and practice, although the procedure of the inquiry itself is not complicated. Generally, the programme followed is that the developer's case is advanced first, by means of expert witnesses who are cross-examined by or on behalf of objectors to the scheme. When this is over – it may take days or even weeks – the objectors advance their own views with witnesses who are in turn cross-examined by the developer. Statements by other interested parties may follow. At every stage the Inspector asks questions as he chooses. When all the parties have been heard, the developer (or Counsel) is allowed the last word in his summing-up and the Inspector makes a physical inspection of the proposed site.

The proceedings are not intended to be judicial in character – the Inspector deliberately keeps them as flexible and informal as he can – but the nature of the conflict between amenity and development tends to polarize the participants. At every public local inquiry many of the contributions – often in fact the majority – will come from members of the public who do not wish to argue about the merits of the developer's proposal, but are simply concerned to ask the developer to mitigate damage to their own interests, or simply to register their opinions. In general, evidence may be submitted to an inquiry by anyone who wishes to do so. However, the doctrine that public inquiries are simply information-gathering exercises on the Minister's behalf cannot conceal the fact that the developer and the principal objectors both want to *win*. The report on the inquiry which the Inspector submits to the Minister generally recommends whether or not the development should be allowed to proceed, and, if so, on what terms. It is this report, and the Minister's ultimate decision, which both sides seek to influence. Indeed the behaviour of the principals before, during and after the inquiry is comprehensible only if the will to win is recognized as central.

It is possible for a developer to influence the outcome of an inquiry long before anyone is aware that he intends to apply for planning permission. For only a developer can know his own plans. He can thus time his planning application or appeal for the most propitious moment. Shell's Anglesey terminal proposal was announced some time after expansion of the company's Stanlow refinery had begun. Since the case for the terminal was to rest on the expanded refinery's greatly increased 'need' for greater volumes of imported crude oil, the timing of the expansion programme itself can be seen to have exerted a powerful influence over both the planning decision and the passage of the private bill. A comparable tail-wags-dog situation almost arose in the Oxfordshire ironstone case over the proposed Newport steel mill.

Once the developer's planning application is lodged, he is still in a strong position. Only he knows why he needs the site, and what the economics of its exploitation are, for he is under no obligation to make known to the public or even to the local planning authority anything more than the fact that he wants to develop a particular site for a simply defined purpose. And while he may be willing to discuss these matters in more detail with the planning authority when he thinks they may grant planning permission, he may decide not to do so when he calculates that his application will eventually be determined by the Minister. Sometimes it will be to his advantage not to reveal his case until the public inquiry takes place, as this will lessen the chance of its being effectively rebutted by the local authority (where the local authority is an objector) or by other objectors to his proposals. However, as the Oxfordshire ironstone case shows, he must balance a strategy of secrecy against the need not to appear uncooperative in the eyes of the Minister. RTZ's experience in Snowdonia seems to indicate that secrecy may not be a good way of winning friends.

But whilst the developer may choose to keep his strongest cards to himself until the last moment, this is not an option open to the local planning authority. The latter must make available its statement of case at least twenty-eight days before the inquiry begins. Furthermore, if third-party objectors intend to put forward suggestions for alternative sites, such suggestions may not be sympathetically entertained by the Inspector unless they have been shown to the developer well in advance of their introduction as evidence.

One reason for holding inquiries locally is to enable the Inspector to gauge local feeling towards the proposals. Wholesale local approval of, or opposition towards, a project might be a factor for the Minister to consider when taking his decision. It will thus be to the developer's advantage to stress any contribution his proposals could make towards the relief of local unemployment. In remote rural areas with high unemployment rates – in North and Mid-Wales, for example – such assurances have great potency, as the Shell Anglesey terminal case and the RTZ smelter and Snowdonia cases seem to show. There is now a growing body of evidence (to which the 1973 report of the Economist Intelligence Unit, *Employment consequences of large-scale construction works in North Wales* is a recent notable contribution) that the employment benefits of such projects may be overstated. But regardless of this fact, the developer who convinces a rural local authority that his project means jobs is half-way home.

Similarly, the developer who consults voluntarily in advance of the public inquiry with the planning authority, the Countryside Commission and the Nature Conservancy Council about ways in which he can minimize damage to amenities will help his case. Indeed, many applicants take a spontaneous interest in minimizing their impact on amenity. It should be noted, however, that a well-timed (and even well-calculated) concession to the environment may strengthen an otherwise contentious proposal. Graham Searle implies this may have happened with the Mawddach Estuary aspects of RTZ's adventure in Snowdonia.

In general then, the build-up to a major public inquiry will see the developer seeking to assuage the concerns of potential or actual objectors, whilst the latter seek, usually in vain, to elicit as much advance knowledge of the developer's case as possible. The months leading up to the Oxfordshire ironstone inquiry proved classically frustrating to a planning authority anxious to know what case it was to face from the applicants.

Once the inquiry has begun, a familiar exchange of arguments unfolds. The developer is concerned to show that the benefits his project will bring to the area outweigh the costs to amenity, while those opposing him will argue the reverse – that the social and environmental costs they and the public at large are being asked to bear are too high to be compensated by the exclusively economic benefits the project will bring. Both sides are by now firmly convinced that right is on their side. The developer is determined to add as many non-economic benefits to his side of the equation as he can reasonably manage – perhaps arguing that the area is not as beautiful as the objectors claim, or that his project will create, paradoxically, a new focus for tourist interest. Similarly, the objectors, to have any real chance of success, must seek to undermine the economic certitudes which are the developer's real strength.

The difficulty for objectors is that they start from an *a priori* dislike of the project. There may therefore be in their attacks on the scheme's economics an element of justifying a prejudice. They must cast around to find alternatives and then explain convincingly both to the developer and the Inspector why it is that the former has not preferred one of these, and why he should do so now. The Oxfordshire ironstone and Shell Anglesey terminal episodes reveal a promising line of argument to have been the claim that the justification for the proposal as presented had been overtaken by events, and that thorough reappraisal of the scheme's economics now revealed its advantages to be minimal. Furthermore, it was suggested, an only marginally more expensive alternative was available, which would have a much less damaging impact on amenity. The success of such a ploy, in an Inspector's eyes, would rest on it's being demonstrated beyond all doubt that such an alternative was realistic. However, this evidence would have to be produced by the objectors themselves; to be effective, it would have to be supported by the testimony of expert witnesses. In this respect as in others, a truly convincing case needs money behind it.

The time and expertise of engineering and economic consultants is valuable, and few amenity bodies can afford them. Exceptional consultants may contribute their service at reduced fees, but generally experts dislike arguing against their own industries. In a public inquiry where the developer is a monopoly such as a nationalized industry, a consultant who appears for nothing as an expert witness on the 'wrong' side may run the risk of damaging his own business interests. Experts may be reluctant to appear as witnesses against the industries in whose technical detail they are expert, unless it is known they are being paid on a consultancy basis; the market relationship puts a neutral aspect on their opposition. Nor is professional risk of this kind restricted to experts on the side of the objectors. ICI appear to have experienced considerable difficulty in finding a botanist to speak out against his peers in the argument over Cow Green reservoir.

The difficulty of finding experts to challenge a developer's proposals combines with the developer's virtual monopoly on knowledge of his own project to have consequences which may be unfortunate for the public interest. The public inquiry (and private bill committee) procedures of examination and cross-examination – the 'adversary' system – are generally held to be the most effective way of eliciting the facts about a proposal. Propositions which go unchallenged tend to be accepted by the Inspector (or committee) as fact. But plainly this system is an effective instrument of inquiry only to the extent that both sides are equally well-informed. Cross-examination which is uninformed will be doubly fruitless; it may leave contentious propositions unchallenged and it may lead the Inspector to feel that because these propositions have not been challenged they are unchallengeable. A developer may allege that no alternative site could possibly suit him, for this or that reason. If the objectors cannot produce witnesses who can convincingly refute his claim, the Inspector will tend to accept the developer's word.

Again, a developer's forecasts about future prospects for his industry or product will naturally tend to support his case for the development in hand. Forecasting the future rates of consumption of raw materials such as clay, copper, water or crude oil is a hazardous business, and it is natural that an Inspector should listen with greatest sympathy to the calculations of those who have a financial interest in getting the future right. However such judgements about the future may not always be correct and the forecasts may subsequently prove to have been infected with wishful thinking. Circumstances may change, and with them, critical variables in the calculations. Thus Shell's initial argument for the Anglesey terminal – that it was in the 'national interest' that there should be a deep-water terminal to accommodate the forecast steady rise in crude oil imports from the Middle East through the 1970s and 1980s – no longer appears valid in the light of North Sea oil expectations over the same period. It is now agreed on all sides that UK oil imports in 1980 will be well below the present figure. Yet in the context of argument about the terminal in 1971–2, the company repeatedly scorned the objectors' argument that North Sea oil prospects had undermined the case for a deep-water *import* terminal. The Inspector (and MPs) who considered the proposal chose to believe Shell's forecasts rather than those of Professor Odell, the objectors' expert. Forecasts also played an important role in the Cow Green and Oxfordshire ironstone cases.

Such technical or speculative questions may go to the very root of a developer's case. Nevertheless, the fact that a public inquiry is a local event makes it an ideal forum for local discussion of the physical impact of a scheme. This fact alone gives it an advantage over traditional private bill procedure. For only those with severe grievances against proposed projects will oppose a private bill; such opposition means arguing, at considerable expense, before a parliamentary committee in London. This is only one of the distinctive features of private bill procedure. •

There is an important sense in which a private bill committee hearing resembles a court action; one side (the petitioners) argues that the other side (the promoters) wants to inflict an injury on its interest. The ambiguity of the public inquiry – where the proceedings are in part adversarial, in part inquisitorial, and even in part public relations – is absent; the private bill committee hearing is unequivocally a contest. The complaints of the petitioners are summarized in a formal petition to the appropriate House of Parliament, and the scope of the hearing is strictly limited to argument on the points made in the petition. To look beyond the terms of the petition, the committee must receive a formal Instruction from the House, directing their attention to a particular matter. Such instructions are unusual, though the Cow Green case contains an effective example.

The hearing takes place in a small committee room in Parliament before a panel of four MPs or (usually) five peers. It is dominated by the presence of parliamentary Counsel for the promoters and, usually, for the petitioners; and the formal quality is heightened by the presence of parliamentary agents (solicitors specializing in parliamentary private business) and transcript writers. However, the relative dignity of the event helps to ensure that the cost to either side can be enormous – transcripts alone can cost £100 a day, and the total cost of presenting a petition almost always runs to thousands of pounds – a cost which can be repeated if a further petition is subsequently lodged in the second House.

The promoters' task before the committee is to 'prove the preamble' of their bill – in other words to show that the merits of the bill outweigh the damage alleged by the petitioners. To do this, the procedure of examination and cross-examination of witnesses is used. The committee must decide whether the preamble is indeed proved, and, if so, whether amendments to the bill might not be desirable, to protect the petitioners' interests. Members of the committee also have the role of advising their House whether the bill would be damaging to the wider public interest. To help them, government departments may submit reports on their views of a bill, at the outset of a hearing, and the committee will take account of them. However, in practice the reports tend to provide little new information, other than the fact that a department broadly approves or disapproves of the bill. For they are usually based on discussions between the promoters and the department before the bill has been laid before Parliament, and so cannot have the benefit of evidence that may come to light during a robust committee stage. The attitudes of the Nature Conservancy Council and the Countryside Commission may also influence the committee's judgement, as these are the statutory bodies most concerned with nature and conservation. And if their disapproval of a private bill proposal is no guarantee that the bill will be rejected, their endorsement can help a promoter by throwing the burden of proof firmly onto the objector. Agencies such as the Commission and the Nature Conservancy Council find themselves in a difficult position, as they are neither government departments nor truly independent bodies, and so are vulnerable to criticism from both sides. But they are naturally reluctant to engage in frequent public controversy – and in a contest such as a private bill committee hearing this fact may unwittingly influence the outcome.

The committee stage is only one of a number of stages through which every private bill must pass. Like a public bill, the private bill must have three readings in each House and the second and third readings provide opportunity for extended debate and votes. Debates are unlikely to take place unless the petitioners have lobbied to precipitate them, for the promoters will be delighted to allow their bill to slip through undebated. The onus will therefore be firmly on the petitioners to publicize and dramatize their complaints inside and outside Parliament, in such a way as to arouse the interest of MPs and peers. This may take time and money. The pages of Hansard reveal only the tip of an iceberg of effort. And at every new stage of a bill's passage, interest must be revived and sustained.

The fact is that even private bills as controversial as those in this book are unlikely to be high on the list of priorities of MPs and peers. The upper House is generally patient and scrupulous in its consideration of amenity matters, but peers are notably reluctant to set their faces against decisions of the elected chamber – a pity, as the Commons may feel little sympathy towards extended consideration of the relatively minor matters with which private bills appear to deal. The same may also be true at committee stage. To the busy MP, days, or even weeks, of listening to arguments about a reservoir may be a trying experience. He has many other pressures on his time. He will be conscious of the fact that it is the petitioners who – by lodging their petition – have precipitated the long proceedings. In this way, though the burden of proof is, in formal terms, on the promoter to justify his bill, in practice the petitioners may find the onus subtly transferred to them as they seek to justify their demands on the time and resources of Parliament.

Both petitioners and promoters may be disconcerted at the extent to which the fates of their respective causes are at the mercy of raw political debate on the floor of the House. When a bill is debated at third reading, few speakers will appear to have any deep familiarity with the issues, and fewer still will have read the transcripts of evidence of the committee hearings. At such times the relatively calm administrative procedures of a public inquiry under the Town and Country Planning Act may seem an oasis indeed.

In recent years, both the administrative and the parliamentary procedures for the scrutiny of major development proposals have themselves come under considerable scrutiny. The present wide respect for the public inquiry system has largely blossomed since the report of the 1957 Franks Committee on Administrative Tribunals and Enquiries and the subsequent creation of the Council on Tribunals. The latter body constantly reviews the rules and conduct of statutory inquiries, and has introduced some significant improvement in the area of procedure. More recently the 1969 Skeffington report on *People and Planning* has considered the need for greater public participation in planning; and the 1974 Dobry review of the Development Control System has been set up to consider, amongst other matters, the supposed problems to which widespread public involvement in planning may have given rise. Similarly, Parliament has its own standing committees (the Committees on Procedure and the Joint Committee on Delegated Legislation) amongst whose concerns is the review of procedural safeguards.

There is so far little sign of any improvement in the capacity of public inquiries or private bill committees to evaluate proposals with a significant technical component, or for which there might be suitable alternative sites. In 1968 a provision was introduced into the Town and Country Planning Act which it was hoped might prove an imaginative solution to these shortcomings of inquiry procedure. In cases of development proposals raising new (perhaps long-term) issues of an unusual character, or complex technical issues, the Minister would be empowered to set up a 'Planning Inquiry Commission'. Such a Commission would be given broad terms of reference and wide powers to consider technical and speculative questions beyond the scope of a conventional public inquiry or private bill committee. The provision now rests at Sections 47–9 of the Town and Country Planning Act 1971. Despite repeated requests, no Minister has ever used it.

An afterthought

How well does the legal and political framework which has been described represent and protect the public interest, particularly in cases such as those this book deals with ? It was suggested at the outset that the very fact of debate and disciplined public conflict is itself a vindication of the public interest. But the limitations of the procedures must be recognized. While admirable for establishing and evaluating the conflicts caused by development proposals when these raise no difficult technical or policy issues, the public inquiry and (except where an Instruction has been given) the private bill committee may not cope well with the broader implications of a proposal. Criticism of government policy is in general held to be beyond the terms of reference of an inquiry or committee. But sometimes the public interest aspects of a proposal cannot be explored without such discussion.

In the present economic climate, for instance, governments of both major parties have shown themselves anxious that Britain's physical resources should be exploited as rapidly and effectively as possible. North Sea oil and gas policies, the mineral exploitation policy implicit in the Minerals Exploration and Investment Grant Act 1972, and the huge planned expansion of the nation's electricity generating capacity (coal, oil and nuclear based) are examples. Despite the wide public debate over the past four years, there is no sign of any slackening in the rates of consumption of imported or indigenous physical resources. Indeed the reverse is the case, as the rates of growth of consumption for most commodities are escalating exponentially, by conscious acts of policy. Yet it is surely improbable that discussion of such policies of maximum exploitation can be excluded from inquiries set up to scrutinize those proposed developments which are themselves direct consequences of those policies. The public at large can only evaluate such policies by their benefits, which are largely economic, and by their costs, which are experienced (often literally) on the ground. To use a ready analogy, it is only now that the costs of the policies embodied in the 1970 government White Paper *Roads for the Future* are becoming clear – as motorways push into every corner of Britain. As a direct consequence, the *need* for particular new motorways (that is, the aptness of the original policy) is increasingly the topic of anxious and angry debate at motorway inquiries around the country.

It may be said in reply, as has been repeatedly said by Ministers, that the only appropriate forum for a challenge to government policy is Parliament. If the policy on oil terminals or mineral exploitation is to be changed, it is Parliament that should change it. And of course this is true. But nevertheless it seems likely that the public inquiry, with its ready accessibility to the public at large, will increasingly provide a forum for the expression of views on policy matters which Parliament will find it difficult to ignore.

Notes

1. 'Minister' is used as a generic term, though in any particular case the Minister may in fact be the Secretary of State.

2. I must declare an interest here, for I was personally involved in the petition against the Anglesey Marine Terminal Bill.

3. 'Bad Neighbour' developments are listed in the Town and Country Planning General Development Order 1973, and include developments such as

public lavatories, sewage plants, slaughterhouses and bingo halls. Special publicity requirements apply when such developments are proposed – as described in Sec. 26 of the Town and Country Planning Act 1971.

4. Britain's ten National Parks are: Brecon Beacons, Dartmoor, Exmoor, Lake District, Northumberland, North York Moors, Peak District, Pembrokeshire Coast, Snowdonia, Yorkshire Dales.

2 Oxfordshire ironstone

Roy Gregory

South of Banbury, the Cotswolds run down into the softer, rolling country-side of north Oxfordshire. This is an area of dignified manor houses set in their parks, substantial farms and picture-book villages. With their thatched, seventeenth-century cottages, some of these villages have in fact become celebrated tourist attractions. It is not dramatic or spectacular countryside. But the wooded hills, the sunken country lanes, the un-expected farmhouse or cottage among the trees, and the characteristic reddish soil of a field under plough, form a landscape of variety and mellow colour. There is a certain homely and tranquil beauty about north Ox-fordshire.

Roots go deep in this part of England. There are families here who have farmed this land for generations; others, more recent arrivals, settled in the district because they liked what they saw. Newcomers or old, most of them are deeply attached to the countryside. In counties like Oxfordshire there are also men of substance and standing, large landowners and independent farmers, determined individuals prepared to give their time and energy in defence of what they value.

A metre or so beneath the folded ridges and meadows lie thick bands of ironstone, an essential raw material for the production of iron and steel. On and off, ironstone has been worked in various parts of Oxfordshire for centuries. One of the prominent ridges near Great Tew is actually named 'Iron Down'. Fifty years ago, a few men working in a quarry might have been regarded as part of the rustic scene; but modern open cast mining on a large scale can hardly fail to change a peaceful rural environment. Trees must be felled and hedges uprooted; mechanical grabs remove the topsoil; explosives are used to loosen the ironstone; and new roads have to be built for trucks to carry the ore to the railways. It is true that, once the ironstone has been excavated, the soil is relaid. But many believe that even the most skilful and conscientious rehabilitation can never wholly restore the countryside to what it was before. As the farmers put it, the bloom goes off the land.

Much of north Oxfordshire is scheduled in the county development plan as an Area of Great Landscape Value. After the war, the County Council decided to confine quarrying to the area near Wroxton, north-west of Banbury, and it was agreed that any attempt to extend mining operations further south should be firmly resisted. In the early fifties, however, the rich, untouched reserves of Oxfordshire iron ore south of

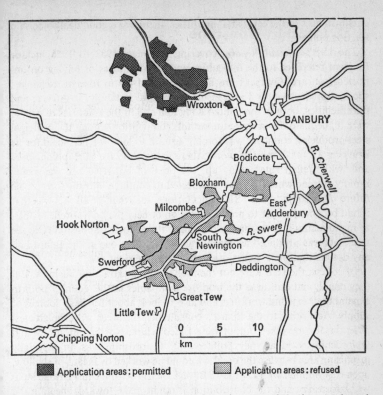

Application areas : permitted   **Application areas : refused**

Banbury were beginning to attract the keen interest of the iron and steel industry.

Iron ore: A policy and its consequences

When steel was denationalized in 1953, the Conservative Government established a new statutory body, the Iron and Steel Board (ISB) to exercise general supervision over the industry. Under the Iron and Steel Act of 1953, it was the duty of the ISB to promote the efficient, economic and adequate supply of iron and steel products under competitive conditions. One of the Board's responsibilities was to keep under review the industry's arrangements for procuring and distributing raw materials, including iron ore. Then, as now, iron ore was available from a good many countries, the major exporters being Canada, Sweden, France, Algeria, Tunisia, Venezuela, Brazil, French West Africa and Sierra Leone. From the outset, however, it was the policy of the ISB to encourage the British steel industry to make the maximum use of home-produced ore. In the circumstances of the early and mid fifties, there was a good deal to be said for this policy.

The ISB's *Annual Reports* covering the years 1953 to 1956 include frequent reference to the difficulties and disadvantages of relying on imported iron ore. Overseas ore had to be paid for in foreign exchange; supplies might be cut off as a result of political instability in Africa; and port facilities, both in the United Kingdom and in the countries of origin, were inadequate. Even more important, competition among the principal steel-producing countries was forcing Britain to look further afield for its iron ore. To make matters worse, there was a shortage of shipping space and, with freight rates going up, the price of imported ore was rising rapidly, a trend which the Board expected to continue into the foreseeable future. According to the ISB's calculations, the result of all this was that it had become cheaper to produce steel on or near the home orefields than to manufacture it from foreign ore. Since it was their responsibility to see that steel was produced as cheaply as possible, no one at the Board had any doubts that their 'home-ore policy' was the right one.

Of course, the ISB were not themselves in the extraction business. But they could, and did, urge the iron ore companies in this country both to expand their existing workings and also to look about for fresh sources of supply. According to the Board's consultants, the areas with the greatest potential for increased output were Lincolnshire, Northamptonshire and Oxfordshire. And as they pointed out, Oxfordshire was an especially promising area because the ore there could be worked by means of shallow, open-cast mining. By 1957 the ISB were clearly setting considerable store by Oxfordshire and the contribution it might make towards meeting the future needs of the steel industry. In a Special Report of that year, they noted that the total United Kingdom output was expected to rise from 16 million t* a year in 1956 to about 22 million t a year in 1962. There was a reasonable chance, they added, that surveys currently in progress in Oxfordshire would enable the industry to exceed 22 million t a year by the latter date, or at least soon afterwards. As on many previous occasions, the Board emphasized that the fullest exploitation of the English orefields, consistent with the maintenance of adequate reserves, was essential for the economic development of the steel industry in the years ahead.

It was at about this time that an important development was afoot in the iron and steel industry. The ISB and the steel companies had begun to consider the possibility of building a new strip mill. Obviously, this would be a project of major economic importance, representing a valuable prize for whichever part of the country was fortunate enough to get it. Naturally, there was a good deal of argument about the most suitable location, the

* t represents the metric ton (tonne), which is 1000 kg.

chief contenders being Scotland and South Wales.[1] Among the individual companies in the running for the new plant were Richard Thomas and Baldwins (RTB), the largest steel firm remaining in public ownership after denationalization.

What part the question of ore supplies played in discussions about the location of the strip mill must remain a matter of conjecture. No doubt there were many excellent reasons for siting at least the major part of any additional steel-making capacity in South Wales; and, of course, their experience and reputation gave RTB a good claim on the proposed steelworks. At the same time, with the ISB attaching so much importance to the use of home ore, the problem of supplies would almost certainly have been raised. Whether South Wales can be described as 'near' any of the big English orefields is a moot point. As far as the ISB were concerned, however, it was near enough. It may be that the ISB asked RTB if they could and would undertake to use a substantial proportion of home ore; alternatively, the company may have volunteered to use home ore in order to strengthen their claim on the new mill. In either event, it would have been for RTB to indicate who would supply the ore, and from where exactly it was to come.

The site proposed by RTB for the strip mill was at Newport, Monmouthshire. If home ore was to be used at Newport, the obvious source was Oxfordshire, chiefly because it was the nearest orefield of any size to South Wales. Moreover, Oxfordshire ore is very easily worked. In some of the other English orefields the ironstone is more than thirty metres down; over much of the Oxfordshire area it is no more than a metre or so below the surface. With only this thin overburden to remove, it would be comparatively cheap to extract. It also enjoyed an important technical advantage. In order to gain the full benefit of a new steel-making method proposed for the Newport works, the phosphorus content of the ore had to be below 0·35 per cent. Of all the home-produced ores, only Oxfordshire ore met this requirement.

As it happened, Oxfordshire ore was already being worked, on a limited scale, in the Wroxton area, north-west of Banbury. Under the joint ownership of Stewart and Lloyds and the Guest Keen steel interests, the Oxfordshire Ironstone Company had begun operations here in 1917, and by the mid fifties had worked about $3·2 \times 10^6$ m². Provided that they could be sure of a market, there was nothing to prevent the Oxfordshire Ironstone Company from increasing their output, for the County Council were not unfavourably disposed towards more extensive ironstone working in this part of the county. From the beginning, RTB were prepared to take part of their supplies from Wroxton. But neither RTB nor the ISB were convinced that the Oxfordshire Ironstone Company could guarantee to meet the full requirements of the proposed strip mill as production expanded in the sixties and seventies. Even had R T B been satisfied that all the ore needed could be guaranteed from Wroxton, it is unlikely that they would have been happy about relying for their supplies on a company owned by one of their competitors: as they saw it, it was essential for them to exercise direct control over most of their home ore, so as to be able to regulate the quality of the iron required for their new steel-making technique.

Naturally enough, the ISB's known policy of encouraging the maximum use of home ore had provided a strong incentive for firms to enter the extraction business. One company that already had the necessary equipment available from their gravel and open-cast coal mining operations was the Dowsett Group. A subsidiary, the Dowsett Mineral Recovery Company, was formed, and extensive surveys were undertaken in the Oxfordshire orefield south of Banbury. Test borings soon confirmed that substantial reserves were available.

It may be that Dowsetts had gone to Oxfordshire simply on the off-chance of finding markets for any ore that they might find. On the other hand, they may have taken an interest in Oxfordshire because they had learned that R T B were looking for ironstone over and above what could be supplied from Wroxton. At all events, there seems to have been an informal understanding between R T B and Dowsetts: if the new strip mill were allotted to R T B, most of the ore would be supplied by Dowsetts from areas to the south of Banbury. There may even have been a suggestion that in due course R T B should buy up the Dowsett Mineral Recovery Company.

A preliminary skirmish

The Dowsett Mineral Recovery Company submitted their first applications for planning permission in April 1957. They were for two areas, the first of about 0.7×10^6 m^2 east of Adderbury, and the second extending over 3.9×10^6 m^2 to the east of Bloxham. Both were good examples of attractive, unspoiled English countryside, though by general consent neither area was of really outstanding scenic beauty. However, it was the Oxfordshire County Council's policy to resist the spread of ironstone working into this part of the county. They opposed the applications, which were then called in for decision by the Minister of Housing and Local Government.

Outside County Hall, these applications would probably have aroused little interest had they not attracted the attention of Major Eustace Robb, the owner of the Great Tew estate. Convinced that the Bloxham/Adderbury proposals were only the thin end of the wedge, early in June 1958

Robb invited a number of his neighbours to a meeting in Tew House. It was an important conclave, for out of it came a formidable local resistance movement in the shape of the Oxfordshire Ironstone Protection Committee. The original purpose of the Committee was simply to represent individual members of the public who opposed the applications. But as the controversy developed, some of its more active members began to play a far more important role than this description would suggest. Before long, it was decided that the Committee should cooperate with the Oxfordshire County Council in preparing the case against Dowsetts, brief counsel, assemble expert witnesses to appear at the expected public inquiry, appeal for funds, and alert and mobilize other countryside organizations, such as the National Farmers' Union, the Country Landowners' Association, Women's Institutes and parish councils.

A public inquiry into the Bloxham/Adderbury applications was held at Bodicote on 16 and 17 July 1958. By comparison with the battle to come, it was no more than a skirmish. Even so, there was an impressive array of objectors. Apart from the County Council and the Ironstone Protection Committee, they included the Chipping Norton Borough Council, the Chipping Norton RDC, the Banbury RDC, eighteen parish councils, nine Women's Institutes, a local committee of NFU members, the Oxfordshire Rural Community Council, the CPRE and two local schools.

Dowsetts' case was simple. It was in the national interest to expand the output of home ore. The ISB had said so in their Special Report of 1957. That report had also indicated that the Board were hoping for 2·3 million t a year from Oxfordshire by 1962, with the possibility of substantial increases after that. The Bloxham/Adderbury areas were by no means exceptionally beautiful, and if the output of Oxfordshire ore was to reach the required level, they would have to be worked sooner or later. Not surprisingly, a representative from the ISB was also at the inquiry to assure the Inspector that Dowsetts' applications had the full support of his Board.

For their part, the objectors argued that the Bloxham/Adderbury applications were only the first step. If Dowsetts were given planning permission here, they would soon be back with more applications in this area. Adderbury and Bloxham might not be outstandingly attractive; but some of the adjacent districts, almost certainly next on Dowsetts' list, were as beautiful as any stretch of countryside in the Midlands. In any case, not even the Bloxham/Adderbury areas should be worked unless it could be conclusively demonstrated that the requisite supplies of Oxfordshire ore could not be provided from elsewhere in the county. Nothing was worse for a district than to be subjected to mining operations that proceeded by fits and starts, and unless there was the guarantee of a sustained demand for ore from these two application areas, this was exactly what would happen. Far better, the objectors maintained, to confine ironstone quarrying to the Wroxton area, where it was already in progress.

This brought them to their other main contention. As far as they could see, even allowing for a substantial increase in the ISB's basic figure of 2·3 million t a year after 1962, the Board's target for Oxfordshire could easily be met from the Wroxton area by the Oxfordshire Ironstone Company. Since that target had been set, the Oxfordshire Ironstone Company had stated that if they were given planning permission for additional areas near their existing workings, they could produce 3 million t a year, provided that the demand justified such an increase in output. There was unlikely to be any problem over planning permission, because the County Council had no intention of opposing applications in the Wroxton district.

Judged by the evidence that they were prepared to put before the inquiry, Dowsetts' case looked decidedly fragile. On the face of things, they had no assured market for their output; or if they had, there was certainly no indication of who they expected to buy their ore. And if, as the evidence suggested, the Oxfordshire Ironstone Company could produce all the Oxfordshire ore for which there was any foreseeable demand, what possible justification could there be for allowing Dowsetts to open up new areas in the attractive countryside south of Banbury? Whatever may have been Dowsetts' hopes or expectations, RTB were not mentioned, even hypothetically, as possible customers. Had Dowsetts been prospecting in Oxfordshire on a purely speculative basis, their silence on these matters would have been only natural. But if, as seems more likely, they had all along been hoping to supply RTB with iron ore for use at Newport, we can only assume that both they and the ISB felt that they could not appear to be anticipating an official announcement from the Government about the operators and location of the new steelworks.

Soon after the inquiry ended, and before the Minister had reached a decision, Dowsetts submitted two further applications, this time for a total of $10·2 \times 10^6$ m², south of their first application areas, in the vicinity of Hook Norton, Swerford, Great Tew and South Newington. Now they were moving into what was undeniably very attractive countryside. The County Council, of course, objected, and informed the Minister that in their view the applications ought to be refused on the grounds that they would cause 'grave and irreparable harm to the amenities of the district'.

Oxfordshire : The penny drops

On 18 November 1958 the Prime Minister, Harold Macmillan, told the House of Commons that the Government had authorized two new strip mills. One was to be built by Colvilles at Motherwell in Scotland; the other was to be constructed by RTB at Newport, Monmouthshire. Both projects, he said, were to be capable of considerable extension, and this was particularly true of the Newport works.

RTB could now begin to plan in more detail. As yet, Dowsetts had not secured planning permission to work their application areas south of Banbury; but, rightly or wrongly, RTB decided to press ahead on the assumption that, in due course, most of the Oxfordshire ore that they needed at Newport would be provided by Dowsetts. Work was begun on the installation of ore preparation plant scheduled to cost about £2 million, and specifically designed to cope with Oxfordshire ore. British Railways were approached, and asked to make the necessary arrangements for freighting large quantities of ore from Oxfordshire to Newport.

At this point there is one aspect of RTB's planning that we must pause over, for later on it was to assume considerable importance. It had never been the company's intention to use 100 per cent home ore. Quite early on, for what were to be described as 'technical and economic' reasons, RTB decided that the optimal blend of home and imported ores would be achieved if they used them in the ratio of 40 per cent from Oxfordshire and 60 per cent from overseas. Given that they had to use a substantial proportion of home ore, it may well be that on their calculations the 40:60 ratio seemed likely to give them the cheapest and most suitable combination. But what must be stressed is this: the *principle* of using a high proportion of Oxfordshire ore at Newport had not been dictated by a careful and open-minded examination of relative costs. As it happened, when the strip mill was at the planning stage, there probably was some cost advantage in using large amounts of home ore. But it was not because they saw the prospect of enormous savings on the cost of raw materials that RTB were proposing to take more than a third of their ore from Oxfordshire: they had agreed to go to Oxfordshire for their supplies in order to conform with the ISB's policy. That policy, initiated some years earlier, was based upon doubts about the wisdom of relying on imported ore, and upon the general proposition that steel manufactured on or near the home orefields was cheaper than steel produced from imported ore. As for the ISB, in supporting applications for Oxfordshire ironstone, it was enough for them that RTB were acting in accordance with the Board's policy.

Although it was now public knowledge that RTB were to build a new strip mill at Newport, nobody outside the steel industry had, as yet, any reason to connect RTB with Dowsetts' applications. But rumours led to private inquiries, and the opposition began to put two and two together. On 29 November 1958, the Oxfordshire County Clerk referred to these rumours in a letter to the Ministry of Housing and Local Government. 'It has come to my notice,' he wrote, 'that there may be an association between the applicants in this case, Messrs Dowsett Mineral Recovery Limited and Messrs Richard Thomas and Baldwins and that it may be represented that iron ore from the Dowsett application areas will be required for the "fourth strip mill" a share of which has just been allotted to Messrs Richard Thomas and Baldwins by Her Majesty's Government. Should this in fact be so,' he went on, 'it would introduce a quite new factor into the situation and I should be glad of the Ministry's assurance that the County Council would in that event be given the opportunity to comment before any final decision was taken by the Minister.'

This new development evidently gave the Ministry a good deal of food for thought. It was not until 30 April 1959, after several months of consultation with other Departments, that they replied to the County Council's representations. Following the announcement of the new strip mill, they said, 'certain facts and considerations' not known at the time of the earlier Bodicote inquiry had come to light. The Minister had been informed that soon after the new steelworks came into operation in 1963 it would need 1 million t of Oxfordshire ironstone a year, and the figure would rise to 3·5–4·0 million t a year by 1965–6. This compared with the estimated output for 1962 (from existing sources in Oxfordshire) of 2·3 million t a year. It was probable, the Minister had been told, that beyond 1966 even more Oxfordshire iron ore would be needed at the Newport works. He understood that consideration had been given to the possibility of meeting these requirements from the existing workings in the Wroxton area. However, the ISB thought it unlikely that the new mill would be able to rely entirely on supplies from there after the first stage of development. In the circumstances, the Minister had decided to reopen the inquiry so that all the interested parties could make representations on the new information which had come to light.

When the Bodicote inquiry ended, the opposition had been uneasy about the outcome, not so much because they believed Dowsetts to have made out a good case, but because the ISB seemed to have such an insatiable, yet at the same time incomprehensible, appetite for Oxfordshire ore. If it was true that behind Dowsetts stood RTB, the situation looked even more ominous. It needed only a little imagination to see a sinister chain of influence in the making. RTB had the Government s backing for their new steelworks. The ISB, another official agency, were apparently telling the Ministry of Housing and Local Government that RTB would have to have a great deal more Oxfordshire ore, far more than the Wroxton area could possibly supply. Presumably the Ministry of Power, the steel industry's sponsoring Department, had already accepted this argument. Dowsetts had by this time submitted applications to work something like

16.0×10^6 m² of the north Oxfordshire countryside. It was known that Dowsetts were in some way connected with RTB. True, the public inquiry was to be reopened, and the opposition would have the chance to challenge the applications. But in the end the decision would rest with the Minister of Housing and Local Government, a member of the Government which was supporting RTB in their important new enterprise at Newport. As the objectors saw it, behind the scenes the Minister of Housing and Local Government was almost bound to be influenced by the views of the ISB and the Ministry of Power. And as they reflected upon coming events, there were some in Oxfordshire who feared that the outcome was a fore-gone conclusion.

What made matters worse was the suspicion that far more was at stake than the fate of the areas for which Dowsetts had submitted applications. If, as the Minister had suggested in his letter of 30 April, RTB were eventually going to need 3·5–4·0 million t of ore a year, then the time would certainly come when even wider tracts of the Oxfordshire country-side would be threatened. Conscious that if planning permission were given for the areas currently before the Minister it would be very much more difficult to protect the rest of the ironstone-bearing land in north Oxford-shire, the County Council decided to press for a thorough and wide-ranging inquiry into the whole question of whether the ironstone deposits south of Banbury ought to be worked. And if the reopened public inquiry was to decide a major issue of principle, they thought it essential that they should know exactly what development programme was planned for the area and exactly what arguments Dowsetts intended to deploy in support of their case.

In a letter dated 26 June 1959 to the Ministry of Housing and Local Government, the Clerk to the Oxfordshire County Council pointed out that they would expect to be told (in advance of the inquiry) which areas Dowsetts intended to work in the years ahead, and how they proposed to transport the ore from the quarries to the railhead. In addition, they would need analyses of the ore from a comprehensive series of trial borings covering the whole of the area involved, together with reliable estimates for the cost of producing the ore. Only if this information was available would the inquiry be in a position to judge whether it was likely to be cheap enough, and of the right quality for use in the new strip mill. As the County Clerk observed, nothing could be worse than to grant planning permission and then discover that the ore was not quite suitable, or that Oxfordshire ore was, after all, dearer than ore from other districts in England, or from abroad. If that were to happen, the areas in question would presumably be held in reserve indefinitely by RTB; or, even worse, they would be subjected to haphazard, small-scale development by

Dowsetts or anyone else who succeeded in buying the mineral rights, and who reckoned that there was some prospect of selling the ore at a profit on the open market. As he reminded the Ministry, the County Council had always argued that, if an area had to be worked at all, it was important that it should be worked steadily and swiftly, so that the people living there could plan ahead, and so as to limit to as short a time as possible the inevitable disturbance caused by ironstone quarrying. The County Clerk insisted that all the information they were requesting was of vital importance, and he asked the Ministry of Housing and Local Government to 'instruct' the applicants to provide it.

Reaction in the Ministry was cautious but not unsympathetic. They pointed out that after the inquiry the Minister would have to decide the applications, taking into account the arguments advanced by both the applicants and their opponents; they could hardly allow themselves to be drawn into collecting information which might be used as a basis for representations put forward by one of the parties to the dispute. On 1 September 1959, however, the Ministry did write to the applicants, telling them that they would be expected to deal with certain specific 'points' in presenting their case.[2] These points bore a strong resemblance to those raised by the County Council. It would be helpful, the Ministry suggested, if the applicants were to prepare a written statement, which could be made available to the Inspector and the Local Planning Authority before the inquiry opened. They were proposing this rather unusual step, they said, because they believed that in this way the case could be dealt with more quickly. If the required information was not produced before the inquiry began, the applicants were informed, the Local Planning Authority might feel it necessary to ask for an adjournment, so as to give themselves time to consider it. The Inspector, added the Ministry, would be bound to take a sympathetic view of such a request. The Ministry also felt that there would be some advantage in dealing with Dowsetts' more recent applications at the same time as the inquiry into the original Bloxham/Adderbury areas was reopened.

The applicants provided the information asked for in a letter to the Ministry of Housing and Local Government of 21 September. They confirmed that production at Newport would begin in 1962–3. Within a short time, they said, more than a million t a year of Oxfordshire ore would be required. By 1965–6 they would need 2 million t a year, and over the following five years their requirements were expected to rise to about 3 million t a year. The blast furnaces at Newport had been designed to use 40 per cent Oxfordshire ore. In using this amount of Oxfordshire ore, they said, they were conforming with the stated policy of the ISB. They intended to treat the area for which applications had been submitted as an integrated working, quarrying the whole of it simultaneously; that is to say, it would not be worked piecemeal, one part at a time. The estimated life of the areas was twenty-five to thirty years. The ore would be carried by rail to South Wales. British Railways had planned the route, and they were already dealing with improvement schemes on certain sections of the line. And, for the Ministry's information, they added that the Dowsett Mineral Recovery Company was now a wholly-owned subsidiary of RTB.

This information the Ministry passed on to the Oxfordshire County Council. The applicants had certainly dealt with some of the relevant factors. But their statement did not go anything like as far as the County Council wanted. They had been told how much Oxfordshire ore the applicants would need at various dates in the sixties and early seventies. But what were the steel outputs to which these tonnages related? Had a definite decision been taken to go beyond the first stage in developing the new strip mill? Could the new steel-making process at Newport operate only on the basis of 40 per cent Oxfordshire ore, or would it be possible for it to use 100 per cent imported ore? If it was true that the Newport works had to use 40 per cent home-produced ore, from where did the applicants propose to get their supplies if planning permission for the current application areas was refused? The estimated life of the application areas, it had been said, was twenty-five to thirty years. Where would the applicants find their ore when these areas were exhausted? In order to form a clear picture of what the operations in Oxfordshire would entail the County Council also asked for a map showing the probable areas that would be worked in each successive five-year period, marking the routes by which the ore would be conveyed from the quarry faces to the railhead. A second map was also requested, showing the positions of all the test boreholes and setting out particulars of the ore analyses, the thickness of the seam and the depth of the overburden at each point.

The opposition were also interested in the reasons that RTB would give for using Oxfordshire ore. RTB had implied that Oxfordshire ore was to be used in order to conform with the ISB's stated policy. The reasoning behind the ISB's policy was something that the opposition could take up with the Board themselves. Nevertheless, they were anxious to find out more about the commercial considerations that were involved. At what price, they asked, did Dowsetts expect to deliver Oxfordshire ore to Newport, and how did this compare with the probable price of ore from alternative sources, imported and home-produced?

In retrospect, it is clear that the opposition were feeling their way, trying to piece together the case that would have to be answered at the inquiry. And from this point onwards, what will become a familiar strategy begins to emerge. In the first place, objectors must try to establish that the proposed development really will inflict serious damage on the local amenities. Usually this is not difficult. But it does call for some foreknowledge of what precisely the developers are planning, so that the objectors can build up and put before the inquiry a credible picture of the disastrous effect that the project in question would have on the environment. But in the second place, if it looks at all feasible, the objectors may also decide to attack the developers on their own ground, in an attempt to cast doubt on the rationale of their policy or decision. Often, they will suggest that it would be in the public interest (and sometimes, indeed, in the developers' own interests) for them to find some other method of meeting their needs, or an alternative site for their project. This, of course, is a much more ambitious ploy, though if it makes headway it can do a great deal to improve the objectors' chances of success.

Given a reasonable amount of information about the applicants' programme, it would be no problem for the objectors to show that ironstone working on a large scale would certainly disrupt the life of the north Oxfordshire countryside. But what about the other side of the strategy? Would it be possible to mount an attack on RTB's decision to use Oxfordshire ore, rather than imported ore? At this stage, it looked a very long shot, largely because RTB could always claim that they were merely conforming with the ISB's known policy. It seemed hardly likely that a County Council and their band of voluntary helpers would be able to shake the fundamental wisdom of that.

To add to the difficulties facing the opposition, by the summer of 1959 a period of economic expansion was well under way. As always in this phase of the business cycle, bottlenecks were becoming painfully obvious, and at one point there were fears that a shortage of steel might hold back the production of cars and consumer durables. It was against this background that, in the autumn of 1959, at the request of the ISB, RTB agreed to accelerate their construction programme at Newport. Understandably, both organizations were even more anxious to dispose of the problem of ore supplies as soon as possible.

On 24 December 1959 the County Council had asked the ISB to explain why they were supporting RTB's plans to use 40 per cent Oxfordshire ore. In their reply, on 7 January 1960, the ISB pointed out that it was not their practice to lay down the specific amount, or proportion, of home ore to be used by any individual company. RTB's decision to use 40 per cent Oxfordshire ore had been taken on technological and economic grounds. The ISB reaffirmed that their policy was still to encourage the maximum use of home ore, consistent with the maintenance of adequate reserves. If Dowsetts were permitted to work their application areas, they would contribute to the additional production of home ore that the ISB considered desirable. More to the point, Dowsett's ore would be needed at RTB's Newport works, for which the Government had made available a loan of £70 million. The new strip mill was now expected to come into operation at the beginning of 1962, or possibly before the end of 1961. Adequate provision must be made for supplying the necessary ore. The Newport project was of great importance to the national economy because of the continuing and increasing demand for sheet and other flat-rolled products required in the production of car bodies and in many other industries. It was essential, they added, that the new strip mill should be brought into operation at the earliest possible date. The ISB were confident that there would be considerable expansion beyond the plans already approved. Right at the beginning, it was vital to ensure that adequate supplies of iron ore were available as soon as they were required. If Dowsett's applications were granted, RTB would be in a position to meet their requirements at Newport as they arose; they would also have the advantage of knowing that a large part of their ore was under their own direct control. As the Board understood it, Oxfordshire ore could be worked with exceptional ease and cheapness. Dowsett ore, they claimed, would be among the cheapest in the country, and certainly cheaper than imported ore.

Another letter from the applicants to the Ministry of Housing and Local Government struck the same note of urgent necessity. On 13 January 1960 they informed the Ministry that the planned output in the first stage of the development had been increased to 1·4 million t of steel a year. By 1962, they said, RTB would need more than 1·0 million t of Oxfordshire ore a year. Previously, they had estimated that they would require 2·0 million t a year by 1965–6; but now they expected to need at least that much by 1964–5. The Ministry would appreciate that, if and when planning permission was granted, a good deal of preparatory work, including the installation of heavy plant and equipment and the construction of access roads and sidings, would still have to be completed before they could actually begin to produce the ironstone. Dowsetts were now estimating that, if they were to be in a position to meet RTB's needs in good time, they would have to start production not later than June 1960. It was vital, therefore, that the Minister should come to a decision on the application as soon as possible. In much the same vein, the applicants told the County Council in a letter of the same date that they were not prepared to make available any more detailed information because the time taken in putting these written statements together would serve only to prolong the delay in reaching a decision.

'Blood from the stone'

A public local inquiry is very largely a battle of arguments. Both sides are anxious to know, in advance, what evidence their opponents intend to rely upon, for then they can seek expert advice, establish their defence, marshal counter-arguments, and work out promising lines of attack. As the developer's case is almost always the more complex, advance information is usually more vital to the objectors. The Oxfordshire County Council now embarked on a dogged campaign to find out just what case the applicants and the ISB intended to put forward at the reopened public inquiry. From the beginning, it was an uphill task. But in their efforts to elicit more information than the applicants were inclined to provide, the County Council always had one strong card to play. They now knew that RTB were in a hurry; and it was a safe bet that the very last thing they wanted was for the inquiry to be adjourned because they had failed to make available enough information before it began. As the reader will by now have realized, rather less is known about the applicants' thought-processes. But apparently they came to believe, at an early stage, that the objectors were trying to dictate the terms on which the battle would be fought. They saw no reason why they should have their case patterned for them in a way that suited the opposition; nor did they feel themselves under any obligation to help out with information which the objectors seemed to think important for their own purposes.

On 21 January 1960, the Ministry of Housing and Local Government told both sides that, in their view, if the inquiry were held at the end of April this would give the opposition a reasonable period of time in which to prepare their case. Since there was to be this further delay, the applicants relented somewhat, and agreed to provide the further detailed information requested by the County Council 'in so far as it was available and relevant to the issues'. This cautious concession did not go down well with the County Council. In a letter of 1 February the County Clerk observed that *all* the information requested by the County Council must surely be available to the applicants; and as to relevancy, it was all relevant. In any case, it was for the Minister, not the applicants, to decide that point.

And now, for the first time, there appeared an explicit formulation of the crucial question that the inquiry would have to answer. 'The decision whether or not to permit the proposed development', wrote the County Clerk, 'must depend to a great extent on the balance between the resulting loss to the nation of amenity, and the resulting gain to the nation, if any, of working the application areas immediately or in the foreseeable future rather than holding on to them as a long-term reserve in case of a national emergency, whether it be military, political or economic.'

As the opposition saw it, there would be no problem about demonstrating the loss of amenity. But what kind of gain for the nation could there be ? Not unnaturally, they assumed that the applicants intended to argue that it would be much cheaper to use Oxfordshire ore than imported ore. After all, the ISB's general policy of encouraging steel producers to use home ore was based very largely on this proposition. And, in their letter of 7 January 1960, the ISB had said, quite unequivocally, that Dowsett ore would be cheaper than any other home-produced or imported ore. If the applicants were going to rely on cost advantage, the issue (it seemed) would resolve itself into one of those teasing questions of value. Was it worth spoiling this beautiful stretch of countryside in order to save whatever might be the difference in cost between steel made partly from Oxfordshire ore and steel made wholly from imported ore ? Or, to put it another way, should the nation pay this price, whatever it might be, in order to save the amenities of north Oxfordshire ?

The opposition had to assume that this difference in cost was substantial and demonstrable. Why else should the ISB and RTB be so set upon using Oxfordshire ore ? Yet if this *was* to be the applicants' trump card, did it really make sense for the opposition to dwell upon this aspect of the case ? It was certainly a question worth asking. But the fact was that, apart from drawing attention to the beauties of the countryside and the dismal effects of ironstone quarrying, there was little else they could do. Furthermore, if they could find out what the cost advantage of Oxfordshire ore was supposed to be, and how this figure had been calculated, they might be able to argue, as objectors often do in these circumstances, that the applicants were exaggerating. There must be a significant cost advantage ; that went without saying. But the smaller it was, the less would be the justification for impairing the amenities of north Oxfordshire, and the better the opposition's chance of success.

Having decided to probe more deeply into this aspect of the applicants' case, the County Council now began to press for detailed information about the comparative costs of manufacturing pig iron from Oxfordshire and imported ores. On 1 February the County Clerk took up this question with the ISB. Recalling the Board's earlier assertion that Oxfordshire ore would be among the cheapest in the country, and certainly cheaper than imported ore, he asked for the figures on which these claims were based. What would be the unit cost of pig iron, he asked, if Oxfordshire and imported ores were used in the ratios 40:60, 20:80, 10:90, 5:95 and 0:100 ?

In Oxfordshire, the answers were doubtless awaited with some trepidation. For all that the opposition knew, they might well turn out to be crushing. When the ISB replied on 12 February, however, all they had to say was that matters like these went rather beyond what they considered appropriate in the preparatory stages of a public inquiry. Detailed questions of this kind, they said, ought to be put, 'if at all', at the inquiry itself. In the circumstances, therefore, the ISB did not think it right to answer the points raised by the County Council. And in reply to a second request for these comparative costs, on 3 March the ISB informed the County Council that because Section 30 of the 1953 Iron and Steel Act prohibited them from supplying information relating to individual firms, they could not provide the detailed figures that had been available to the Board when they reached their conclusions about the cost of Dowsett ore compared with that of other home-produced ores.

If the ISB were not permitted to disclose this information, the obvious move was to go direct to the firm concerned. On 18 February the County Clerk put the same questions about comparative costs to Dowsetts. The response came several weeks later in a letter of 11 March. In a 'supplementary statement' the applicants now dealt with a good many of the points that had been raised in earlier letters from the County Council. RTB's revised timetable for the Newport works was confirmed. They agreed that it would be technically possible for the new steelworks to use only imported ore. But, they said, the proposed use of Oxfordshire ore conformed with the ISB's policy, which called for the maximum use of suitable home ore. Oxfordshire was the nearest orefield to the Newport works from which suitable ore could be obtained in the quantities required. All the deposits that they intended to work were near the surface, and close to a railway. Both production and freight costs were therefore expected to be the minimum possible. As they had made clear at the Bodicote inquiry, they were thinking of extending their operations to a further large area round Deddington. They were also carrying out surveys in the districts adjacent to their current application areas. It was expected that in the Hook Norton and Iron Down areas the ore would be transported by heavy-duty dump trucks on specially prepared roads leading to the railheads. In the interests of amenity, they had decided not to use what would have been very conspicuous crusher installations in any of the application areas. Instead, a modern ore preparation plant was under construction at Newport.

This was all very interesting. However, as the County Clerk pointed out in his acknowledgement on 17 March, the applicants had completely ignored the County Council's questions about comparative costs.

The County Council were also anxious to find out more about the ISB's attitude to another issue that was clearly going to be of some importance at the inquiry. Did the ISB feel any sense of responsibility for the effects of iron-ore mining on the countryside ? Not much, it seemed. In his letter of

1 February, the County Clerk had suggested to the ISB that the application areas were of great natural beauty, and in this respect they might be unique among the iron-ore bearing districts. Since the deposits were scattered, a larger area would suffer loss of amenity than would be the case elsewhere. The ISB's reply merely pointed out that the Board's statutory duty was to promote an efficient, economic and adequate supply of iron and steel products, including iron ore. The natural beauty of an area of contemplated development, they said, was hardly a factor that the Board could properly take into account.

It was now well past the end of April, the time suggested by the Minister for the public inquiry. The County Council were still not satisfied with the amount of information they had been given, and the applicants were apparently unwilling to provide any more. In an effort to speed up the decision, on 26 May 1960 the Minister himself met representatives from both sides and, as a result of this meeting, a month later the applicants produced another set of plans for the opposition to brood over. This latest dossier included two maps, one showing diagrammatically the probable pattern of areas to be worked in each successive five-year period, and indicating the direction in which the ore was to be transported from the working faces to the railway sidings, and the other showing the positions of all the boreholes in the Hook Norton and Iron Down application areas, together with a schedule setting out details of the analysis, the thickness of ironstone and the depth of the overburden at each borehole.

If the applicants thought that this would satisfy the opposition, they were to be disappointed. On 6 July the County Clerk returned to the attack. The diagrammatic map was dismissed as of little use : to form a clear picture of what was planned, he wrote, nothing less than a six-inch to the mile [about 0·1 metre to the kilometre] map was required. More important, he reminded the applicants that they had still not provided any information about the comparative costs of producing pig iron from Oxfordshire ore and imported ores.

It would seem that until now the opposition had been pursuing this question of costs more in hope than with any real expectation of discovering a serious weakness in the applicants' case. So as to be able to put up a reasonable show at the public inquiry, in March 1960 they had commissioned the Economist Intelligence Unit to examine the economic arguments for using Oxfordshire ironstone at Newport. The report was delivered early in May. It now began to dawn on the opposition that they might well have latched on to something of critical importance.

The opposition would have to assume, suggested the report, that RTB would claim some cost advantage from using 40 per cent Oxfordshire ore. In other words, they would say that this gave them cheaper steel than any other ratio of home to imported ore. But, the report continued, the choice of this ratio must have been based upon calculations made some considerable time before. In the previous few years there had been significant changes in some of the variables that RTB would have taken into account. As the report pointed out, the price of imported ore had begun to go down, shipping freight rates were no longer rising, and the cost of rail transport within the United Kingdom had increased. So that, whatever might have been the case for using a high proportion of home ore at Newport several years earlier, in the circumstances of 1960 it was almost certainly a great deal weaker. It might no longer make sense to use as much as 40 per cent home ore at Newport: the optimal proportion could well be 30 per cent, or even less. And if less Oxfordshire ore was needed, it might be that the Wroxton orefield would suffice after all.

The Economist Intelligence Unit's report did not merely question RTB's proposed 40 : 60 ratio; it also implied that the ISB, the fount of wisdom, might be wrong in sticking to their policy of encouraging the greater use of home ore. In 1955, it recalled, world reserves of iron ore had been put at about 83,000 million t; the most recent estimates, by contrast, suggested that reserves amounted to more than four times as much as had previously been thought. There was certainly no need for anyone to worry about future supplies from abroad. Moreover, the worldwide shortage of shipping and the high freight rates of the early fifties had given way to a surplus of tonnage and appreciably lower rates than had been expected. These trends might not continue so markedly in the future; but there was no reason to fear a recurrence of the type of shipping difficulties experienced in the previous ten years. If all this was true, why were the ISB persisting with their policy? The answer, suggested the report, was inertia. 'In an industry which abounds in joint organizations and controlling bodies', it observed, 'it may take a long time before a certain policy, a policy of home-ore development, for instance, is accepted and agreed upon by all parties concerned and it is to be expected that policies, once adopted, will not be lightly reversed, even if the reasons which originally led to their adoption no longer apply.'

For the opposition, this made encouraging reading. It still seemed too much to hope for; but was there just a chance that the applicants were reluctant to release the relevant data because they realized that the figures would do little or nothing to help their case?

When he wrote to the applicants on 6 July, the County Clerk repeated his earlier requests for information about RTB's estimates for the cost of producing steel from home and imported ores. 'Clearly,' he wrote, 'these comparative costs were a most important factor in reaching the decision to use 40 per cent Oxfordshire ironstone and 60 per cent foreign ore and, since that decision was taken some time ago, it is presumed that further estimates have been made from time to time to ascertain whether the 40:60 ratio continues to be a sound one from the point of view of the interests of Messrs Richard Thomas and Baldwins Ltd, and of the country.' And in the hope of being able to get to grips with these elusive figures, soon afterwards the County Council retained a chartered accountant to advise them on the economic aspects of the applicants' case. On 13 July the County Clerk wrote again to the applicants, suggesting a meeting between their representatives and the County Council's accountant to examine RTB's cost estimates.

The reply, received on 28 July, surprised and puzzled the opposition. According to the applicants, cost advantage did not form the basis of their case. Of course, they said, if the County Council wanted to make estimates, that was their business. Most of the necessary information, they thought, would be readily available without reference to Dowsetts or RTB. However, if the County Council required specific factual information that only the applicants possessed, they would be glad to consider whether they could provide it. In the circumstances, neither Dowsetts nor RTB thought that a meeting with the County Council's accountant would be appropriate.

This was a disconcerting piece of news for the opposition. Time was slipping by, and now it was being implied that they had failed to understand the case that would have to be answered at the inquiry. When the County Clerk replied on 2 August, a note of desperation began to creep in: 'If the cost advantage of the use of a high proportion of Oxfordshire ore in steel production at Newport does not form the basis of your case, what does ?' The answer must have left him as baffled as ever. The policy which dictated the proposed use of Oxfordshire ore had been explained by the ISB in January 1960, said the applicants; the specific proportions of imported and Oxfordshire ores to be used at the new steelworks had been determined by technical considerations which would be explained in detail at the public inquiry.

There it was in black and white. But evidently the opposition still could not bring themselves to believe that, in the end, the applicants would not rely on arguments about cost advantage. On 29 August the County Clerk returned to this point yet again, and asked the applicants to say, quite specifically, whether an alleged cost advantage did or did not form any part of their case. Whatever the answer, he went on, the fact remained that in January 1960 the ISB had claimed that Dowsett ore would be among the cheapest in the country, and certainly cheaper than imported ore. Presumably cost advantage was part of the reason for the ISB's support for Dowsett's application. And, so far as the national interest was concerned, the cost advantage (or disadvantage) of Oxfordshire ore was obviously one of the factors that would have to be taken into account when the application was finally determined. For this reason, the County Council thought it essential to establish in advance of the inquiry the precise extent of any financial savings from using Oxfordshire ore. They were still unable to prepare their case, and time was fast running out. If the applicants were not prepared to provide the necessary information by the middle of September, he wrote, and were not prepared to agree to a meeting with the County Council's chartered accountant, then the Council would feel obliged to ask the Inspector to adjourn the inquiry.

Nor was there much additional clarification on the question of costs to be had from the ISB. On 19 September the Board provided the County Council with a draft statement of the evidence that was to be given on their behalf at the public inquiry. The statement explained yet again why the ISB were encouraging the more extensive use of home ore, and why they were supporting RTB's applications. But so far as comparative costs were concerned, it was couched in carefully guarded language. 'Richard Thomas and Baldwins Ltd have advised the Board', they said, 'that according to their estimates the cost of producing steel at Llanwern (Newport) would be greater if Oxfordshire ore were not used in its production. The Board agree with the Company that there should be a cost advantage in the use of Oxfordshire ore, but cannot say what the precise amount will prove to be.'

Hitherto, hints of further delay had always been followed by additional instalments of information. At this point, however, the applicants dug in their heels. On 5 September they told the County Council that they were not prepared to produce a more detailed map of their development programme. As to the question of costs, whilst Dowsetts and RTB had naturally 'had regard to' the economic advantage to themselves of their proposals, a detailed comparison of costs formed no part of their case in respect of the planning application. A full statement of the technical considerations involved in the 40:60 ratio would be produced at the public inquiry and not before. If the County Council still felt that they had not been given enough information, they added, no doubt they would refer the matter to the Minister's Inspector as soon as possible.

The opposition needed no invitation and, on 10 September, the County Clerk wrote to the Ministry of Housing and Local Government claiming that the County Council had still not been given all the information they considered essential. He emphasized that they attached very great importance to the question of costs. In their view, 'the only factor which could possibly justify the destruction of the amenities of the Great Tew area would be an overriding national need, clearly demonstrated, to use the iron ore in this area, and this must mean that costs must be one of the issues to be fully debated at the inquiry.' It was vital, therefore, that the County Council should know (in advance of the inquiry) the cost advantage, if any, of using Oxfordshire rather than imported ore at the Newport works. The only way in which they could get this information was for their accountant to discuss the relevant figures with the appropriate officers of Dowsetts and RTB. In consequence, they wanted a meeting with the Ministry officials involved, the Inspector and the applicants' representatives, at which the Ministry could give a clear indication of what information they thought should be made available to the County Council before the inquiry. The Ministry of Housing and Local Government, however, were not to be drawn further into the preliminary arguments, and on 21 September they informed the County Council that the Minister thought it undesirable for him to intervene now that he had appointed the Inspector to hold the inquiry. He regretted, therefore, that he could not arrange a meeting of the kind proposed. The Inspector, too, felt that it would not be proper for him to join in discussions at this stage.

By now, the date of the inquiry had been fixed for 8 November 1960. While their solicitors and the County Council had been locked in arguments about the applications that were already in, Dowsetts had continued with their prospecting in the Oxfordshire countryside. On 25 August they submitted a further planning application for additional land in the Milcombe area. It was subsequently agreed that this application should also be considered at the forthcoming inquiry.

There was still time for one more disagreement, this time about the status of the witnesses that the applicants proposed to rely on. In support of their case, they had decided to call R. A. Hacking, RTB's Director of Research, W. E. Smith, the General Manager and W. J. A. Knibbs, the Managing Director of Dowsetts – by now renamed RTB (Mineral Recovery) Ltd. The County Council argued that this was not good enough. They contended that the Managing Director of RTB ought to be at the inquiry, for it was the working programme of the parent organization – not that of the subsidiary mineral company – that was relevant to the major issues of national policy involved. RTB, they maintained, ought to be represented by someone who could speak with authority about the company's development programme, and not by a member of their research staff, supported by representatives of the mineral company. This contention was rejected by the applicants: their witnesses, they said, would be fully competent to speak with authority on all matters that they regarded as relevant to the applications.

A similar exchange took place between the County Council and the ISB. The ISB had decided that their spokesman at the inquiry was to be

J. R. C. Boys, the head of their Development Division. The County Council wanted a full-time member of the Board, and not an officer, to give evidence on behalf of the ISB. It was clear, they said, that the ISB's support for the applicants was a matter of great importance. This support apparently arose out of the Board's general policy of encouraging the maximum use of home ore. Evidence should therefore be given by a member of the Board, someone who had been responsible for formulating this policy, and who could explain exactly why it had been adopted. The ISB, however, would have none of this. In the first place, they said, they had been advised that no member of the Board could be in a position to give evidence as to why any particular policy decision had been taken by the Board, since he 'could not take it upon himself to say what particular factors influenced the minds of other members of the Board participating in the formulation of the policy decision.' Consequently, they could not agree to the presence of a full-time member of the Board at the inquiry. Their second reason was less metaphysical, but it did suggest that the two sides were approaching the inquiry with very different ideas as to what did and did not come within its scope. 'The Board do not accept, in any event,' they wrote, 'that it is appropriate that the Inquiry should constitute itself as an Inquiry into the policies of the Board, and take the view that the policy of the Board on relevant points is a matter of fact, and represents a factor to be considered at the Inquiry with other relevant factors.'

From the ISB's point of view, this attitude may have been reasonable enough. After all, *they* were not seeking to extract ironstone from the Oxfordshire countryside. Why then should they be obliged to justify and defend their policies to the Oxfordshire County Council at a public local inquiry ? On the other hand, if it was to be one of the mainstays of the applicants' case that they were conforming with the ISB's policy, and that policy was to be beyond challenge, then plainly the opposition were going into the inquiry with the odds stacked heavily against them.

The public inquiry

There was no doubt about the strength of feeling in Oxfordshire. While the County Council were engaging the applicants at the official level, leading members of the opposition had been busy in the villages and hamlets. Throughout the spring and summer of 1960 they were hard at work, addressing public meetings, parish councils and Women's Institutes, and explaining the effect of ironstone quarrying on the life of the area. Their efforts were supported by the local press, particularly the *Oxford Times*, which gave full coverage to these meetings and ran a series of feature articles drawing attention to the beauty of the countryside in the threatened districts. From time to time interviews were recorded with people living in the more picturesque villages. Some of them held out hair-raising prospects. The vicar of Swerford, for example, predicted that, if the applications succeeded, the effect would be 'to blast Swerford off the map'.

By the autumn of 1960, north Oxfordshire was thoroughly stirred. Almost every local organization with any conceivable interest in the countryside, had lodged an official objection. Apart from the Oxfordshire County Council, the bodies opposing the applications included the Banbury RDC, the Chipping Norton RDC, the Banbury Borough Council, the Chipping Norton Borough Council, the North Oxfordshire Ironstone Areas Protection Committee, twenty parish councils, forty-four Oxfordshire Women's Institutes, the Oxfordshire branches of the NFU and the CLA, the Oxfordshire Rural Community Council, the Oxfordshire Playing Fields Association, the Oxfordshire Association of Parish Councils, the Banbury Ornithological Society, the Banbury Historical Society, the Banbury Business and Professional Women's Club and two local schools. The landowners, and other owners of mineral rights in more than two-thirds of the area involved, objected. In addition, a number of national amenity and recreational organizations, including the National Parks Commission, the CPRE, the Royal Fine Art Commission, the British Travel and Holidays Association, and the Ramblers' Association, also came to the support of the local opposition.

On 8 November 1960 the much-delayed public inquiry opened in Banbury Town Hall. It was expected to take five days; in fact, it lasted for ten. Held under Section 12 of the 1947 Town and Country Planning Act, the inquiry was concerned with the applications of Messrs Richard Thomas and Baldwins (Mineral Recovery) Ltd to mine and work ironstone and other minerals in six areas in Oxfordshire between Hook Norton on the west and the county boundary near East Adderbury on the east. Altogether, the applications covered an area of about $19 \cdot 0 \times 10^6$ m² though the working areas themselves, from which the ironstone was to be excavated, covered only $11 \cdot 5 \times 10^6$ m². The applicants were represented by J. P. Widgery, QC, and G. Eyre; the Oxfordshire County Council were represented by R. V. Cusack, QC, and B. T. Neill; J. Arnold, QC, appeared for the Protection Committee. The Inspector was H. F. Yeomans.

Opening for the applicants, Widgery made it clear that as Dowsetts had now become a subsidiary of RTB, to all intents and purposes it was RTB, the parent company, who were there seeking planning permission. RTB, he said, needed no introduction. It was a company in which Her Majesty's Government had a very substantial interest. Whether it was called a nationalized industry or not was immaterial: the fact was that the Government was a major shareholder. RTB's works at Newport, he went on, had been designed to meet the growing demand for thin, flat-rolled steel products, which were required for making car bodies and consumer durables such as washing-machines and refrigerators. The new strip mill would also bring more employment to South Wales. It would take fifteen years to complete; but the works had been planned to come into operation in stages. So far as Stage I was concerned, it was hoped to begin production in September 1961, building up to an output of 1·4 million t a year by April 1962. In Stage II, it was envisaged that output would rise to 3 million t a year by 1964–5. Beyond that, there might well be further expansion, with output rising to 6 million t a year by 1975.

To produce steel in these quantities, RTB would need a great deal of iron ore. They hoped to be able to begin feeding ore into the Newport works by March 1961. In Stage I they would need 1 million t of Oxfordshire ironstone a year, in Stage II 2 million t a year, and eventually they might well require 4 million t a year. As yet, no firm decision to go beyond Stage I had been taken; but RTB regarded Stage II as virtually certain.

From the start, Widgery explained, RTB had assumed that a substantial proportion of their iron ore would come from Oxfordshire. Why Oxfordshire ? The basic reason, he said, was that it was Government policy to use home ore. This had been a policy decision, involving considerations of foreign politics, foreign exchange and other questions that went far beyond the competence of any single steel producer, however big. These were matters for the Government to decide. 'It was not our decision,' he said, 'and I am not here with evidence to support the rightness or not of that decision; it was a decision at Government level.' Given the policy decision to use home ore to the fullest possible extent, said Widgery, Oxfordshire was the obvious choice for supplies. It was fairly close to Newport, and its chemical constituents were particularly suitable for combining with foreign ore in the type of steel-making processes designed for the Newport works.

It was quite true, he said, that the Oxfordshire Ironstone Company could provide RTB with 0·5 million t of ore a year immediately, and 1·0 million t a year three years later. In fact, RTB intended to take part of their requirements from Wroxton. But even if they took the full potential of the Wroxton area, there would still not be enough to meet their long-term needs. In any case, RTB were anxious to keep a proportion of their supplies under their own control, so that they could regulate the quality of the ore supplied to Newport. In order to match chemical variations in the imported ores, they had to have at least five ore faces open simultaneously; they could not just confine themselves to one place at a time. It was for this reason that they were seeking consent to work over such a large area.

As to the question of costs, RTB had no intention of disclosing their detailed estimates for the differences that might result from using imported and Oxfordshire ore in various proportions. They had, of course, made estimates. But Widgery had been instructed not to reveal these figures in public because they were of great commercial importance, and RTB's competitors would be delighted to learn about them. However, if the Minister of Housing and Local Government wanted their costings on a confidential basis, they would be prepared to make them available to him. They were certainly not going to produce them at the inquiry.

Developers are as much entitled to try to undermine the objectors' claims as vice versa. Turning to the opposition's case, Widgery conceded that if the applications were granted there was bound to be some interference with amenity and agriculture. But, he suggested, it was easy to exaggerate the natural beauty of the countryside that would be affected. There was a good deal of difference, he said, between the amenity values of individual application areas. Judging from afar, some people were under the impression that the whole area was comparable with Great Tew, which admittedly possessed great charm, and which the applicants would ensure was not damaged by their workings. But, at the other end of the amenity scale, there was the Milcombe area, a relatively featureless plateau adjoining an extremely unsightly installation of wireless aerials on a former airfield. Moreover, it was quite wrong to think, as some people evidently did, that iron-ore workings would destroy all the trees in the area. Trees, he claimed, tended to grow on the edge of the ironstone deposits, and so would not be much affected. 'The effect of mining on the trees,' he declared, 'would be so small you would not notice the difference.' Then there was the other popular misconception, that the fall in the level of the land after restoration would leave the farms and cottages on pedestals. 'The idea that homes will be left as castles in the air,' said Widgery, 'is quite unfounded.'

The applicants' case was now developed and defended by their four witnesses. First came Hacking, the head of RTB's central research laboratories. To the surprise of the opposition, he announced that in Stage I of the development at Newport the ratio of Oxfordshire to imported ore would be not 40:60 but 30:70. RTB would revert to the former proportion in Stage II and thereafter. He agreed that it would be technically feasible to use 100 per cent imported ore at Newport. But, he claimed, the ratios that they were proposing would mean cheaper steel. And now, for the first time, there was some precise, quantified indication of what this cost advantage might be. According to Hacking, RTB would be able to produce pig iron 3 per cent (or 0·06p per kg) cheaper if they used the 30:70 ratio. Presumably he meant 3 per cent cheaper than if they relied entirely on imported ore, though this was not made clear. In any event, Hacking could not himself explain how RTB had arrived at this figure. It was based, he said, on calculations made by the company's accountant. The accountant was not at the inquiry, for the simple reason, it was implied, that RTB did not attach any great significance to this cost advantage.

Their next witness was Boys, who came to explain why the ISB were supporting the applications. The ISB's policy, and the reasoning behind it, have already been explained. When it came to cross-examination, Boys was hard pressed to justify the Board's position on several important issues[3]. The ISB advocated the maximum economic use of home-produced ore, he said, because home ore resulted in cheaper steel. But was it not a fact, asked Cusack, that in recent years the price of home ore had increased, whilst that of imported ore had gone down ? Boys conceded that this was so ; but, he said, there had also been a tendency for inland freight charges to go down, because the railways were prepared to give mineral traffic favourable rates. Then there was the question of maintaining adequate reserves, including strategic reserves. Oxfordshire ore, as everyone agreed, was near the surface, and easily extracted. While foreign ore was available at reasonable prices, asked Cusack, was this not just the type of ore that ought to be kept for use in an emergency ? In an emergency, Boys replied, it would be easier to expand supplies rapidly in an area that was already being worked. But what would happen, asked Cusack, when the Oxfordshire deposits had been used up ? They might indeed last for another thirty-five years, as Boys said. But what then ? Again, there was the matter of distance between the Newport works and the Oxfordshire ore. Was it not a new departure to have a steelworks using as much as 40 per cent home ore when it was more than 160 km from its source of supplies ? The Steel Company of Wales had been taking their ore from Oxfordshire, and so had other South Wales firms, said Boys. But then, as counsel pointed out, the Steel Company of Wales had found it so uneconomic to use Oxfordshire ore that they had now stopped.

The third witness for the applicants was Smith, the General Manager of RTB (Mineral Recovery) Ltd. Much of his evidence was concerned with the effect on the countryside of ironstone workings and the methods of extraction that the company intended to use. He denied the suggestion that even after restoration the contours of the area would be completely transformed into a flat prairie. But he agreed that the amount of farmland put out of agricultural use at any one time would be not about 0.2×10^6 m^2 (as Widgery had claimed) but more like 0.8×10^6 m^2 in the first five years, rising to 1.8×10^6 m^2 twenty-five years later. He admitted that it would certainly be possible to see the quarries from public roads in the area, and these quarries, he agreed, would undeniably inflict a temporary scar on the countryside. It was also true that there would be a good deal of noise from detonations. Smith explained at some length how the company would do its best to mitigate the disturbance and shock. The explosions required for loosening the ore would not occur simultaneously; they would be phased out. But as counsel tartly observed, whilst the sound of detonations might be music in the ears of mineral recovery men, even phased-out explosions could hardly fail to disturb and annoy the local residents.

Last of the applicants' witnesses was Knibbs, Managing Director of RTB (Mineral Recovery) Ltd. It fell to him to explain why – if they were so set on Oxfordshire ore – RTB were not making more of an effort to meet their needs from the Oxfordshire Ironstone Company's Wroxton workings. RTB's attitude towards Wroxton has already been described. In their view, the Oxfordshire Ironstone Company could not guarantee sufficient ore in the long term; and even if they could, RTB wanted their main source of home ore under their own control. Counsel for the Protection Committee put a much more sinister interpretation on RTB's policy, though it was an interpetation that reflected a very genuine fear among the local opposition. RTB, he suggested, were anxious at all costs to avoid a contract for Wroxton ore. If they once entered into a long-term contract with the Oxfordshire Ironstone Company, he said, they would have to take all the ore that they had contracted for, even though it might have become uneconomic to use any Oxfordshire ore at all at Newport. If RTB were not bound by contract, he suggested, as soon as it became uneconomic to use Oxfordshire ironstone they would simply abandon their workings. Knibbs could only reply that since he was not a Director of RTB these matters were quite outside his jurisdiction.

It was now the turn of the objectors to develop their case. Their strategy was first to dwell upon the amenity value of the application areas; second, to demonstrate the grave and irreparable damage that the proposed ironstone workings would inflict on the natural beauty of north Oxfordshire; third, to suggest that the preservation of these amenities was in the national interest; and fourth, to argue that these valuable amenities should be destroyed only if it could be proved, beyond doubt, that other considerations outweighed the desirability of preserving them. The onus, they suggested, was on the applicants to show that their case was so watertight, so unassailable, and so proof against criticism, that in this instance it was in the national interest to sacrifice amenity. To a lesser extent, the opposition also argued that there would be a serious, albeit temporary, effect on agriculture.

As to the quality of the north Oxfordshire countryside, the opposition's principal witness was M. W. Robinson, the Oxfordshire County Council's Planning Adviser. The application areas, he said, stretched across several kilometres of unspoiled and mature landscape. Scenically, this was one of the most attractive districts in the county. And the natural beauty of the countryside was enhanced by its charming villages and ironstone cottages. The Great Tew area, he emphasized, was of particularly high aesthetic value, consisting as it did of steep-sided valleys, beautifully timbered, and forming an especially pleasing landscape. A large part of central Oxfordshire was scheduled in the County Development Plan as an Area of Great Landscape Value. He had reason to believe that the National Parks Commission was considering the designation of the Cotswolds as an Area of Outstanding Natural Beauty. The eastern boundary of that area came to within 3 km of the western extremity of the proposed excavations, and in his opinion, the application areas east of Hook Norton and on the southern slopes of Swerford Heath and Iron Down might well have been included in this Area of Outstanding Natural Beauty, had they been adjacent to it.

What would be the effect of ironstone working on this lovely stretch of countryside ? From their experience in the area north and west of Banbury, he said, they knew that opencast mining, even after restoration, left the countryside bleak, bare and uninteresting. The absence of trees and hedges gave it a desolate and characterless appearance, and he did not see how this effect could be avoided. Even when some timber reappeared many years later, the natural contours of the land would have been distorted into something alien and unattractive. And, of course, in the immediate future the outlook was much worse. Massive pieces of machinery would be left standing about in the countryside ; there would be periodic explosions ; and trucks and lorries would be continuously shuttling backwards and forwards. Robinson was prepared to admit that, so far as agriculture was concerned, in time the land could be brought back to something like full production. But from an aesthetic point of view, the attractiveness of an area worked over for ironstone was invariably destroyed. If there had to be open-cast mining in Oxfordshire, he argued, it should be confined to the area north of Banbury ; there were nearly 12×10^6 m^2 of untouched ironstone land there, he said, and the Oxfordshire County Council had raised no objection to quarrying in that part of the county.

In the course of his evidence, Robinson drew attention to other considerations which, he maintained, ought to be taken into account in cases of this kind. Beauty that nobody ever sees was perhaps of limited value. But one of the characteristics of the north Oxfordshire countryside was its accessibility : the main roads were chiefly on high ground, and provided excellent vantage points for large numbers of visitors. The English countryside was a diminishing asset ; it was vital, therefore, to preserve what was left. It was no use arguing that only the acknowledged beauty spots ought to be saved, for carried to its logical conclusion this theory would mean that only the beauty spots would remain for public resort and enjoyment. In those circumstances, he asked, how long would they continue to be beauty spots ?

On the question of trees, the inquiry also heard evidence from C. M. Harris, the Oxfordshire County Council's Forestry Consultant. This project, said Harris, would be nothing short of vandalism. Trees were an accepted part of the Oxfordshire scene. You could fell a large oak or elm or beech and bulldoze it away in a day; but no power on Earth could replace it in less than a hundred years. The applicants had suggested that they could extract ironstone from round the trees without harming them; even if this was an economic proposition, the effect would be to lower the water-table, and this alone would probably be enough to kill trees even as much as 15 m away from the workings. After the land had been restored it might prove very difficult to replace all the trees that had been destroyed, because where the fresh soil was very shallow, the roots of the newly-planted trees and hedges would soon reach impervious clay strata. Under these conditions, plants would certainly deteriorate and probably die.

The Oxfordshire County Council had plenty of allies prepared to testify to the beauty and interest of the application areas. The National Parks Commission's witness confirmed that the landscape affected was comparable to much of the Cotswolds, which the Commission proposed to designate as an Area of Outstanding Natural Beauty. The loss of natural beauty here, said the Commission's witness, would be grave and irremediable, because however skilful the restoration it would leave the character of the countryside permanently changed. The Council for the Preservation of Rural England took much the same line: their representative had visited areas said to have been restored after ironstone working, and compared with the surrounding land they looked bare, impoverished and characterless. It would be a national calamity, declared the CPRE's witness, if Great Tew and Swerford were spoiled.

The Banbury and Chipping Norton Borough Councils drew attention to the importance of the tourist industry for the area, whilst the Banbury and Chipping Norton RDC's were particularly worried about the possibility of the workings being abandoned if they became unprofitable in the future. This was a fear that was shared by the Treasurer of Christ Church, Oxford. The college, he said, had had some experience of ironstone operations in the past. He recalled that in 1917 they had signed a lease with Baldwins for certain workings. There was then a reshuffle and the lease was assigned to another company, which had come to the owners in the 1920s with a hard luck story, and offered them a choice between a reduction of 30 per cent in royalties or the abandonment of the workings. The same situation might be repeated here. It was some measure of the intensity of feeling against these proposals, he added, that Christ Church and the other land- and mineral-owners in the area should oppose the applications and voluntarily turn down royalties that might amount to £4 million.

Though clearly of secondary importance by comparison with the amenity objections, there was also opposition to the applications on agricultural grounds. The Oxfordshire branch of the NFU argued that the proposed workings would inflict financial loss and personal hardship on the farmers in the area. They did not claim that restoration was impossible; but it would be many years before the soil was in good heart again. And in the meantime there would be a direct loss of land as a result of the opencast mining, and constant interference with the efficiency of farm working as the quarry faces advanced. The NFU were supported in their objections by the Oxfordshire branch of the CLA and by Major Robb, who pointed out that so far as his tenants were concerned the prospect of iron-ore workings would cast a blight on farming land and would certainly discourage the necessary capital investment.

There was certainly a strong case for preserving this stretch of the north Oxfordshire countryside. And there could be no doubt that local opinion was overwhelmingly against the applications. Nevertheless, as the objectors judiciously conceded, there are times when even the strongest feelings must give way to overriding necessity. Excellent though the case for preservation might be, possibly the applicants had even better arguments, that would demonstrate beyond any shadow of doubt that it really was essential, in the national interest, for them to extract ironstone from this attractive and unspoiled corner of England. The opposition now turned their attention to the case for the applicants.

The attack was based chiefly on the findings of the Economist Intelligence Unit and on the expert evidence of P. Sargant Florence, the former professor of commerce at the University of Birmingham. Sargant Florence argued that, if the new strip mill had been sited in Oxfordshire or the south Midlands, the use of Oxfordshire ore would have been logical enough. But it was more than 160 km from Oxfordshire to Newport; and since the port facilities there were so good, the new steelworks was ideally situated to use imported ore. As for the ISB's policy decision to encourage the maximum economic use of home ore, this (he said) had been overtaken by events. The case for using home ore in large quantities might have been sound enough even as late as 1956 or 1957; but within the previous two or three years the situation had changed so much that the Board's policy no longer made sense, at least as far as the Newport strip mill was concerned.

When they had settled their policy, said Sargant Florence, the ISB must have taken three main factors into account. They were: the price of imported ore, the price of home ore, and railway freight rates. What had happened under each of these heads since 1956?

So far as the price of imported ore was concerned, he said, it was clear that, after what had turned out to be a misleading rise in 1957 (the year of the ISB's Special Report), the trend had been rapidly downwards. Taking 1956 as 100, the price index had moved as follows: 1957: 105, 1958: 95, 1959: 86. By contrast, the price of home-produced ore had steadily risen, the index reading: 1956: 100, 1957: 108, 1958: 113, 1959: 123. Within the previous few years, Sargant Florence pointed out, railway freight rates had also gone up. There had been a rise of 10 per cent in August 1957 and another $7\frac{1}{2}$ per cent in October 1958. This upward movement was likely to continue, he said. With the Newport works 185 km away from the application areas, a small increase in freight charges could make a big difference to the cost of home ore at the strip mill.

As for the availability of foreign ore, he reminded the inquiry that the last United Nations Survey of world iron-ore resources had been carried out in 1955. It was now clear, he said, that this Survey had seriously underestimated the extent of world reserves. Yet, presumably, that was the only estimate available to the ISB when they formulated their policy and prepared their Special Report in 1957. And presumably this was the estimate that the Board had had in mind when they decided that RTB's new steelworks should use a substantial proportion of home ore. 'Whatever justification there may have been in the past', declared Sargant Florence, 'for a greater exploitation of home ore on the ground of difficulties in obtaining imported ore, this clearly does not apply now.'

Then there was the impact on the balance of payments of using imported ore, another argument that was supposed to tell in favour of the ISB's policy. On the visible side of the trade account, he conceded, it was obvious that there would be some adverse effects. However, any losses there might very well be offset in other ways. The British Government's policy was to give aid to countries like Mauretania to help them develop their iron-ore industries. But trade was a better policy than aid, he claimed, and if we imported raw materials from underdeveloped countries we would probably open up new markets for our own exporters. Moreover, to assure these underdeveloped countries of a market for their commodities was to improve the prospects for political stability, which, in turn, would help safeguard future supplies of iron ore. There would also be a gain on the so-called 'invisible' side of trade account, he suggested. This would take the form of payments for the use of British shipping, together with a financial return on British investment in some of these overseas sources of iron ore. They ought to remember, he added, that this part of Oxfordshire was a favourite resort of American tourists; it was areas like this that attracted them to England in the first place. A good many English tourists also visited north Oxfordshire. Some of them might well choose to go abroad if the local countryside was ruined.

By this point, Sargant Florence was clearly down among the makeweights of his evidence. The Inspector was still thinking about his earlier arguments, and he was evidently anxious to make sure that he had grasped the full import of what the eminent economist was saying. The next few moments were to be among the most important in the whole of the inquiry, as the Inspector carefully took Sargant Florence back over the main points in his evidence. Would it be possible, asked the Inspector, to draw up a simple balance-sheet setting out the total economic cost of extracting iron-stone from Oxfordshire, and comparing this with the cost of importing the necessary supplies from abroad ? The answer to that, Sargant Florence replied, depended on whether the Inspector was including loss of amenity under economic cost. The point was, he continued, that economists like himself often used the expression 'real costs' to include psychological costs ; the loss of beautiful scenery certainly would be a psychological cost. The trouble was, of course, that costs of this kind were not easy to quantify. In this particular case, however, the problem of putting a money value on loss of amenity hardly mattered, because the applicants had failed to establish that their scheme had any advantages even on those criteria that were measurable. Three years earlier, he said, there probably had been some economic advantage in using home ore rather than imported ore. But by 1960 the costs of home and imported ore were much the same. When amenity was also thrown into the scales, there could be no doubt where the balance of advantage lay. Anyone could see, he implied, that it did not lie in RTB's scheme to dig up the Oxfordshire countryside in order to extract ironstone that they could get just as cheaply from abroad.

It now remained only for counsel to sum up in their final speeches. From the opposition there was more criticism of RTB for not sending better-informed and more authoritative witnesses in support of applications that were supposed to be so vital to them. As they reminded the Inspector, only one witness had come from the parent company itself, and he was a technical expert, not in a position to deal with matters of policy. He had been joined by two executives from the subsidiary company, and these 'three musketeers,' as Cusack described them, 'had been sent forth by their superiors, lurking somewhere in Monmouthshire, to capture this vast stretch of Oxfordshire countryside.' True, there had been one representative from the ISB, and he had been a fair and helpful witness. But his knowledge and authority were clearly limited.

From the very beginning, the opposition claimed, the ISB had maintained that their policy of encouraging the maximum use of home ore was based primarily on its cost advantage over imported ore. In the light of the evidence heard at the inquiry, the ISB's policy now looked decidedly suspect. But even if the general policy was sound, the ISB had never instructed RTB to use Oxfordshire ore at Newport. That was a decision for RTB, and it certainly did not follow that the company was obliged slavishly to adopt the ISB's policy even when, patently, there was no cost advantage in their particular case.

As for the applicants' assertion that the 30:70 ratio would mean a 3 per cent saving in the cost of producing pig iron, that claim was totally unsupported by evidence. How could the applicants possibly put forward a precise figure like this? They had admitted that no freight rates had yet been negotiated with the British Transport Commission; they had not yet agreed rents and royalties with about thirty-six landowners in the application areas; and they had not yet entered into a contract with the Oxfordshire Ironstone Company for the quota of iron ore to be drawn from the Wroxton area. With all these unknown quantities, it was quite impossible for the applicants to make a reliable estimate of any cost advantage from the use of Oxfordshire ore. No wonder, it was implied, that RTB had been so reluctant to disclose, far less discuss, how these calculations had been made. And small wonder that there was no one from RTB at the inquiry to be cross-examined on them. The Minister was entitled to conclude that RTB's costings were sheer guesswork. Even if these figures had any meaning at present, they would be completely unreliable as a guide to costs in thirty-five years' time. The applicants had suggested during the inquiry that figures could be supplied in confidence to the Minister. To do this would be to perpetrate a fraud on the public; if the Minister needed further information the only legitimate way of obtaining it was to reopen the inquiry.

The last word was with the applicants. In his closing address, Widgery argued that the Minister had four questions to consider. First, were the ISB right in adopting the policy of making the maximum economic use of home ore? Second, if the policy was right, were the applicants correct in saying that they had to look to Oxfordshire for the ore they needed? Third, could the necessary ore be found in the Wroxton area? And fourth, if the ore could not be found in the Wroxton area, did the amenity arguments outweigh the applicants' case?

The fundamental question, Widgery insisted, was the first. Was the ISB's policy right in the national interest? When the Newport works were planned, RTB had been asked to conform to the ISB's policy, and they were content to base their case on the correctness or otherwise of that policy. In the last resort, it was for the Government, and not the applicants, or the public inquiry, to say whether or not the ISB's policy was sound. How could any steel producer, however important, say whether the national interest required the maximum use of home ore? There was, for example, the question of the balance of payments. To use home ore would save foreign exchange, and only the Minister, in consultation with other

Ministers, could decide how much weight should be given to this argument. On a matter of this kind, he said, the final decision could not possibly depend exclusively on the evidence given at the inquiry, because the Government had specialists to advise them on balance-of-payments questions. The same considerations applied to Sargant Florence's evidence as to the need for 'trade not aid'. The Government was not going to look to a public local inquiry for advice on a policy question like this, and it would have been pointless for RTB to call witnesses to deal with it. Exactly the same could be said of the evidence that the objectors had submitted about the desirability of leaving home ore as a strategic reserve. This was not a matter for amateur strategists in RTB or at the inquiry.

The opposition had argued that it could not be right for RTB to adopt the ISB's policy in this particular case because, whereas the Board's policy had been adopted in order to save on the costs of producing steel, the applicants had not shown that Oxfordshire ore would mean cheaper steel at Newport. This objection entirely missed the point, he said. It was important to be clear that the ISB's policy was *not* 'the use of home ore when that produces the maximum of economy'. Rather, the policy implied (in Widgery's words) 'that you use as much home ore as you can until the time comes when it is uneconomic. That is to say, until the time comes when you are losing money as a result.' The first approach, Widgery suggested, would entail that you use home ore only when you can show a substantial cost advantage by doing so. All along, the objectors had been putting this argument into the mouths of the applicants, whilst in reality this was not their position at all. This was why the question of costings was not important. 'Costings become insignificant,' said Widgery, 'when our case is recognized to be what it is – namely that we understand the ISB to direct the maximum use of home ore up to the point when it ceases to be economic to do so. For it to be economic in that sense', he went on, 'does not require any specific cost advantage. Indeed, it does not require any cost advantage at all ; it merely requires that by and large there should be no cost disadvantage. Anyone who suggests that the use of this ore would be uneconomic must ask, "Why in that case are RTB making such a fuss about getting it ?" We are not here for amusement,' he declared, 'we are here becase we want the ore.'

So, unless the ISB's policy was misguided (and this was not a matter for RTB or for the inquiry), the applicants were right to use 30 per cent and later 40 per cent home ore at Newport. Once the broad policy was accepted, the choice of Oxfordshire ironstone was virtually automatic, because it was the nearest orefield to the Newport works, and it also had the necessary phosphorus content. Nevertheless, it might still be said that the applicants should take what they needed from the Wroxton area.

Everyone agreed that Wroxton ore would have to be supplied by the Oxfordshire Ironstone Company. The question was, how much could they be safely relied upon to produce for the new strip mill ? On 3 March 1960, said Widgery, the Oxfordshire Ironstone Company had told the County Council that they could supply RTB with 0·5 million t of iron ore immediately, and, given consent for their additional planning applications, they could expand supplies to 1·0 million t a year by 1963. It was true, as had been said at the inquiry, that since then they had ceased to supply ore to the Steel Company of Wales. Even so, there was nothing to show that the Oxfordshire Ironstone Company could meet the needs of the Newport works. The County Council could have called representatives of the company as witnesses to substantiate their claim that Wroxton could supply the necessary ore. But this had not been done. The fact was that in the near future RTB would require 1·0 million t a year, and the Oxfordshire Ironstone Company could guarantee only half that figure. And assuming that the strip mill moved on to Stage II – as there was every reason to suppose it would – the potential output of the Wroxton area would be left far behind.

If the Minister agreed that the basic policy still held good, Widgery concluded, then Oxfordshire had to supply the ore ; and the Wroxton area could not supply anything like the calculated need of the new strip mill in the future. Thus, inevitably, the applicants had arrived at the application areas so vigorously defended at the inquiry. For their part, RTB believed that the objectors were exaggerating the effects of ironstone working on the local amenities. It was only natural that they should. But since every other consideration pointed so inexorably to this particular area, the question facing the Inspector and the Minister was this : would the proposed ironstone workings really inflict so much damage on the countryside that the applicants' case ought to fail at this last hurdle ?

On 18 November 1960 the inquiry came to an end. Having toured the application areas to see for himself, the Inspector retired to write his report. The anxious defenders of the north Oxfordshire countryside and the steel men lurking in Monmouthshire now awaited the verdict from Whitehall.

Echoes in Parliament

While the Inspector pondered upon what he had seen and heard at Banbury, rumblings from the Oxfordshire countryside reached Westminster. At Question Time on 28 November Neil Marten, the Member for Banbury, asked Richard Wood, the Parliamentary Secretary to the Minister of Power, how much RTB had already spent on capital development specifically designed to handle Oxfordshire ironstone. The company had so far spent £250 000, and it was committed to spending another £1 350 000,

Wood replied. He had been told, he added, that if it became necessary, the plant already installed could be used to deal with ore from other sources. Why had this expenditure been authorized before the result of the inquiry was announced? asked Marten. Was it not true that RTB were trying to influence the outcome of the inquiry? The Minister of Housing was certainly not going to be blackmailed, Wood retorted, if that was what Marten was suggesting. In any event, he added, the Minister had been told that if the decision should go against RTB they would have incurred very little nugatory expenditure.

Soon afterwards, a far more formidable challenge to the Government was mounted in the House of Lords. On 1 December Lord Lucas of Chilworth asked the Lord Chancellor (Lord Kilmuir) if, in view of the widespread concern that had been aroused, he would refer the whole matter of the north Oxfordshire inquiry to the Council on Tribunals. Lucas did not want to influence the Inspector's report, or the Minister's decision. But he thought that there should be a full investigation into what had occurred before and during the inquiry, so that the Council on Tribunals could rule on whether or not the procedure had been in accordance with the spirit and the precept of the Franks Committee's report, which had called for openness, fairness and impartiality at statutory inquiries.

Lord Lucas went on to accuse the Ministry of Housing and Local Government, the ISB and RTB of withholding every scrap of vital information that the objectors needed for the proper conduct of their case. He recalled that at the inquiry counsel for the applicants had begun by claiming that they were only carrying out the policy of the ISB and had then gone on to make the 'fallacious, dangerous and quite erroneous statement', that the ISB 'stood in all regards as a Government Department', and therefore were not answerable for their policy to a public inquiry. He reminded the Lords that the applicants had refused to give any information about their costs, but had said that these figures could be supplied in confidence to the Minister after the inquiry was over. Again, during the inquiry one of the applicants' witnesses had said, or implied, that £2 million had already been spent on equipment specially designed for Oxfordshire ore. That now turned out to be quite untrue.[4] Only a few days earlier, a Minister had told the House of Commons that only £250 000 had been spent, and that there would be very little wasted expenditure if planning permission were refused. If there had been a barrister in charge of the inquiry, a man experienced in taking evidence, none of this would have happened. As it was, added Lord Lucas, the objectors had been obliged to spend £5000 in trying to answer a case that had never been put.

He was supported by Lord Salter, the President of the Town and

Country Planning Association. In cases of this kind, he said, there was usually the problem of weighing the expected economic advantage against the prospective destruction of the beauties and amenities of the countryside. But in this instance the applicants had refused to indicate how much economic advantage they hoped to gain from their proposals. In his view, the applicants had been reticent because they themselves were conscious of the weakness of their own case.

In reply, the Lord Chancellor said that he was distressed to hear Lord Salter dealing with the merits of the case, even though he knew that the Inspector had not yet reported to the Minister. It was quite improper, he went on, to try to put pressure on the Inspector and the Minister in this way while the case was still *sub judice*. Lord Salter interrupted to observe that a public inquiry was not the same as a court of law : and if critics waited until the decision was announced it was always too late to express an opinion. The Lord Chancellor was not impressed. He reaffirmed that the Minister would never be influenced by evidence that had not been available to both sides in the dispute ; that, he said, would be contrary to natural justice, and he would never be a party to proceedings of that kind. Until the Minister had the Inspector's report, it would be premature to consider referring the case to the Council on Tribunals. In the meantime, he would look into the criticisms of the way in which the inquiry had been conducted.

The Lord Chancellor told the House the outcome of his inquiries in answer to a Parliamentary Question on 13 April 1961.[5] He did not feel that a reference to the Council on Tribunals would be justified. Lord Lucas had suggested that the Minister of Housing and Local Government was under pressure because RTB had already committed themselves to considerable expenditure. There could be no question, said the Lord Chancellor, of the Inspector's or the Minister's judgement being influenced by the fact that expenditure had been incurred before the inquiry, or by the statement made by counsel for the applicants that the Government had a financial interest in the parent company. 'The developer who embarks on expenditure in such circumstances', he went on, 'is assumed to be aware of the risk he is running, and developers often refer to commitments of this sort, particularly in mineral cases. On such matters the manner in which they present their case at the inquiry is for the developers themselves to decide, but no weight is given to arguments of this sort in reaching a decision.'

Lord Lucas had maintained that vital information had been withheld by the ISB, RTB and the Ministry. It was obviously in the applicants' own interest, said the Lord Chancellor, to support their application by making available as much relevant information as possible. But it could not be held against them if they took the view that there was a limit to the information they were prepared to give. So far as the Ministry of Housing was concerned, when an application was called in the Minister could elicit before the inquiry only as much information as the applicants were willing to supply. They could not be required, before the inquiry, to elaborate their description of the proposed development. This was their task at the inquiry itself, and the view taken by the Inspector would depend largely upon the applicants' ability and willingness to justify their proposals. In this particular case, the Lord Chancellor went on, the company had prepared a written statement which had been made available to the County Council and to the Inspector. They had gone further, and entered into correspondence with the County Council. If the applicants had failed at the inquiry to support with detailed evidence their generalizations on comparative costs, this should not be regarded as depriving their opponents of an opportunity to attack them in cross-examination, but rather as reducing their own chances of obtaining planning permission. In short, he said, the applicants had gained no advantage from not producing further information.

Lord Lucas, however, was not satisfied, and on 20 April he formally asked the Council on Tribunals to consider various unsatisfactory features of the procedure both before and at the inquiry. Subsequently, the Oxfordshire County Council associated themselves with his request. But long before the Council on Tribunals had looked into the procedural issues raised by Lord Lucas, the anxiously awaited result of the battle of north Oxfordshire was announced.

The verdict and after

The Inspector's report was presented to Henry Brooke, the Minister of Housing and Local Government, on 10 January 1961. As is usual with reports of this kind, it began with a description of the area involved, and summarized the arguments and counter-arguments advanced by both sides at the inquiry. The Inspector then set out his own observations and conclusions. The applicants, he said, had not made out a case on the grounds of cost advantage. True, one of their witnesses had claimed that to use Oxfordshire ore in the proposed proportions would save 3 per cent on the cost of producing pig iron at the Newport works. That witness, however, had not personally been responsible for making these calculations, and he had not been able to say how the company's accountant had arrived at this figure.

As the Inspector saw it, one relevant fact that had emerged from the exchanges on costs was that if there was any advantage at all in using Oxfordshire ore it was very small, and could easily be reversed if economic conditions changed. If the working areas were opened up, and then became unprofitable, there was a risk that they might be abandoned. Or- alternatively, if the relative prices of home and imported ore should fluctuate in the future, the workings might be intermittent, and the period of working could be prolonged.

In the Inspector's opinion, there were four arguments in favour of granting the applications. First, there was a demand for Oxfordshire ore in the steel industry. Second, the prosperity of the steel industry was important to the national economy. Third, the potential consumers of the ore at the Newport works expected to make a saving in production costs as a result of using this ore. And fourth, the use of home ore, either from the application areas or from elsewhere, meant a saving on the nation's import bill.

On the other hand, there were two main arguments against granting planning permission. First, the proposed workings would interfere with agriculture over a long period and would impair the efficiency of farming operations. And second, they would certainly injure the amenities of the area. The Inspector had been favourably impressed by the continuity in the character of the villages from Great Tew to East Adderbury, the ironstone walling being the predominant link. The proposed workings would undoubtedly cause severe damage to the rural amenities : there was no question that they would destroy natural features and create a great deal of noise and disturbance. The damage would be more severe in the area south of the river Swere ; but the working of any part of the application areas would lessen the attractions of the district as a whole. As the quarry faces advanced across the countryside there would be two sorts of terrain. Ahead of the workings people would see mature farmland ; behind them there would be rather bare, restored land at a lower level. What with mechanical face-shovels, giant dumper trucks, the other plant used for removing overburden, railway sidings, and periodic explosions, there would be a considerable amount of noise. The Hook Norton and Iron Down area had specially impressed him. 'It is not exaggeration,' he wrote, 'to say that this part of the application areas is beautiful country, and that from an aesthetic point of view, iron ore workings would be a calamity.' The applicants had said that they would restore land progressively as the working faces advanced. But however successful restoration might be as regards reshaping the land, it would be many years before the landscape reached maturity, and even then it would be difficult to disguise changes of level where worked-out land adjoined roads and buildings.

The applicants had established that there was a demand for this ore. But they had conceded that the demand could be met in other ways. There was no evidence, the Inspector added, that the needs of industry made it essential to work these areas. In his view, the balance in terms of economics, including agricultural considerations, was uncertain.

Then came the crucial value-judgement. If there was any small economic advantage to be gained from extracting the ore from all or any of the application areas, the Inspector concluded, it was outweighed by the injury to amenity. He therefore recommended that all the applications should be rejected and that planning permission should be refused, on the grounds that the extraction of iron ore would cause serious damage and loss to agriculture and would inflict severe injury on the rural amenities by destroying natural features and by creating noise and disturbance.

It was not until 8 May 1961 – four months after receiving the Inspector's report – that the Minister of Housing and Local Government announced his decision. Part of the delay may perhaps be attributed to the Lord Chancellor s investigations. The Minister accepted his Inspector s recommendations and rejected all the applications.

In his decision-letter the Minister made it clear that in his opinion the applicants had failed to establish that it was essential to work the areas in question. Since the workings were *not* essential, it was a question of weighing the objections against the economic argument put forward by the applicants. There were two objections. They were damage to agriculture and injury to the amenities. So far as agriculture was concerned, a part of the land (a relatively small part) would be taken out of agricultural use for the full working period. On the other hand, the interference with agriculture caused by the extraction of ironstone would be for the most part of a temporary nature, and in any case would be largely overcome, as working proceeded, by the progressive restoration of worked-out land. In the Minister's opinion, therefore, the effect of the proposed development on agriculture would not have been, of itself, a sufficient reason for withholding planning permission if a strong case for the applicants had been made out.

But taking the agricultural considerations together with the injury to amenities, the Minister thought that ironstone working should not be permitted in these areas (especially in the very attractive areas south of the river Swere) without clear evidence of an overriding economic need. He was not convinced that there was such a need in relation to the whole, or any part of the land in question. Nor did he think that enough attention had been given to the possibility of drawing additional supplies from the Wroxton area.

And there ended this protracted struggle over the use of about $16 \cdot 0 \times 10^6$ m^2 of the north Oxfordshire countryside. The Minister's verdict was received with delight and relief in Oxfordshire. The battle was over, and the opposition had won.

Only the postscripts remained to be written. Insisting all along that he had been concerned with the procedural aspects of the inquiry, and not with the merits of the case, Lord Lucas refused to withdraw his reference to the Council on Tribunals. The Council delivered its opinion in the Annual Report for 1961. There were no grounds for serious complaint, it thought, though when the Government had a specific financial interest in a planning application there was something to be said for appointing an independent Inspector, as was usually done with proposals to establish or extend a New Town. But in general, the Council on Tribunals endorsed the arguments put forward earlier by the Lord Chancellor. On the alleged failure of the applicants to make available all the necessary information prior to the inquiry, it suggested that if developers did not produce evidence, that might show the weakness of their case, but it did not demonstrate that there were any deficiencies in the inquiry procedure.[6]

As for the steel industry, it no doubt felt entitled to some guidance from the Government about the policy that it ought to follow in the aftermath of the Oxfordshire decision. This came in a letter from the Minister of Power to the chairman of the ISB in the spring of 1962. It was the Government's intention, wrote the Minister, that the steel industry should use whatever ore was considered, on balance, to be most economic. The producers ought therefore to be free to make use of home ore from a particular site whenever it was clear after a careful examination (if necessary at a public inquiry) that agricultura, amenity, scientific and social objections did not override the case for its use on economic and balance-of-payments grounds. The Government did not accept the argument that our national resources should be reserved for an emergency. Foreign ore could be drawn from widely separated parts of the world; and furthermore, the Government had been told that it was easier to increase production quickly from areas already being worked than to open up new quarries. Though the Government did not wish to make light of the inconvenience of ironstone working to individual farmers, from the national standpoint arguments drawing attention to the loss of agricultural production did not appear to carry much conviction. From a narrowly economic point of view, iron-ore mining was a more profitable use of land than growing crops or raising stock. And in any case, ironstone extraction involved only a temporary loss of agricultural output, because the land could soon be restored to its original use after the ore had been taken out. But, said the Minister, 'the real possibility of doing irreparable damage to beautiful parts of the country must certainly be avoided.'

And what of RTB, deprived of their Oxfordshire application areas? The heavens did not fall. According to the ISB's Annual Report for 1961, RTB had begun negotiations for increased supplies from the Wroxton area. As compared with what had originally been intended, they also expected the Newport works to be able to use rather more imported ore.

Notes

1. In view of what was to happen subsequently, a leading article in *The Times* of 14 June 1957 is of some interest. It acknowledged that there was strong political support for building another steelworks in Scotland. On the other hand, South Wales had better and cheaper coal, and was rather better placed in relation to the market for sheet steel. There was general agreement, it continued, that more use should be made of home ores, so as to reduce the cost of producing steel. Voicing what it obviously thought were obvious truths, it observed that a strip mill in Scotland or South Wales would use imported ore; if the most economic use was to be made of home ore, it concluded, Northamptonshire would be the best place for the new works.

2. All correspondence on the applicants' side was, in fact, dealt with by a firm of solicitors. By this stage Dowsetts had been taken over by RTB, and it must be assumed that the parent company was now involved in preparing the case for the applications. In the text, the expression 'the applicants' should be taken to refer to RTB and Dowsetts jointly. On the other side, all correspondence was handled by the Oxfordshire County Council, as the Local Planning Authority concerned. After the Bodicote inquiry, however, the chief objectors worked in close cooperation, eventually (in February 1960) forming an advisory committee (consisting of representatives of the County Council, the Protection Committee, the NFU, the CLA, the Parish Councils Association and the Chipping Norton and Banbury RDCs) to coordinate their efforts. In the text, the expression 'the opposition' refers to this united front.

3. Before he gave evidence, there was an argument between opposing counsel about Boys's status as an official of the ISB, and the extent to which he was to be cross-examined. For the applicants, Widgery maintained that Boys could not be questioned on the thinking behind the ISB's policy. He pointed out that paragraph 318 of the Franks Committee's *Report on Administrative Tribunals and Enquiries* had recommended that officers of Government departments should confine their evidence to matters of fact, and should not venture into questions of policy. This, he said, had been accepted by the Government. It was true that the ISB were not, strictly speaking, a Government department. Nevertheless, the principle remained the same : an officer could not be asked to say how his department or organization had decided upon its policy. To question Boys about the reasons for the ISB's policy would be to ask him to look into the minds of all the constituent members of the Board, and this would clearly be unfair and impossible. Counsel for the objectors rejected this argument. Cusack argued that the ISB were not a Government department, and Boys was not a civil servant. If Boys was to give evidence-in-chief, outlining the ISB's policy, then the objectors ought to be able to cross-examine him on it. He reminded the inquiry that the Oxfordshire County Council had anticipated this difficulty when they had

suggested that evidence on behalf of the ISB ought to be given by a full-time member of the Board. If Widgery's contention was accepted, said Cusack, the ISB had a position of immunity enjoyed by no other public or private body in the country. Suppose, he said, the application had come from a private company, and a director had come to the inquiry and said, 'Oh well, it's the policy of my trade federation that such and such a thing should be the case. You must not ask questions why : you must not question the trade federation.' If Boys could not answer questions on policy formation, said Cusack, then the Inspector should require someone else to come from the ISB who could. That person, suggested Cusack, should be Sir Robert Shone, the executive member of the ISB. In the end, it was agreed that Boys should be cross-examined in the usual way, and that if Widgery objected the Inspector would rule on the admissibility of the question.

4. In fairness, it should be added that both the applicants and the ISB deny that any such statement was made at the public inquiry. The misunderstanding arose, they claim, because of inaccurate reporting in the press, due in part to bad acoustics. It is certainly true that in the official transcripts of evidence several passages are so garbled as to be quite incomprehensible.

5. By now, the Minister of Housing and Local Government had been in possession of the Inspector's Report for something like three months. The Minister's decision had not yet been announced.

6. This argument is open to two objections. In the first place, any information that the applicant deliberately chooses to keep back is not likely to be evidence that he thinks would help his case. On the contrary, if anything is deliberately concealed, it will be information that might help the objectors. In these circumstances, applications might succeed because the developer has managed to suppress information that would have weakened his case. Secondly, and admittedly this is much less likely, the applicants might simply misjudge the situation. They might conceivably hold back evidence, either because they wrongly judge that it will harm their case or because they think it unimportant, when, had it been available, it might have improved their chances. In these circumstances, the applicants would not be the only losers, for it is clearly not in the public interest that objectors should succeed because a developer has misguidedly or inadvertently failed to produce all the evidence necessary to enable the Minister to reach the right decision.

3 Copper in Snowdonia National Park

Graham Searle

In the southern part of the Snowdonia National Park, at the confluence of the Afon Wnion and Afon Wen, is to be found a typically dispersed North Wales community. The loose-knit village has as its focus a Nonconformist chapel, and as its name the biblical, Capel Hermon. It was here – twelve kilometres or so north of Dolgellau – that the future of Britain's National Parks might have been resolved.

Capel Hermon itself comprises farmsteads or *hendres* (winter houses) nestling in the pastureland or *fridd* of the valley bottom, the whole picture being framed by rugged uplands over which the sheep wander and graze in the summer months. Since the adoption of pastoralism, North Wales farmers have been sheep farmers with only the husbandry of highland cattle – the Welsh Mountain Black – serving to add a degree of diversity to the pattern. Up to a few decades ago, many of the sheep were left high up the mountain side all year round, but these tough *wether* sheep (as they are known) gave tough mutton. With refinement of tastes and the luxury of choice of the post-war years, it was the more tender meat which attracted the housewife ; so now all the sheep are brought off the mountain to spend the winter months in the kinder pastureland below.

Not so long ago, the farmers themselves used to follow their stock up and down the mountain with the changing seasons, and for each lowland hendre there was an upland *hafod* which was the summer home of the farmer and his family. Nowadays, while sheep farming is still the rule, the greater mobility of the farmer has enabled him to dispense with this seasonal migration ; today all his affairs are conducted from the hendre in the valley.

But today his affairs are not only those of the sheep farmer. Hill farms such as those in North Wales have become increasingly uneconomic and, in the face of higher costs and smaller returns, the sons of this generation are drifting away from the land into the city which appears, at least, to promise more diverse and more lucrative employment. This trend and the financial pressures on the hill farmers prompted diversity – either into the tourist trade, with camp sites and bed-and-breakfast, or (sometimes) into work with the Forestry Commission, which offers full-time employment and grants tenancy of a farm, enabling farmers to work in their own time. In many cases the North Wales farmer has become both forester and small-scale hotelier or camp-site operator into the bargain. In this way he is at least able to retain a measure of the independence to which he has been

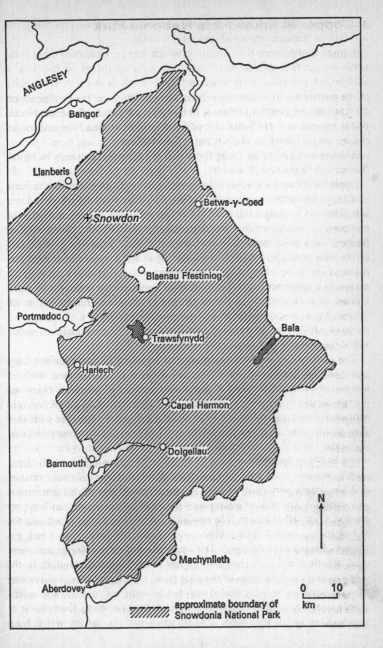

ANGLESEY

Bangor

Llanberis

+ *Snowdon*

Betws-y-Coed

Blaenau Ffestiniog

Portmadoc

Trawsfynydd

Bala

Harlech

Capel Hermon

Dolgellau

Barmouth

N

Machynlleth

Aberdovey

0   10
km

////// approximate boundary of
Snowdonia National Park

accustomed. Although not rich in the narrow fiscal sense of the term, the hill farmer remains employed and retains pride.

However, this is not the position in which many members of other rural communities find themselves. Apart from growing things on the land, it was getting things out of it which provided North Wales with its stability of employment. The extractive industry – mining and quarrying – has always been of great importance, and recent arguments about large-scale metal mining in Snowdonia cannot be appreciated unless the attitude of the people to mining is at least partly understood.

Mining and quarrying are in the blood of many of the people of North Wales. Up to the end of the First World War, the whole area we now call Snowdonia formed a traditional mining province; concentrations of lead, zinc, gold and copper were sought after, and their veins followed and dug out. There is scarcely a hill in North Wales without a hole in its side – the evidence of former mining, its smallness of scale dwarfed by the natural panoply of well-cropped hills and rugged ridges. Since the holes themselves were small, so too were the heaps of waste or spoil which the operation of the mines disgorged on to the surface; and it is this spoil which serves as a reminder of the days of metal mining. For, once in a while, a change in a watercourse, whether natural or man-inspired, results in the stirring up of a spoil heap and a consequent mobilization of metal ions, some of which – as we were reminded in Conwy, where escaping cyanide killed the oyster fishery – may prove toxic.

The other major extraction industry to be found in Snowdonia is slate quarrying and, although this does not involve the question of toxicity associated with metal mining, it does raise a number of problems of its own – some aesthetic, some economic, and all of them social. Slate mining is in serious decline; quarrying in North Wales is in a more depressed state now than at any time since it began late in the 1700s, and it is the very fact that up to the 1940s the industry had flourished so magnificently for a century and a half that makes its decline as socially damaging as it is. In the nineteenth century, when the now-enormous slate quarries of Caernarvonshire and Merioneth were really opened up, there existed a ready market for the raw material. The task of quarrying was labour intensive, demanding very great skill as well as brawn. The raw face was worked by hand, without the aid of high-powered drills; hand augers made the holes into which explosive charges were dropped. The work was not only arduous and more than a little risky, it required an almost brotherly understanding of the vagaries and idiosyncrasies of the slate itself. Quarrymen were paid not by the number of holes they drilled nor by the hours they put in, nor indeed by the quantity of slate they brought down, but rather by the volume of usable slate which they were able to win from the quarry walls. Such experts were they – drillers often travelling long distances from quarry to quarry to perform their minor miracles – that their efforts resulted in an amazingly high usable-slate-to-waste ratio. With the later introduction of mechanized drilling, which was quick and cheap, things were to change: the quantity of waste material was multiplied tenfold, and it is this as much as anything which has resulted in the vast areas of slate waste which intrude into the very heartland of Snowdonia. The waste is slow to become vegetated; indeed until the natural agents of erosion have ground the shimmering slabs to dust and rubble, grass will not be able to reclothe slate-strewn mountainsides. So porous is the layer of slaty waste that nothing will grow on it, although tree seedlings of oak and birch can grow between the slates provided they can find both a rooting medium and freedom from the voracious attentions of sheep and hares. Areas such as Blaenau Ffestiniog (which, because of this legacy of dereliction, was excluded from the Snowdonia National Park and about which more is said later) could be reclaimed at a cost of several millions of pounds, and at least be screened at a cost of about one million. But, while the aesthetic costs incurred by destructive development can be quantified, the social costs are less tangible, though really no less apparent.

After the Second World War, there came on to the market a great variety of alternatives to slate products – other insulators, roofing materials and tiles combined to knock the bottom out of demand for slate. Plastic-based compounds enjoyed in addition a lightness which bestowed upon them great savings in freight costs; and some could be made close to the areas of maximum demand rather than having to be quarried in the inaccessible mountains of North Wales. One by one the quarries contracted, then closed; one by one families which for generations had had their roots in the villages of the region moved away to the towns and to what jobs were available there; one by one the once profitable townships, which had sprung up with a vulnerable dependence on the benevolence of the slate industry, went into decline. Now, only a generation later, there is increasing rural depopulation, regional unemployment, and the frequent incidence of youngsters having left school years ago only to join the ranks of the unemployed, before graduating to those of the unemployable.

It is this former dependence upon a few vulnerable industries which is so often at the root of current regional depression, itself a malaise to which the attraction of short-term highly capital-intensive civil engineering schemes (such as power stations or reservoirs of the sort which are frequently the politician's first response to the problems of Scotland, North Wales or North-East England) provides no real cure. But it is the seeming hopelessness of their situation which makes some at least of the inhabitants of Snowdonia clutch at the straw which another dam or a large-scale mining operation will provide. Even if the construction phase of such 'development only lasts for ten years, then that at least provides ten years employment for some – a fact not to be dismissed lightly by tourists who see mountains in Snowdonia but who seldom appreciate the needs of men who live in the mountains' midst.

This, then, is the background against which we must examine what happened when the largest mining company in the world formulated plans to put what would have been Britain's largest opencast mine in what remains one of Britain's most beautiful landscape areas. Some councils, trades associations and political groupings were in favour of new and large scale mining, and some were against. It is not the task of this chapter to criticize either view, but simply to present the history of one case which threw into marked relief the various arguments for and against large-scale opencast mining in the Snowdonia National Park.

National Parks

In May 1972 a BBC 'Horizon' team produced a documentary programme on the question of opencast mining in Britain's wildlands, which they entitled 'Do you dig National Parks?' In the programme, an employee of Noranda-Kerr (a Canadian consortium which is exploring in Snowdonia) was asked whether he found the idea of large-scale mining in Britain's National Parks at all worrying, and he answered – perhaps narrowly, but strictly correctly – that 'the National Park was here long after this was a mining field.' Similarly, Sir Val Duncan has quite correctly observed that, in England and Wales, 'mineralization is most likely to occur in the more attractive and remote areas often designated as National Parks.' So, while there remain many valid criticisms of the way in which Rio Tinto-Zinc (of which Sir Val is chairman) and other companies have pursued their goal of exploiting the mineral potential of the United Kingdom, that they have chosen to concentrate their quest for metals on the National Parks is neither surprising nor Machiavellian. That these areas are mineral provinces was well known long before they were designated National Parks, and that some might later want to mine them extensively was foreseen before the National Parks and Access to the Countryside Act became law in 1949.

The world's first National Park was established in the USA at Yellowstone in 1872, and moves to establish such areas in the UK can be traced back to 1884. Things moved at their usual pace, and it was in 1931 that the Addison Committee and in 1942 that the Scott Committee repeated the demand for British National Parks. The Dower Report of 1945 developed the case and went as far as defining what a British National Park should be:

an extensive area of beautiful and relatively wild country in which, for the Nation's benefit and by appropriate national decision and action :

a) the characteristic landscape beauty is strictly preserved;
b) access and facilities for public open-air enjoyment are amply provided;
c) wildlife and buildings and places of architectural and historic interest are suitably protected, while
d) established farming use is effectively maintained.

The Hobhouse Committee of 1947 echoed the need for strict preservation of landscape and went further by proposing a nationally-administered capital programme of land improvement and purchase within the Parks. But the 1949 Act which established British National Parks was less bold and, while it defined the purpose of designating National Parks and Areas of Outstanding Natural Beauty as being the preservation and enhancement of natural beauty and the promotion of open-air recreation and the study of nature, it proposed no means by which such protection could be afforded to the Parks. Moreover, it left their financial and administrative control to local authorities. There was to be no central National Parks Agency, and – unlike National Parks in the USA – the land (and its mineral rights) were to remain in private ownership.

Thus the safeguards recommended by the Dower and Hobhouse Reports, designed to afford the National Parks of England and Wales some degree of protection from, for instance, the incursion of opencast mining activities, did not appear in the Act, although this likely source of conflict was referred to before the legislation was enacted. In the second reading debate in the Commons, the then Minister of Town and Country Planning, Mr Lewis (now Lord) Silkin, enunciated a clear set of conditions which were to be complied with before large-scale mining was to be permitted in the Parks :

It must be demonstrated quite clearly that the exploitation of those minerals is absolutely necessary in the public interest. It must be clear beyond all doubt that there is no possible alternative source of supply and, if these two conditions are satisfied, then the permission must be subject to the condition that restoration takes place at the earliest possible opportunity.

In this statement the Minister echoed the recommendations of the Hobhouse Committee ; but since 1949 such statements have suffered successive dilutions on successive occasions until in 1971 Lord Sandford, Minister of State for the Environment, was able to amend 'absolutely necessary in the public interest' to read 'on balance, the national interest justifies', to dispense with the condition dealing with alternative sources of supply, and to modify 'restoration takes place at the earliest opportunity' to 'every care is taken to require whatever screening and restoration works are practicable'.

The original purpose of National Parks has also suffered some deliberate, and some accidental, confusion to the extent that in 1971 Sir Val Duncan of RTZ felt bound to explain, somewhat misleadingly, that Britain's designated areas are regions of 'rocky and hilly country which is not suitable as a living area for a large population and much of it has therefore been set aside as National Parks'.

While National Parks are not generally understood, and while largely due to planning restrictions imposed by their various County and Park Planning Committees they remain beautiful, stimulating and (in an increasingly urbanized society) even more important foci for leisure pursuits and recreation, the manner of their administration has on the whole contributed little to their management and much to the confusion which surrounds their purpose. The Peak District National Park (which falls largely in Derbyshire) was the first to be established, and has been run from the outset by a single Park Planning body – the Peak Park Planning Board. This, like its equivalent in the Lake District National Park, is a Joint Planning Board made up of appointees of the county councils involved and of the Secretary of State for the Environment. (As with all Park Committees and Boards, locally nominated members outnumber those centrally appointed by the appropriate Secretary of State in the ratio 2 : 1.) These Joint Boards are the actual planning authorities for the Parks; and the Peak Park Planning Board (having greater power of precept on the county authorities than has the Lakes Board) employs its own full-time director and staff.

Four National Parks each lie wholly within a single county (these are Dartmoor, Northumberland, North York Moors and Pembrokeshire Coast) and are administered by a specially appointed planning committee of the county council. However, in the remaining four Parks, which each lie within more than one county, the administrative machinery is unduly cumbersome. In Exmoor, Brecon Beacon, Yorkshire Dales and Snowdonia each county has its own seperate Park Planning Committee. Thus in Snowdonia there are Caernarvonshire, Denbighshire and Merionethshire Park Planning Committees. These are then supervised by a Joint Advisory Committee which draws members from each county ; and this body (as its name implies) is solely advisory and has no executive powers. Such a situation – especially in areas with low rate returns – seems likely to make more difficult the planning authorities' task of recognizing the national perspective in planning for the Parks. Only the Peak Park Planning Board has sufficient freedom and – most important – sufficient money to behave in the manner originally envisaged by the proponents of the National Park idea.

The National Parks Commission (later the Countryside Commission) had for long been arguing that the Peak District provided the model on which other Park administration should be patterned, when (in 1969) the Report of the Royal Commission on Local Government in England (Redcliffe-Maud) was published. This Report supported categorically the establishment of special authorities like the Peak Board to run the Parks. So too did the Longland Report, which embodies the opinions of the Countryside Commission and contains a detailed analysis of the weaknesses of alternative forms of Park administration. But the Government was to ignore the advice given to it. In February 1971 the White Paper *Local Government in England* (Cmd 4584) announced less radical amendments to Park administrations. Broadly speaking, the Peak and the Lakes would continue as before, and the rest would be run by single National Park Committees which (in multi-county parks) would be made up of representatives of each county concerned. Each National Park would have its own National Park Officer who would be an employee of the county council (or one of them). The exact status of the National Park Officer is not clearly defined, and there seems to be no provision for the employment of staff specifically for the Park, nor indeed provision for any measure of fiscal independence from the counties.

When applied to Snowdonia (since the provisions obtain in both England and Wales) the reforms have less meaning than in some other Parks for, under local government reorganization, Snowdonia will anyway become a single-county Park falling exclusively within the new Gwynedd authority. It will thus have a National Park Committee with an officer who will presumably report to the Gwynedd County Planning Officer. Administration will certainly be simplified; but the Park will not achieve the measure of independence which has afforded the Peak Park such success.

At the time of writing, however, that is for the future. Rio Tinto-Zinc's ambitions in the Snowdonia National Park were dealt with under the old and more cumbersome system.

Rio Tinto's diamond drills

The interest of Rio Tinto-Zinc in the mineral potential of Snowdonia first became apparent in 1966 when that company began to negotiate terms with the mineral rights' owners in the Coed-y-Brenin (King's Forest) area in the south of the Park. Studies of the nineteenth-century literature which dealt with the extraction of copper from that part of the forest centred on Capel Hermon suggested to the company's geologists that large-scale copper mining might prove a commercially viable proposition. As G. J. Sharp (RTZ's chief geologist in Merioneth) later explained in a company report, they had been particularly interested in an account of the old Turf Copper works near Capel Hermon, where the extraction of copper was achieved in a somewhat crude but effective manner; peat which had been naturally enriched with copper was stripped from a 28 000 m² bog, burnt in kilns and the ashes shipped to Swansea for smelting. In one year a profit of £20 000 was made from the operation. Capel Hermon seemed interesting.

Upon completion of the literature search, RTZ (actually its exploration subsidiary Riofinex) began drafting geologists into the area to undertake prospecting. This they did in a legitimate but extremely secretive fashion, and one which resulted in the local community treating their activities with a great deal of suspicion.

Early in 1968 a Dr M. Mehrtens of RTZ, in his capacity as a private citizen operating from a Somerset address, applied for planning permission to set up a caravan laboratory in the area. His purpose was ostensibly academic: 'The caravan would be used solely as an office and laboratory for analysis of natural substances in connection with the scientific study of geochemical dispersion of elements in rocks and streams in the district.' His researches were complemented by those of a team of field geologists who in May began drainage and soil sampling over an area of about 8 km² between Afon Mawddach and Afon Wen. When asked for whom they were working, the geologists explained to farmers that they were no more than a group of scientists keen on soil sampling. But, in attempts to be as inconspicuous as possible, they developed a marked tendency to encroach upon the land of tenant farmers without first seeking permission – a practice which led to them being collared and identified as employees of the largest mining company in the world – Rio Tinto-Zinc. It is curious, but not so surprising, that, for all its secrecy, RTZ was not able to conceal either its identity or its purpose (for it was known they were after copper) from the tenant farmers of Capel Hermon; but – as one farmer remarked – 'When you dress a wolf in sheep's clothing, don't try to fool a shepherd with him.' In attempting to do so the company made itself immediately unpopular amongst the community.

Why then did the company not take the farmers into their confidence from the outset? Why was there such insistence on the maintenance of secrecy? The normal answer advanced by mining companies is that commercial practice dictates that one mining company does everything in its power to conceal its activities from another lest the latter realizes that the former is on to something and decides to compete in the same location. In real practice, however, an exploration geologist or rock mechanics man working, say, for Norrander-Kerr on one side of a hill not only knows what his opposite number from a rival company is doing on the other side, but is positively keen to tell anyone who professes an interest exactly what his competitor is up to. Nothing seems to please a prospector more than to keep mum about his own operations but to discover and spill the beans about those of his rivals. But this still does not explain the need to attempt to conceal what is happening from the local residents. When asked whether this sort of secrecy was really necessary, Mr Roy Wright (vice chairman of RTZ) said that it was not – indeed that it was no more than 'a habit in the mining world'. Secrecy, however, as we shall see, did bestow one dubious benefit on RTZ which tends to make Mr Wright's statement seem less than candid – for the less that was known of their operations then the more likely it was that they could proceed with the next stage without interference from the local and county councils.

In the course of 1968 RTZ discovered that the Turf Copper prospect formed but a small part of a much larger geochemical anomaly ; and geophysical work which was begun late in 1968 indicated that 'low-grade copper mineralization of importance might exist'. By January 1969 RTZ had embarked upon what proved to be one of their most controversial undertakings in the course of the Capel Hermon affair. Without making application to the County Planning Office for permission, or even informing them, the company began drilling, first in the Coed-y-Brenin and later in open country. Farmers and the Forestry Commission were approached for permission to drill on their land. Where access was granted drilling went ahead, but in some cases it was refused. Cyril Jones, a Capel Hermon tenant farmer, refused to have anything to do with RTZ when he heard that they did not have planning permission to drill on his land, and in consequence the company's drilling contractors went ahead with a series of holes all along the field boundary of his land and uncomfortably close to his house. Since official planning permission had not been sought, no restrictions were placed on the work of the drillers, and sometimes drilling went on all day and all night, regardless of the needs of the sheep, which were about to drop their lambs, and of the residents, whose sleep was constantly interrupted by the whine from the rigs.

RTZ has maintained throughout (and apparently still maintains) that it had complied with the Town and Country Planning Act 1962, and that permission to drill was not required ; and it was not until nearly a year later – in December 1969 – that the County Council was informed by the company of its activities in the Hermon area. In April of that year RTZ's drills located the body of low-grade copper mineralization which had been indicated by its surveys. In June 1969 a third party – not RTZ – tipped off the County Planning Office that holes were being drilled in the forest. But between June and December, when the Council was officially informed, the County Planning Office did not issue an enforcement notice restraining the company. The reasons for this are curious. As was subsequently shown, Merioneth Planning Office was decidedly of the opinion that drilling operations (since they constituted engineering operations) needed planning consent. They therefore sent a representative to Coed-y-Brenin to establish what was happening there. When he, Mr Lazarus, met the drillers, they informed him that their operations would be completed in one week's time. This information he communicated to the Planning Office which decided (understandably) not to bother with an enforcement notice since the activities were to cease so soon. But it appears that, when the drill operators told Mr Lazarus they were finishing in a week, they were referring not to the whole programme, but rather to the time during which one particular drill rig would continue working in one particular location. Each of the four rigs moved around roughly every month, and the drilling programme proceeded, unrestricted by the Planning Office even though it seems likely that they would have known unofficially that work was still being undertaken. It was not until 20 January 1970 that representatives of RTZ and Merioneth County Council actually met.

The 'calling in'

The copper drilling programme was not the only one to be pursued by RTZ in Southern Snowdonia in the course of 1969. At about the time the drills were starting up in Capel Hermon, geologists were busily taking sediment samples from the tributaries leading into the Mawddach Estuary. The prize this time was gold.

The Mawddach Estuary runs from Dolgellau to Barmouth and lies almost entirely within the Snowdonia National Park. The prismatic qualities of the meandering river throw a kaleidoscope of colours at the eyes of those who see it. Tennyson, Ruskin, Shelley and many others have heaped praise on this 16 km stretch running westwards to the north of Cader Idris. Ruskin is on record as saying: 'There is but one finer walk in Europe than the walk from Dolgellau to Barmouth, and that is the walk from Barmouth to Dolgellau.' To say that it is beautiful is to do the estuary scant justice; to have predicted an outcry when RTZ's interest in mining alluvial gold from beneath the silt was made public would have constituted no more than an articulation of the obvious.

When, in January 1970, RTZ personnel met with members of the Merioneth County Planning Office, they explained that work had been undertaken in an attempt to prove the presence of winnable gold in the estuary and copper in Capel Hermon. The County Planning Officer, Cyril Tuck, stressed that the company had need of planning permission for drilling in Capel Hermon and recommended that they filed an appropriate application forthwith. Between January and April 1970, representatives of the County Council and RTZ held a series of meetings in which the company laid great emphasis on the employment benefits which could accompany later mining operations. Drilling continued, and no application for permission was filed. By April the County Planning Office was concerned that, although outline schemes of the manner in which mining might proceed if the deposits proved viable had been described, RTZ had provided the Office with nothing on paper. The County Clerk therefore informed the company that, unless it gave details in a written form, he himself would write up his notes of what had been said and present them for the information of the Council. On 6 April (with twenty-four holes having been drilled at and around Capel Hermon) RTZ prepared two papers, one entitled 'Exploration at Coed-y-Brenin', dated 6 April 1970 and bearing the name of G. J. Sharp, and one entitled 'Proposed Exploration for Alluvial Gold in the Mawddach Estuary, Merioneth, Wales', bearing neither date nor details of authorship. These were sent to the County Clerk and were received on 29 April 1970.

The Mawddach paper stated quite clearly that 'while detailed proposals for an eventual full-scale dredging operation cannot be developed at this stage, the likely methods and implications have been considered'. These methods included the deepening of the main channel of the Estuary, the construction of a gravel embankment across the Estuary mouth (with sluice gates and salmon ladders and perhaps carrying a road), and the operation of a dredger 96 m long, 24 m wide and 24 m high. The dredging operations would take 10–20 years and tailings (waste) would be discharged over previously dredged areas. The report recommended that the dredger's 'colour can be chosen to blend in with the background', and concluded that 'contrary to common opinion, far from detracting from local amenities, the operating dredge could become a tourist attraction'.

The Coed-y-Brenin report was less dramatic, stating only that 'should a mining operation result from the exploration work, there is little doubt that it would be on a large scale'. These two documents were to cause RTZ some considerable embarrassment in the months to come.

Throughout the discussions which led to the submission of these papers to the County Planning Office, the Merionethshire staff were generally sympathetic but a little sceptical of RTZ's plans for the area. The papers included no mention of employment opportunities but, at the same time that they were sent, RTZ was involved in similar discussions with the Dolgellau Rural District Council, which was understandably extremely preoccupied with job prospects and initially very sympathetic to RTZ. Again the company played on the question of employment and, although it again proved reluctant to commit promises to paper, it did address a full meeting of the Rural Council where its predictions of 1000 temporary jobs and 500 permanent ones were minuted. As Bryn William-Jones, Clerk to that Council, explained quite candidly, it was the company's estimated staff requirement – and that alone – which won it the Council's support.

On 28 April 1970, Rio Tinto-Zinc submitted applications to the Dol-gellau RDC for shallow geological drilling to a depth of 450 m in the Coed-y-Brenin, and to Dolgellau RDC and Barmouth UDC for shallow geological drilling to a depth of not more than 90 m in the River Mawd-dach estuary bed. The applications were passed to the Merioneth County Council for consideration. On 12 May, the Merioneth Park Planning Committee was informed of an application 'out of accord' with the County Development Plan, and on 29 May Mr Tuck, the County Planning Officer, wrote to the Secretary of State for Wales asking for the application to be 'called in'. Permission for drilling had still not been granted, but drilling continued unchecked.

The procedure whereby applications can be 'called in' is straight-forward; if a particular application for planning permission is deemed by a local planning authority to be of national importance, then that authority can ask the responsible Minister, at his discretion, to 'call in' the applica-tion and to deal with it himself. This the Minister will do if he agrees that the matter under consideration is indeed of national importance. On 13 July 1970, the Secretary of State for Wales indicated that this was his view of the RTZ application by directing that this should be referred to him. The application was passed over on 24 July. But no restraining order was issued to Rio Tinto-Zinc. Hence, although the Secretary of State had announced his intention personally to deal with RTZ's application for permission to do what it was doing anyway, the company continued to drill.

Meanwhile, in June 1970, the County Planning Committee were trying to make up their minds whether to support or to oppose the granting of planning permission. On 12 June, the Snowdonia National Park Joint Advisory Committee met, and were advised by their planning consultant, Professor Allen, to recommend to the Merioneth Park Planning Com-mittee that they should oppose the granting of permission. The major concern of the County Planning Officer was whether, although per-mission would be confined to the drilling of boreholes for the purposes of exploration, the granting of such permission could be construed as sup-porting possible exploitation afterwards. That the application had been called in appeared to suggest that this might be the case; a Minister would not spend time deciding whether a few score holes should be drilled unless the possible implications of successful drilling were uppermost in his mind. On 15 June 1970, Mr Tuck received a letter from Sir Lyn Ungoed-Thomas which convinced him that permission should be opposed. Writing from the Royal Courts of Justice, Sir Lyn argued: 'This is the thin end of the wedge; the consent inevitably carries the implication that, if it is worthwhile, permission for development will be granted'. When Mr Tuck put this point to the Clerk of the County Council, who was also a solicitor, the Clerk replied that this might well be the case. The County Council resolved to oppose RTZ's application.

The normal course of events which is followed after the calling in of an application is for the Minister responsible to announce a public inquiry at which both proponents and opponents of a particular development can communicate their views to the presiding inspector. In the run-in to the inquiry, interested parties assemble their case. Thus in July and August Rio Tinto-Zinc conducted an opinion survey in the Capel Hermon area; visitors were asked why and how frequently they visited the place and what they would think of a proposal to mine copper. Interestingly, the results of this survey were never published, although undoubtedly, had they been favourable to the company's proposed activities, they would have provided useful ammunition at the ensuing inquiry. It can only be concluded that the answers received differed from those for which the company hoped.

By October 1970, the fact that RTZ was still drilling without permission, three months after the Secretary of State had undertaken to decide whether they should, had become a source of embarrassment to the Welsh Office. Accordingly, RTZ was instructed to stop drilling. The contractors had by then been drilling in and around Capel Hermon with neither planning control nor permission for nearly two years. Drilling finally ceased in November, by which date the company's tally was forty-eight holes – no mean feat in Snowdonia, where an ordinary farmer must run a gauntlet of planning procedures to get permission to put up a shed.

When RTZ made its application to drill, it forwarded to the County Council maps of the area around Capel Hermon in which it was interested. On 23 October, it had to revise its application, since the original area had included National Trust land. Negotiations with the Trust over mineral rights had met with failure and hence the Trust property had to be excluded. On the same day the Welsh Office gave notice of the public inquiry. Advertisements to this effect appeared in local papers in November, and an inquiry was scheduled for 15–18 December, to be held in the Assizes Court in Dolgellau.

Tinker and Byers

In the months leading up to the public inquiry, a tremendous amount of attention was focused by conservation organizations and the national press on the question of whether opencast mining on the scale envisaged should be permitted in a National Park. The Rambler's Association, the Youth Hostels Association and many others lined up against RTZ. Friends of the Earth (FOE) set up a research team to campaign against the granting of permission to mine. Articles appeared in the *Sunday Times*, the *Observer*, the *Guardian*, the *Liverpool Daily Post* and all the local papers which command a readership in North Wales. The articles themselves and the letters which followed voiced abhorrence at the idea of digging up Snowdonia and Rio Tinto-Zinc was (often irrationally) portrayed as a company which cynically spent a great deal of money on propaganda about its concern for the environment whilst at the same time, and in a secretive fashion, setting about dismantling it. Things came to a head in November with the publication (on the 12th) in *New Scientist* of an article by Jon Tinker entitled 'Snowdonia cops it'.

Tinker wrote the article following a meeting which he had with Lord Byers, who was then the RTZ director with responsibility for exploration, chairman of Riofinex (which subsidiary company was conducting the investigations of Capel Hermon and the Mawddach), ex-chairman of the Liberal Party and leader of that Party in the House of Lords. According to Tinker, Byers told him over lunch in the RTZ boardroom that he 'would loathe to see opencast mining in *all* our National Parks. But in two or three it would be OK.' But another, more important, line led Tinker to guess correctly the outcome of RTZ's prospecting applications. Byers apparently said (and did not later deny): 'We can go anywhere else in the world for our gold; so far as I'm concerned you can have the Mawddach.' Tinker put two and two together and came up with four; the Mawddach scheme was the cover for the much more important copper development in Capel Hermon. By making applications for drilling rights both in the Mawddach (which they had not drilled) and in Capel Hermon (which they had), the company was successfully concentrating the great weight of public indignation on the former, less hopeful and less lucrative prospect. The public inquiry would concentrate on the Mawddach and, whatever decisions were reached about limitations on drilling, if the go-ahead were given in both localities, all of the resources available to the conservation organizations would be employed in defence of the estuary. Capel Hermon would be lost by default. The FOE team, however, had reached a similar conclusion and resolved to focus all their attention on the Capel Hermon prospect.

A final point of interest which arose in the Tinker–Byers conversation was that, according to RTZ, it was actually encouraged to prospect in Capel Hermon by the late Ministry of Technology.

Three weeks later, *New Scientist* gave Lord Byers a page in their magazine in which to reply to Tinker's accusations. Counter-accusations of misreporting, misrepresentation and journalistic invention flew thick and fast, and Byers took specific exception to Tinker's statement that there existed at Capel Hermon, 'thousands of millions of tons of low-grade ore with a copper content of 0·5 per cent'. He concluded: '*New Scientist*'s biology correspondent has apparently divined this by some technique other than deep drilling, unknown to mining companies, which would make him a public benefactor if he divulged it, and render the present planning inquiry unnecessary.' But, evidently unbeknown to Byers, Friends of the Earth, Tinker and very few other interested parties, had got hold of RTZ's 'confidential' report on the Capel Hermon copper prospect, in which the surface dimensions of the ore body were given. Also RTZ had told the County Council the likely pit-depths and indicated the likely copper-richness of the ore. Elementary calculations based on this information led to Tinker's conclusion; it was not based on what Byers had said, but neither was it journalistic invention. However, it later became clear that Tinker's figures relied on what proved to be an optimistic forecast of copper concentration; had he said hundreds of thousands of tons at 0·3 per cent, he would have been spot on.

Lord Byers was understandably angry that he had been quoted as saying that, whilst he did not like the idea of parts of all National Parks being dug up, he thought it would be OK in one or two. This he described as 'a fabrication and at odds with the views I hold'; but, when challenged to make clear the views which he did hold, Byers declined to respond. 'RTZ policy is crystal clear', he wrote. 'We are conservationists. We are also miners.' Further than that he could not go.

Some time after his original article appeared, Jon Tinker received a letter from MinTech's successor, the Department of Trade and Industry, in which Lord Byers's claim that the old Ministry of Technology had actively encouraged RTZ's interest in Capel Hermon was refuted. The letter runs: 'RTZ commenced work on their copper prospect as far back as 1966. Their interest in North Wales was the result of their own thinking and researches ... RTZ have not been advised by MinTech about the question of planning permission for exploratory borings or any other aspect of their operation.' Things seemed anything but 'crystal clear'.

The public inquiry

On 15 December 1970 the public inquiry opened in Dolgellau. Mr C. Hilton, Her Majesty's Inspector, Sir Andrew Bryan, mining assessor, and Dr E. H. Francis, geological adviser, took their places before the various supporters and opponents of the drilling application. Representatives and witnesses of the company, the County Council, Local Councils, Amenity Societies, farmers and landowners, lawyers and pressmen crowded the hall. The Inspector could not speak Welsh, the press could not write because they did not have a table (and complained bitterly), comfort went out of the window when the last participants came in the door, and the people at the back could not hear. The scene was set for the final irony; for no one could agree what they were there to discuss.

Mr Martin Thomas, the lawyer representing the Mawddach Association (an amenity society concerned with the conservation of the estuary) stressed that his clients felt strongly that the inquiry should concern itself not solely with the question of whether a few small-diameter holes should be drilled, but with the possible and likely effects of permission being given for dredging, were the estuary bed to be proved to hold minable gold. His clients (and the same held true for those opposing developments at Capel Hermon) were of the opinion that now was the time to consider the wider implications of the potential mining programme. Mr Goodfellow, the Queen's Counsel retained by Rio Tinto-Zinc, expressed the opposite view: 'We propose ... to restrict our submissions and our evidence to those matters which, rightly or wrongly, we believe to be relevant to these applications.' In the case of Coed-y-Brenin (Capel Hermon), RTZ sought permission to drill 'approximately forty to fifty holes' in an area of 2475 acres [about 10^7 m^2], using mobile derricks (which would take on average twenty-eight days to drill each hole, the maximum depth of which would be 450 m). The declared purpose was to 'seek to obtain information as to the extent and quality of copper mineralization within this application area'. Since the company did not have the necessary information, it could not – at this stage – decide whether to apply for permission to mine. Counsel therefore concluded that any questions relating to mining fell outside the scope of this inquiry. The same argument for the drilling alone to be considered was applied to the application to drill to a depth of 90 m in the 1775 acres [about 7×10^6 m^2] of the Mawddach between Penmaen toll bridge and the Barmouth railway bridge.

Mr Goodfellow then gave the reasons why his clients had drilled in Coed-y-Brenin without the benefit of planning permission: 'We did not believe – and we do not believe – that we strictly need ask for planning permission for these particular drilling operations.' The 1962 Town and Country Planning Act defines the types of developments for which planning permission need be sought, one type being development by way of operation and the other by way of change of use (of land). Mr Goodfellow affirmed that the drilling constituted an operation as defined in part of Section 12 (i) of the Act, where reference is made to the 'carrying out of building, engineering, mining or other operations in, or over or under land'. But, Mr Goodfellow argued, in the course of drilling a hole to a depth of 100 feet [30 m] and removing the core, one is only shifting five cubic feet [0·14 m^3] of earth, 'which is roughly equivalent to what could be put in an ordinary garden barrow'. A 1500 foot [450 m] hole would only account for fifteen barrowloads. Since the degree of change to the land is minimal it was decided (by the company) that planning permission need not be sought.

R T Z's counsel proceeded to explain that, if his interpretations of the law were not right, 'some very curious consequences might follow. Because if one goes out into one's garden to dig a little to put one's compost in, and digs it [sic] five feet [1·5 m] long by three feet [0·9 m] wide by five feet [1·5 m] deep, you [sic] move the volume of material which is broadly equivalent to a drill hole of 1500 feet [450 m] in depth . . . if what I have been submitting is not right, then before you dig a compost pit in your garden, you ought to apply for planning permission.'

Now Mr Goodfellow is, of course, free to hold whatever opinions of the law he chooses, and if he wishes to regard drilling, which is clearly and strictly an engineering operation, as no more than a sophisticated way of removing a few barrowloads of earth, then so be it; but in his later remarks he made clear that in certain cases drilling does require planning permission. For instance, deeper drilling (to 6000 feet [1200 m]) for oil or natural gas does (in Goodfellow's opinion) merit an application for permission; shallower drilling (to 1500 feet [450 m]) for copper does not. This somewhat curious argument echoes that of Lord Byers when he wrote in the *New Scientist*: 'Legal advice taken by R T Z indicates that the initial shallow scout drilling with small rigs does not require planning permission, but concentrated and deeper drilling does do so.' Yet R T Z chose to file an application for drilling to 90 m in the Estuary, while at the same time choosing to drill without permission to greater depths in Coed-y-Brenin. If R T Z was indeed advised that it was all a matter of degree and that depth was the important criterion, then its actions indicate that it chose to ignore this advice.

Mr Goodfellow concluded his opening address by emphasizing that, whether they needed to or not, his clients had applied for permission to drill and were prepared to deal with questions related to the drilling, but were not prepared to discuss hypothetical questions relating to later mining. He disagreed with the Local Planning Authority's contention that 'the present applications cannot be considered separately from the probability of exploitation and extraction of minerals'. The witnesses he would call were competent to speak on the effects of the drilling alone. If others wanted to address themselves to hypothetical questions then he had no objection, but the applicant company would not do so. However, Mr Watkin Powell, acting for the County Council, insisted that it would be absurd to restrict the scope of the inquiry in such a way as to exclude from consideration the likely effects of successful drilling programmes, which effects would require massive amendment to the current development plan.

Unless the Inspector directed him otherwise, he intended to cross-examine witnesses on issues not confined to mere matters of drilling and preliminary exploration. In this he was supported by two other solicitors representing interested parties. Mr Thomas (for the Mawddach Association) observed that in the case of a recent inquiry held to decide whether (in the Dulas Valley) permission should be given for trial borings designed to provide information needed to assess the feasibility of constructing a dam there, the wider implications of drilling were in fact considered, and the application refused. He was of the opinion that the wider aspects of the current applications should be similarly examined.

The Inspector, on the other hand, felt bound to follow the conflicting precedent set in the case of an application made by Home Oil of Canada for permission to undertake exploratory drilling for oil and natural gas in North Yorkshire – the so-called Westerdale case. Here, although the Inspector reported on the possible repercussions of a successful exploration programme, the Minister chose to disregard the Inspector's conclusions on these matters and concluded that the 'application falls to be considered solely in its own terms'. Mr Hilton agreed with this ruling when applied to the case before him, and thought it likely that, if he were to report on wider issues (which he would allow to be discussed), his findings on these matters would be disregarded by the Minister.

There then followed an interesting exchange of views between the opponents of the application and RTZ's counsel. Mr Powell (for the County Council) contended that the reason for the calling in was that the drilling operations formed a part of a development which threatened the policy of the National Parks and Access to the Countryside Act. The issue was of national importance precisely because it involved more than just a few holes in the ground. When Mr Goodfellow stood firm, Powell raised the question of the two reports prepared by RTZ which dealt, in the case of the Mawddach, with the methods which could be employed in dredging operations and, in the case of Coed-y-Brenin, with mining. These documents had been received by the County Council as long ago as April 1970, dealt with more than just the drilling programmes, and were highly relevant to the conduct of the inquiry. Had these documents been forwarded to the Secretary of State?

Mr Goodfellow was not pleased that Mr Powell chose to refer to these reports: 'Of course the Secretary of State has not been given any such document, nor will he be given any such document, because it is irrelevant.' The documents were provided to the County Council on a confidential basis. 'I am bound to say that, having regard to the basis on which they were originally provided, I am somewhat surprised to find my friend Mr Powell has been instructed to refer to them publicly, but he has and there it is. My instructions are to the contrary and quite clear.' In discussing the question of confidentiality, Mr Powell cited a letter written by RTZ to the County Council on 12 March 1970 which read : 'I hope to let you have a brief resumé of the statements made on behalf of RTZ during the early part of next week. This will be in draft form for you to approve so that it can be submitted with the planning applications which are in course of preparation. I apologize for the delay.' Mr Powell was clearly of the opinion that the document referred to was one or other (or both) of the Reports received in April. Mr Goodfellow was adamant that this was not the case and that the letter referred to 'possible draft statements in relation to matters relevant to this inquiry', though precisely what these were he did not say.

After the lunchtime adjournment, the argument about what was and was not relevant was renewed. It was proposed that, since the Secretary of State had called in the application and hence clearly considered the matter as of national importance, the inquiry should adjourn pending a decision from the Minister as to the desired scope of the inquiry. Mr Goodfellow replied : 'If we are right, it will be quite wrong that the decision on this inquiry should be delayed because people want to get a decision from the Secretary of State about matters which, on this view of the matter, are irrelevant at this stage.' The Inspector decided not to adjourn, to allow people both to address themselves to whatever they considered relevant, and to refuse to address themselves to those matters which they considered not to be relevant. He would take notes and report on all that was said. The Minister would decide whether to take notice of the various parts of his report.

What the Inspector did not make public was that there actually had been a conference held at the Welsh Office the previous October, to decide the procedure to be adopted at this inquiry, and at which matters such as the scope of the inquiry must surely have been discussed. The procedural wrangle in Dolgellau, which took up more than one half of one day of a four-day public inquiry, raises some interesting questions. The 1962 Town and Country Planning Act requires the determining authority (in this case the Minister) to take into account 'the provisions of the development plan, so far as material to the application and ... any other material considerations.' It is apparently for the determining body itself to decide what construction should be placed on the word 'material'. In the case of the Dolgellau inquiry, if, on receipt of the Inspector's report, the Secretary of State for Wales were to form the opinion that questions of possible mining were themselves material, he would then have to decide whether the information contained in the report provided sufficient basis for a decision. The Inspector's report would (and did) contain reference to the beauty of the Mawddach and of Capel Hermon, their amenity and tourist value, but would not (and did not) contain evidence of the methods of mineral extraction which could be employed (since RTZ refused to reply to questions related to such extraction). The Minister would thus be unable to decide upon the merits of the application to explore, and would presumably have to order another inquiry to elicit relevant information. The decision of the Inspector to permit the applicant company to confine itself only to the narrower question of drilling presented the Minister with a simple choice : either to consider drilling in isolation from the possible effects of successful prospecting, or to reconvene the public inquiry. The discretion of the Minister in these matters is absolute, and any attempt to challenge his decision on the grounds that he has misdirected himself on a point of law – that is, to show that all material considerations had not been taken into account – would probably mean an appeal to the House of Lords. The appellant would have to have standing in law (be seen to be an injured party), and would in practice have to be affluent enough to fight the thing through. Hence it would seem that judicial review of decisions made is severely circumscribed.

The Dolgellau inquiry proceeded, and the application to drill in the Mawddach Estuary was considered first. Mr Greenleaves, the RTZ geologist called to give evidence on the estuary proposal, was closely cross-examined by the representatives of RTZ's opponents, not least on the questions of possible dredging and the release of toxic metal salts from tailings in the course of this operation. Since dredging and its ecological consequences were beyond his competence, Greenleaves could not provide specific answers, but he did stress that the odds were about 100 : 1 against the gold deposits being proved commercially viable. The chances of mining copper from Capel Hermon were by comparison very much greater, but the idea that the company had filed application for drilling in both areas in order to draw fire away from the Capel Hermon prospect he said was totally without foundation, adding that 'in many ways there are disadvantages in considering them together'.

Greenleaves was on the stand all afternoon and, apart from his exchanges with Mr D. R. Jones (acting for Dolgellau Rural District Council, who were favourably disposed to the company's intentions) was subjected to a barrage of questions which he had affirmed he was unable to answer, and which resulted in this final interchange with RTZ's counsel, Mr Goodfellow :

Q Mr Greenleaves, perhaps we can just get it clear: you are not a dredging expert ?

A No, sir.

Q You are not an ecologist ?

A No, sir.
Q Nor an expert on wild life ?
A No, sir.
Q Nor a chemist ?
A No, sir.
Q Nor a marine biologist ?
A No, sir.
Q Just a poor geologist ?
A Yes, sir.

The question-and-answer session, as recorded, is both understandable and touching, but primarily serves to illustrate the frustration caused to the objectors who sought reassurance about wild life, toxic metal salts and so on. If RTZ's witness could not comment on these matters then, in the objectors' opinion, the company should put up other witnesses who could. The objectors were determined that all possible implications should be discussed and to this end, in the course of his cross-examination, Mr Powell had skilfully placed before the witness the report which RTZ was so keen to keep confidential and which dealt with possible dredging applications. As Mr Greenleaves left the stand, Mr Powell moved to 'put in' the document, that is, to give it to the Inspector to pass on to the Secretary of State. He argued that, since it had been referred to in cross-examination and was before the witness, it had to be accepted as part of the evidence. The first day ended with Mr Powell convinced that the document had gone in, and with Mr Goodfellow determined to debate the matter before it did.

The second day, however, did not commence with the renewal of that particular discussion. Instead, Mr Goodfellow called a chartered surveyor, Mr A. J. Duncan, who had familiarized himself with the Mawddach proposals on which he was to be examined. Mr Duncan affirmed quite positively that proposals of the type made by RTZ were 'never the subject of individual applications'. Evidently, drilling for gas, oil and potash might be the subject of such application, but in his experience of drilling for 'limestone, loadstone, sand and gravel', small-scale drilling fell outside the scope of drilling applications, so RTZ did not really need to apply for permission to drill in the Mawddach. Why this should be so when no specific reference is made in the Act either to the scale or to the nature of the material being investigated was not made clear. Indeed, in his submissions, Mr Duncan pointed out that an application for drilling by the Institute of Geological Sciences (IGS) was in fact granted by the Merioneth County Council, and the drilling here was larger scale – more akin to the sort of drilling used in evaluating potash. The inference was that, if the planning authority gave the nod to the IGS, why should they make so much fuss over RTZ's proposals. One reason had, of course, already been made plain: the Council did make a distinction between the implications of academic research and commercial evaluation. However, there is also a second reason for looking at the two applications in different lights. The drilling to which Mr Duncan referred was for a single bore hole whereas, in their application, Rio Tinto-Zinc did not restrict itself to any number of holes: the application was open ended. Finally, the fact that the IGS proposal was the subject of an application illustrates that both the County Council and the IGS are of the opinion that the drilling of a single (admittedly deep) hole required the granting of permission. If the applicant company wanted to maintain that it was really all a question of scale of operations involved in a proposal which dictated whether permission was required, then – for them – this precedent was a singularly unfortunate one. A planning authority which deemed that a single deep hole required permission could not be expected formally to turn a blind eye to the drilling of an unquantified number of shallower ones, and neither did it.

In the course of Mr Duncan's testimony, which was as hamstrung as that of others by the witness's inability to address himself to broader issues, a further interesting point was made. The witness advanced the argument that 'the advantage to be gained, not only by the company but by the country as a whole, in furthering the geological knowledge of the area, would seem to me far to outweigh any possible argument that these operations . . . ought not to be permitted for amenity reasons.' Counsel cross-examining Mr Duncan did not have at his disposal the means of taking issue with him on this affirmation, but Mr Francis, the mining assessor, did ask him what he meant by it. Duncan suggested that since this was not his field (even though it was he who had made the statement), the question should be referred to the RTZ geologists – either to Mr Greenleaves, who had been called in connection with the estuary, or to Mr G. J. Sharp who would be dealing with Coed-y-Brenin. The actual position is that information gained from bore holes over 30 m in depth is given to the Institute of Geological Sciences in confidence, and is not made public without the approval of the company concerned. The country as a whole does not have unrestricted access to this data; and neither would objectors to later mining proposals.

The desirability of acquiring greater geological knowledge of the structure of the National Park was also raised by the County Planning Officer, Mr Tuck. Up to June 1970 and the meeting of the Snowdonia National Park Joint Advisory Committee, Mr Tuck was of the opinion that drilling should be permitted in the interest of such acquisition of information. But soon afterwards Mr Tuck began to reconsider his position and, following the advice given to the Advisory Committee by their planning consultant, Professor Allen, and the letter received from Sir Lyn Ungoed-Thomas, the county planner changed his mind. He took the view that the application to drill could not be considered in isolation from potential mineral extraction. The County Council resolved to oppose the application and advised the Minister to call it in.

The County Planning Officer regarded the exploration and exploitation phases as inextricably linked parts of a single development, and argued that, if prospecting were successful, there would be irresistible pressures to win whatever was there. Such was the devastation caused to neighbouring areas by earlier extractive industry, that it was his opinion that to permit the inception of a fifteen-year programme which would destroy the estuary would constitute a great mistake. For the sake of profit, and profit for fifteen years – the figure given to Mr Tuck by RTZ – an entirely alien intrusion threatened the area, posing 'a sad fate to overtake an estuary which has been famous for centuries for its beauty'.

Mr D. F. Jones, representing the Dolgellau Rural District Council, which supported the application, made much of Mr Tuck's change of mind and accused the County Planner of refusing to 'stick to his guns'. As Tuck replied, his choice was between appearing 'feeble and vacillating' by changing his mind in the light of new information or advice, or appearing 'stubborn and obstinate' by refusing to do so. But on one matter he took issue with the Dolgellau RDC. They had written that 'in lending its support (to the RTZ application) ... the (Dolgellau) Council is fully aware of the unwelcome and indeed unwarranted publicity which this application has engendered.' With those sentiments, Mr Tuck had no sympathy whatsoever. No matter what the views of the Council may be, he concurred with the findings of the Skeffington Committee that the widest possible publicity should be given such matters – a point emphasized by Professor Allen in his evidence which followed.

Professor Allen was of the opinion that drilling for minerals in National Parks was contrary to the intentions which led to their designation – whereupon Mr Goodfellow promptly quoted a part of page 39 of *Government Selected Planning Appeals* for 1963 : 'Minerals can be worked only where they are found. The fact that proposed workings may be situated in a National Park or an area of outstanding natural beauty is not in itself sufficient to justify refusal of permission.' To that, Professor Allen could only reply that there was an urgent need for the Countryside Commission to 'establish on a national scale a policy (covering mineral development) which would apply to all National Parks.'

Mr D. F. Jones, for Dolgellau RDC, put it to Professor Allen that he was concerned about the well-being of visitors to the area to the exclusion of that of the residents even if the latter 'cannot get bread to eat and cannot work to get that bread'. Professor Allen's reply adequately sums up the case made by RTZ's opponents on the question of mining as a source of employment :

I am as concerned about the welfare of the people of South Merioneth as I hope you are. Let us make it quite clear that the problem of depopulation of upland areas is not peculiar to South Merioneth. It is a national problem and it is for this reason that I am strongly supporting any move for industry to be introduced into the National Park which is suitable for a National Park. This is the whole of my point. I am not suggesting there should be unemployment here or that there should be no opportunities for employment, but I would like to see the kind of employment in which the young child at school can study at school with the hope of getting progressive employment, with progressive promotion, within his own county. That is very different from providing a few years' work for the lower-paid workers of the county who will then at the end of the period of employment go back on the dole. I am looking for permanent employment with progressive opportunities for promotion. . .

It was Professor Allen's contention that greater overall benefit accrues from smaller-scale long-term stable employment than can be brought by shorter-term forms of job provision.

As evidenced by the cross-examination conducted by Mr D. F. Jones, it was not only the opponents of drilling who were vitally concerned with the implications of successful exploration. On the third day of the inquiry, Mr D. W. Williams, County Secretary of the Merioneth Branch of the NFU bore this out. His County Committee was in favour of the proposal to drill the estuary since successful drilling might eventually (with the installation of barrages, and operation of dredgers) reclaim parts of the estuary for agricultural purposes. Mr Williams lamented the fact that where once there was 'waving corn and the hum of threshing machines you now have bullrush and wild duck'. To those objectors who, while liking waving corn, also appreciate bullrushes and wild duck, Mr Williams view seemed narrow, but his position was understood ; he was a farmer, and he wanted more land to be farmed. Since Mr Williams was able only to attend the inquiry on this single occasion, he was permitted to comment at this stage on the Capel Hermon copper prospect. Here, however, his desire to conserve farming interests seemed less apparent. Admittedly, Mr Williams made it clear that long-term questions must be carefully considered before giving an opinion, but his statement that Capel Hermon's 'plain full-time farming interests are now very slight' indicated to Capel Hermon tenant farmers who would be ousted from their holdings in the event of mining that they should expect little help from the NFU apart from advice about the appropriate level of compensation. 'Agricultural erosion has occurred in the area in question some quarter of a century ago with the vast Forestry Commission plantation at Coed-y-Brenin,' Mr Williams said. Were mining to complete the process of erosion, the NFU seemed unlikely even to express concern.

There followed statements by interested parties either supporting or opposing the estuary drilling programme, one of which, that of Mr I. M. Jones for the Barmouth Council, was of particular interest since his was one council which supported the proposals. Mr Jones made it clear that the Barmouth Council shared the opinion held by the County Planning Officer before he became convinced that drilling was the thin end of the wedge ending in large-scale gold extraction. Were the Council to have been similarly advised it might have been that their attitude would have been different. The implication was clearly that RTZ would be foolish to rely on Barmouth Urban District Council for support in the event of applying for permission to dredge.

That part of the inquiry dealing with the estuary ended in the mid-afternoon of the third day with the evidence of those 'conservation' organizations – the YHA, the Ramblers' Association and the CPRW – each of which opposed both drilling and the possible development of large-scale extraction.

In his evidence on the Capel Hermon copper prospect, Mr G. J. Sharp (of RTZ) described the functioning of diamond drilling rigs, the operation of each of which requires ideally 25 m^2 in which to house pipe storage, a portable shelter, pumps and the drill itself. Mr Sharp affirmed that evaluation of cores already taken was not complete, so no hard information on what had been found was available. The duration of each hole-drilling exercise had been found to vary between nine days (for a 90 m hole) and 109 days (for a 250 m hole); sometimes the crews had worked a night shift but normally a twelve-hour day was worked from 07·00 hours to 19·00 hours. The noise of the drills had in no case been distinguishable from background levels at distances greater than 180 m.

Mr Sharp admitted in cross-examination that his company had accelerated their drilling programme since applying for permission to undertake drilling; between January 1969 and April 1970 they drilled twenty-four holes, and between April and December 1970 managed another twenty-four. Complaints had been received from local residents about the conduct of the drilling operations, but Mr Sharp considered these to be 'generally minor'.

Beyond agreeing (somewhat reluctantly) that, if copper were to be extracted, the form the mining would take would be opencast, Mr Sharp was unable to comment on possible mining plans. But he was able to say that in the many months (including the tourist season) during which he had worked in the small area around Capel Hermon, he had seen no more than five visitors. This submission greatly surprised many objectors present at the inquiry, not least a representative of the Merseyside Naturalists' Association, who four times each year leads expeditions of fifty people around precisely that area. Finally, on the question of whether the drilling application was open-ended in that it specified neither the number of holes nor the total duration of the programme, Mr Sharp agreed with the Inspector that the application was of a somewhat open nature and did not even specify the number of rigs to be operated at any one time. Counsel for RTZ immediately suggested, subject to later instruction, that the Inspector himself consider imposing a limit on the number of rigs and the duration of the programme – an idea which was welcomed by Mr Powell (for the County Council) who nevertheless reaffirmed his clients' rejection of the whole drilling proposal. After receiving instructions, Mr Goodfellow proposed four rigs for twelve months in Capel Hermon and two rigs for the same period in the estuary. It was further proposed that the drills should run from 07·00 to 19·00 hours, six days a week.

The next witness to be called by the applicants was Mr A. J. Duncan, the surveyor, who repeated most of the opinions he had previously given in connection with the estuary application ; he saw no reason for the company to have to apply for permission to drill and no grounds on which, such applications having been made, permission should be refused. Mr Duncan believed that to refuse drilling in a National Park on the grounds that it was noisy would lead logically to the County Council also prohibiting many farming and forestry activities which were also noisy. Furthermore Mr Duncan said that 'from his own inspection' the area did not receive many visitors, though under cross-examination he had to admit that he had been to the area only four times – twice outside the holiday season – and that he had no way of telling which of the people he saw were visitors and which were not. His argument that there were, outside the holiday season, 'virtually no visitors' did not hold up very well to cross-examination.

Mr Simpson of the Merseyside Naturalists' Association questioned Mr Duncan on whether permission was in fact required for drilling and whether decisions made after a public inquiry are binding. If Mr Duncan advised RTZ that they did not need permission, did that company intend to proceed with drilling even if the Secretary of State refused their application to drill? 'Will they say we never needed permission, so carry on?' On this matter, neither Mr Duncan nor the Inspector offered guidance and Mr Goodfellow went as far as suggesting that if he wanted an answer to that, Mr Simpson should take counsel's opinion – a taunt which could equally be directed at the tenant farmers, none of whom could afford a fraction of Mr Goodfellow's fees. Mr Goodfellow himself had no comment to make. Similarly when Mr Simpson asked Mr Duncan about a survey conducted by RTZ in the Capel Hermon area, the response he received was less than helpful. At first, Mr Duncan denied all knowledge of a public opinion survey (of visitors' views on opencast mining coming to the Park), but later admitted that he did know of 'a sample survey and inquiry organized by RTZ', he thought in 1968 (actually 1970). He was not aware of the survey's findings and no evidence based on them was to be put in by the company.

The Dolgellau Rural District Council were very strong supporters of RTZ's Capel Hermon proposal. Councillor D. J. Williams informed the inquiry that, in the opinion of Dolgellau RDC, the minor drilling proposals fell to be considered in their own right; but it is clear from his testimony that it was the potential for large-scale mining which attracted his support. Councillor Williams declared South Merionethshire to be both underdeveloped and underpopulated: 'The Rio Tinto proposals at least afford the hope that, if approved, there may be a reversal in the population trends during future years.' The tourists who do come, don't bring money into Dolgellau, he argued, since most of them stay on caravan sites which yield little revenue and which are self-contained with their own shopping facilities.

Every attempt to attract industry into the area has, by and large, failed. . . The Council has always supported the concept of heavy industries based on the natural resources of the area, as the only realistic solution to the problems with which we are faced. . . The Rio Tinto proposals, if proceeded with successfully, can re-establish a viable economy to the area. . . There are far too many people who regard the County of Merioneth as some form of Indian Reservation inhabited by the Welsh equivalent of the Blackfoot, Sioux and Apache Indians. . . We believe that if the Government wishes to conserve certain areas to the detriment of the development of those areas then there should be compensation to the area to be conserved.

The Rural District Council's views were put forcefully and well. Of the six parish councils, four supported the position of Dolgellau RDC, one was undecided, and one – Llanfachreth – opposed the drilling. The only qualifications Mr Williams had to place on his statement in the light of cross-examination were that tourism did in fact make a distinct contribution to the Council's income via rates on bed-and-breakfast accommodation and the like, and that – while it was true that no new light industries had been established in the Rural District within the past fifteen years – the Urban District of Dolgellau had in fact succeeded in attracting such industries. But clearly the main point which Mr Williams wanted to make was well made; a disproportionate amount of attention was focused on the visiting population to the detriment of the resident. Mr Bryn Jones of the Dolgellau Urban District Council confirmed that his Council similarly supported the application for drilling, but had no comment to make on the separate question of mining.

Spokesmen for the Council for the Protection of Rural Wales, Friends of Snowdonia, the West Wales Naturalists' Trust, and the Nature Conservancy voiced their objections to the drilling. The Conservancy was particularly concerned about a designated site of Special Scientific Interest (SSSI) which was situated within the Coed-y-Brenin area in which RTZ were interested. The SSSI contained a rare oceanic (Atlantic) flora of mosses and liverworts which require high atmospheric humidity, mild winters and cool summers. The Natural Environment Research Council (of which the Conservancy was a part) were prepared to withdraw their objection provided they were consulted by RTZ before holes were sunk; they reserved the right later to object to any mining plans which may develop.

It was now Mr Simpson's turn to contribute to the proceedings, this time as witness for the Merseyside Naturalists' Association rather than as cross-examiner. He had been working (sponsored by the British Trust for Ornithology) for a number of years specifically in Coed-y-Brenin and his evidence included all manner of fascinating observations of the local wildlife; he had identified 350 species of flowering plants, innumerable mosses, liverworts, ferns and lichens, eighteen of the thirty-six British species of butterflies, six of the eleven British species of reptiles and amphibians, two species of bats, twenty of the twenty-seven British mammals – all within the RTZ area. Most important, his prime responsibility was the documentation of the numbers of nesting pairs of birds of different species, and the results of his research indicated that there had been a marked decline in the numbers of nests and of bird species since the inception of RTZ's drilling programme. At this point Mr Goodfellow saw fit to interject: why hadn't Mr Simpson tackled Mr Sharp on this point when the RTZ geologist was on the stand, and why hadn't Mr Simpson given Mr Goodfellow copies of all the maps and charts he was producing? Mr Simpson said that he had been told only to put in a proof of evidence to the Inspector, which he had done. The Inspector pointed out to Mr Goodfellow that Mr Sharp could always be recalled. But Mr Goodfellow would not be placated; he needed time to examine the maps and to talk with Mr Sharp. The Inspector offered to lend him his own copies and explained that people without the benefit of counsel's advice are bound not fully to understand the procedure of public inquiries, and a degree of latitude must be afforded them. The latitude was too much for RTZ's counsel: 'There comes a point when the fact that you are represented professionally,' said Mr Goodfellow, 'ought not to put you at an unfair disadvantage, and I am suggesting respectfully that that point has now come... Mr Simpson had better make up his mind whether he is going to make one of these plans available to us or not, because if he is not I shall say here and now I object and that would be an end of the matter.' Mr Simpson had no spare copies so the Inspector repeated his offer to lend his copy to Mr Goodfellow, and instructed Mr Simpson to make no further reference to the decline in nesting pairs of birds 'for the moment'.

After the luncheon adjournment Mr Goodfellow challenged Mr Simpson's maps of where and when drill rigs had operated within the bird-census area. He further suggested that drilling was not the only cause of disturbance, and (rightly) that 1969 had been a generally bad year for the breeding of summer migrants like the whitethroat. But Mr Simpson stood firm and stated that, in his opinion, and that of the British Trust for Ornithology, the drilling programme was an extremely important factor. So Mr Goodfellow resorted to the old chestnut which, with miscellaneous modifications, is used to convince the non-believer that industry and wildlife are invariably compatible: 'It has been known for birds actually to nest in one instance at the top of the kind of drilling rig which you can see in photograph Number 2 in our album. Does that astound you?' the QC inquired. No one was astounded.

Mr Meredith Roberts, an old Capel Hermon hill-farmer who looks hewn from the hills themselves, spoke for the local community. He described life in Capel Hermon, the farmsteads, the two chapels, the new community centre in the old school, and all that would be lost if mining were to come to the valley. He also contrasted the two proposed types of land use for the area:

The financial gains from agriculture and afforestation no doubt look puny when compared with the wealth to be reaped by mining the copper ore. So also does the insignificant number of farmers and small holders at present employed compared with the hundreds that would, presumably, be employed in the mining. But agriculture can last for ever if wisely practised and leaves the land richer in the end. The same presumably, is true of afforestation... But the mining of an area only lasts until the ore-lode is exhausted – about twenty years is mentioned in this case. After that the miner has no further interest in the place but moves on in search of the next minefield.

It was between these conflicting uses that one had to choose.

Following Mr Roberts, other Capel Hermon tenants described the effect on them of the drilling undertaken so far. Both Mr Cyril Jones and Mr Wyn Thomas had originally permitted RTZ's drill teams to come on their land in the belief that no planning permission was required. When they learnt that this was not the case and when they saw the mess caused by the operations, they decided to refuse permission for further holes. In the opinion of Mr Thomas, the behaviour of the drill crews then amounted to intimidation. The crews began damming a stream which fed the house with water and proceeded to drill seven holes along the boundary of Mr Thomas's property, one within 45 m of his front door. Mr Sharp sorted out the problems caused by the interference with the stream, but the rigs still caused considerable annoyance by working a seven-day week and sometimes all night. Whatever compensation payments were made to the farmers by RTZ, they were obviously not thought to be commensurate with the aggravation involved.

A number of individual objectors and one supporter then made statements; petitions and letters (including an objection from the Countryside Commission – the Government agency responsible for administering the National Parks Act – and one from Mr Walter Bor, then President of the Town Planning Institute) were handed in. Mr Tuck, the County Planning Officer, took the stand and was challenged by Mr Goodfellow on the success of his office in attracting light industry to the area in order to offset the high unemployment. Mr Tuck replied that he thought their record of three new plants and considerable expansion of a fourth to be a fair performance. About 100 jobs had been created (the current unemployment figures for the Barmouth Exchange, which covers a considerable area including the whole of Dolgellau, were later reported as being 102 and fifteen female). Mr Goodfellow declared that the policy of the County Council was to say : 'Never ever must new minerals in any circumstances be won or worked in the National Park' – a statement which was more than a little wide of the mark since, as Mr Tuck pointed out, the County Council had quite recently permitted small-scale underground mining close to the area in which RTZ were interested. It was all a question of the scale of operations envisaged.

The summing up speeches of Mr Powell and Mr Goodfellow were, by their very nature, repetitious. Each quoted non-binding precedents to support his own view either that wider implications must be considered or that they must be excluded. Mr Powell had a final crack at RTZ for their refusal to provide appropriate witnesses to discuss possible effects of mining. Mr Goodfellow replied :

We may be a large Corporation, we may have committed the unforgivable sin of being successful and having created wealth. We may have a large capital. We are content to abide by the results when the facts are known, so far as they can be known. We do not say to the preservationists, 'Go away, there is nothing to be said on your side.' Why cannot they have the grace, why cannot they have the dispassion, why cannot they have the fairness to deal with matters in the same way ?

Hamstrung as it was by the diametrically opposed opinions of its scope, the inquiry had proved less than satisfactory.

Changing opinions

The Report of the Inspector was finally forwarded for decision to the Secretary of State for Wales on 29 March, and from the end of December 1970 to July 1971 there was a great deal of press speculation about the outcome.

The Environmental Correspondents of national newspapers (a new strain of journalist successfully reared from cultures prepared in European Conservation Year) were unanimous in their disapproval of RTZ's intentions. But more interesting were the attitudes of mining correspondents; as one would expect, these were generally of the opinion that domestic mining was worthy of encouragement, and thought that RTZ had been given an unduly rough ride.

As the debate in the country and the letter columns intensified, it became possible to detect changes of heart amongst some mining journalists, the most notable example of which is provided by the writings of Edwin Arnold, the much-respected mining correspondent of the *Daily Telegraph*. On 12 February 1971 he filed the following as part of an article entitled 'Aladdin's caves lying under Britain's National Parks':

I am a staunch advocate of British mining development because I see it as an unparalleled way of effecting continuing and lasting balance of payments savings through import substitution ... Import savings of a minimum £200 million annually and on a regular basis can only make our economy that much richer and stronger. And without financial strength the total quality of our national life must decline in the long run. No country, in my view, is so rich that it can afford to ignore the potential of its mineral resources.

Mr Arnold further said: 'RTZ went along to Coed-y-Brenin with three diamond drill rigs and put down fifty holes under a General Development Order (GDO) which allows a company to drill anywhere in the country (National Parks included) providing the rig does not stay on the same site for more than twenty-eight days.' Actually, though, even if this interpretation of the relevant Act is correct, RTZ did admit that some holes took considerably longer than twenty-eight days to complete; but Mr Arnold – if he was aware of this – chose not to draw attention to it. The correspondent was firmly on the side of ripping out whatever Snowdonia's Aladdin's cave had to offer. One year later the same journalist was to write an article which, under the headline 'Keep the mines away from our beauty spots', represented a complete volte-face. Mr Arnold became convinced that – whatever he had formerly said – mining in Snowdonia was utterly undesirable.

To understand the reason for such a change of mind – a change which came not only to Mr Arnold, but also to many who formerly supported mining developments – one has to examine the course of the 'anti-mining' campaign subsequent to the public inquiry. Throughout 1971 the debate about what would be best for the Park and the indigenous populace became progressively more sophisticated. In April the columns of *The Times* provided space for an interesting exchange of views between the Council for the Protection of Rural Wales and the Welsh Nationalist Party, Plaid Cymru. In his letter, Mr Dafydd Elis Thomas – Policy Director of the Plaid – whom one might have expected to have gone over-board in favour of RTZ, felt bound to stress that 'in an ideal economic strategy for Merioneth, RTZ would not be among the kind of industries to be attracted here.' Mr Thomas found himself caught in a cleft stick, one branch of which pointed in favour of mining for reason of job creation while the other opposed the aim of an English company to exploit Welsh metals for private profit. The position of the Welsh Nationalists as a whole mirrored this dilemma; it seemed that, whatever they did or said, they could not win, and certainly could not at the same time satisfy both their supporters in job-hungry Blaenau Ffestiniog and those in Capel Hermon and Llanfachreth. But a genuine worry of Mr Thomas's was that which had been voiced by opponents of the scheme: how long would RTZ's jobs last? – would they really provide the stability of employment the county needed? By their refusal to be drawn on such matters, RTZ had failed to give their potential supporters the information needed to argue their case; the mention in private of thousands of job opportunities was no substitute for public declaration of what was likely to be involved in a mining scheme.

In the following month, however, RTZ was to make a public declaration about what it was doing in Snowdonia, and indeed was to spend many thousands of pounds making sure its views were placed before the public in full-page advertisements in many national and local, weekly and Sunday newspapers. The occasion was the Annual General Meeting of the company on 19 May, and Sir Val Duncan chose to devote by far the largest part of his address to 'the environment'. The headline chosen for the ads was 'Natural Resource companies have special responsibility . . . not to destroy the environment'.

Sir Val was feeling bullish. Having explained that you can only win metals where they occur and can't pick and choose your site, he defined the choice which had to be made: 'Whether ecological and environmental considerations should always take precedence over raw material demands which are entirely essential for rising living standards in a world enjoying [sic] a major population explosion.' The RTZ chairman argued that simply to mine abroad (and 'export our pollution') and to refuse to under-take similar operations at home is no answer, and smacks of double standards. But (according to Sir Val) in its activities abroad, RTZ is extremely mindful of its effect on environment; the Palabora copper mine next to South Africa's Kruger National Park was a prime example of what could be done. Its effect on wildlife is anything but adverse: 'Indeed a family of hippos has taken up permanent residence in the tailings dam,' explained Sir Val. RTZ's critics could be excused for wondering how God's creatures survived before the advent of the mining industry; if it wasn't bird's nests up drilling rigs it was hippos behind the dam.

The reason for Sir Val Duncan choosing this time to pay public attention to the environmental issues was provided by the apparent likelihood of success in Capel Hermon. The debate had to be brought home. 'I think there is a particular problem relating to the United Kingdom, because of the density of the population in these small islands,' ran the ad. 'It so happens that the areas in which base metals are most likely to be found are in general in the rocky and hilly country which is not suitable as a living area for a large population and much of it has therefore been set aside as National Parks.' Coed-y-Brenin it explained, 'is located in a National Park, not many miles from the traditional mining area of Blaenau Ffestiniog.'

It was this part of his speech which aroused most anger amongst the conservationists. Sir Val Duncan well knew the reason for the establish-ment of National Parks and their purpose (the National Park Act explains this clearly), and his implication that 'Park' was just a tag given to an area when no one could think of what to do with it was disingenuous. It would also have been more candid for Sir Val to explain that Blaenau Ffestiniog with its rolling oceans of slate waste and dereliction, did not itself fall within the Park; indeed it was specifically excluded, so great was its legacy of dereliction. Sir Val Duncan explained that he looked forward to in-formed public discussion of the question posed in Snowdonia, but his own references to the area were neither informative nor accurate.

Within days of the RTZ Annual General Meeting a well-timed counter-blast appeared in the *Ecologist*, and received almost saturation coverage in the national press. The importance of the article, which was by Friends of the Earth (FOE) was twofold. Firstly the authors described in detail the history of the project and dealt with each of the specific arguments which had then been advanced in support of mining (and which had included a somewhat lame thesis about copper being a strategically im-portant metal to which the reply was 'then why squander it in peace-time?'). Secondly, and more importantly, it was made clear in the five pages of copy that FOE was prepared to lead the attack on RTZ in the

National Parks. The latter was very important, for it meant that other national conservation organizations reading the *Ecologist* and the press identified FOE as the focus of research and campaign strategy, and were able, by giving practical and financial assistance, to dovetail into the growing debate. FOE's opinion was made plain : 'Britain is neither rich enough to afford to sell Snowdonia, nor poor enough to need to.' FOE's aims were also clear and its style of operations by June 1971 was well recognized; the plan was to raise enough money to pay the four-man research team they had already established and which was concentrating specifically on large-scale mining in designated areas of the UK. The staff, led by Simon Millar, were politically and technically competent to run the show. To the credit of many who cared about the future of Britain's National Parks, FOE managed to raise the money needed to put their plan into operation.

'Rock Bottom'

By June 1971, there had still been no pronouncement from the Welsh Office about RTZ's drilling application. Then in July things moved fast. On 8 July, the Department of Trade and Industry announced a £50 million scheme under which mining companies would have access to public money to help them in their exploration programmes within the UK. Thirty-five per cent of their expenditure on prospecting for 'any natural deposits capable of being lifted or extracted from the earth' could be obtained from the public purse, and would in practice only become repayable in the event of permission being given for later mining.

The dice appeared to be heavily loaded against those who sought protection for Britain's landscape heritage, not least because a prominent lobbyist in favour of the exploration incentive scheme had been Rio Tinto-Zinc. The sceptics did not have long to wait ; one week after the DTI's announcement, the Secretary of State for Wales gave the go-ahead to drilling in Capel Hermon and the Mawddach. The programme was to last for twelve months and was to be limited at any one time to the six-day week daytime operation of no more than four rigs on the hillside and two in the estuary. The decision, stressed the Secretary of State, did not carry the implication that mining would be permitted.

Precisely one week after this, RTZ announced that, together with half a dozen other mining houses it had set up an 'independent commission on mining and the environment' under the chairmanship of Lord Zuckerman, former Chief Scientific Adviser to the Government. Other members were Viscount Arbuthnot, Professor C. Kidson, Max Nicholson and Professor Sir Frederick Warner – undoubtedly a team with considerable experience of planning and environmental questions but one which had no direct experience of problems caused by opencast metal mining operations. The commission's brief was 'to make recommendations designed to reconcile economic and technical considerations with other requirements of national policy, especially those concerning physical planning and the environment in terms of amenity, recreation and scientific interest and historical interest.' Their appointment, however, was greeted with howls from amenity societies and from the press. Why, it was asked, if the commission is independent, were non-mining organizations not consulted about its membership and terms of reference? Why were there no members with whom either conservation bodies or the people of Merioneth could identify – whom they could trust to give fair weight to their opinions? The outcry was perhaps over-loud but it did result in the appointment of Sir Jack Longland, a member of the Countryside Commission, as an additional commissioner. More important though, the establishment of the Commission provided RTZ with something they badly required: a screen behind which to hide from the glare of publicity directed at their activities in Snowdonia. For the next fourteen months, RTZ could (wrongly but effectively) refer to the question of mining in National Parks as *sub judice*. That question, they were able to say, was for Zuckerman to decide. But the question was never put directly to the commission and, when it reported, it was to have no specific recommendation to make about mining in the Parks.

Over the next few months, drilling continued in Capel Hermon, and a great deal of interest in RTZ's activities was shown by television companies. Indeed, for a time camera crews were as numerous in the hillsides as were drilling rigs, with different teams putting together programmes on what was there to be won and there to be lost.

In the estuary, however, it was the absence of drilling rigs which excited journalists' imaginations. Was Jon Tinker right in his *New Scientist* prediction that the gold-dredging was just a blind to get permission to go after copper? It began to seem so, especially when Sir Val Duncan appeared on 'Panorama', the BBC 1 documentary programme, vowing that his company would not dredge for gold if to do so would result in significant disturbance to the estuary. Since the scale of operation would have to be enormous and since dredging would inevitably result in massive disturbance, RTZ-watchers concluded the gold-scheme had been dropped. A similar calculation of probabilities had resulted in ITV's 'World in Action' team concentrating exclusively on the copper prospect. The FOE researchers had by now become a fairly sophisticated outfit designed to make things as easy as possible for journalists interested in the issue to put together well-researched articles and programmes. Two researchers were detailed to work with 'World in Action' and the resulting broadcast in September – 'A Subject called Ecology in a place called Capel Hermon' – showed the value of this approach. Thanks to the work of John Sheppard the producer, tenant farmers who stood to lose their homes with the coming of a mine began to believe they had a chance. By declining an invitation to participate in the film, RTZ did themselves no good in the eyes either of supporters or of opponents in Merioneth.

Meanwhile the Zuckerman Commission had not got off to a very auspicious start. Lord Kennet, himself a former Minister in the Labour government and President of the Council for the Protection of Rural England, announced that the CPRE would not give evidence to a commission which had been set up without consultation by bodies with a single vested interest in its deliberations. Others agreed with him. Friends of the Earth decided that more mileage could be made from the publication of well-researched evidence than from refusal to offer any. Its submission 'Rock Bottom – Nearing the Limits of Metal Mining in Britain' was presented on 18 January 1972. The decision was a correct one ; the report was described by Kenneth Allsop as 'obligatory reading', was very well reported, and succeeded in defining many of the problems surrounding the development of opencast mining in the UK.

'Rock Bottom', which is better read than paraphrased, dealt with every consideration which, in the opinion of the authors, merited the attention of a Commission such as that chaired by Lord Zuckerman ; but, before doing so, it took issue with the manner in which the work of the Commission was to be undertaken. It was felt strongly that for this body to accept evidence from mining companies which was given in confidence and which would not later be published would lead to *ex cathedra* conclusions based partly on facts withheld from public discussion. Such a course was the enemy of full public appreciation of the factors involved – precisely the sort of approach the Skeffington Report had sought to discourage. There was a good case – since justice should be seen to be done – for Lord Zuckerman to urge the government to establish an obviously independent and official commission to examine the issues raised. The Zuckerman Commission, FOE's evidence argued, should consider the avoidance or postponement of resource depletion as one of the 'requirements of national policy' with which they were to be concerned. Failure to do so, and any accompanying determination to deal solely with cosmetic ameliorations of mining disturbance, would constitute a refusal to come to terms with the underlying factors upon which exploitation might proceed. The re-use and recycling of metals 'to buy the time required to overcome social inertia and make more fundamental changes' was hence of paramount importance. Also the terms of reference of the Zuckerman Commission were such as to suggest that at all times and in all locations conservation and mining were capable of compatability; this was not regarded by 'Rock Bottom' as being the case, and the authors expressed the hope that 'if in certain cases you (the Commission) agree with us, your terms of reference allow you to say so'.

The report stressed the magnitude of the likely scale of metal mining for low-grade ores – a scale hitherto not envisaged in the UK. It listed nineteen specific criticisms of the procedure and conduct of public inquiries; presented the advantages which would be derived from a Government agency (the Institute of Geological Sciences) themselves conducting the research required in the formulation of a sound resource-exploitation policy; and highlighted the conflict caused by simultaneous designation of some areas of the UK both as development areas and 'protected' ones. The purpose of National Parks and the conflict caused by illicit drilling operations were similarly scrutinized. Most particularly, likely problems caused by the liberation of toxic metal ions in the course of mining were underlined as a prime worry of many critics of large-scale metal-mining in the UK, and one which the Commission should examine in some detail. The arguments advanced in 'Rock Bottom' were to become those on which the bulk of RTZ's critics were to concentrate in the next twelve months.

Films, books and meetings

On 24 February 1972 the Mineral Exploration and Investments Act (which gave mining companies up to £50 million for exploration) became law. Less than four weeks later, RTZ formally announced their abandonment of their gold prospect in the Mawddach Estuary. Their announcement, however, met with a hostile and accusing press – much to the bewilderment of Sir Val Duncan himself. Trevor Fishlock in *The Times* immediately stressed that the decision provided 'a relatively small crumb of comfort', since the primary interest of RTZ was the copper lying beneath Capel Hermon. The industrial correspondent of the *Guardian*, Victor Keegan faithfully reported the decision:

Sir Val Duncan, chairman and chief executive of RTZ said yesterday in Cardiff: 'We have come to the conclusion that, even if gold were to be present in substantial quantities, we cannot win it in that estuary – which is one of the most beautiful in the world that I know – without such disturbance to this natural amenity as would be unreasonable'.

He left it to Judy Hillman, the *Guardian* planning correspondent, to point out three days later that many observers had 'always expected the company to sacrifice the gold search as a price for a better reception for the possibility of opencast copper mining in the national park itself'. Somehow RTZ appeared to be failing to get that better reception, and their bewilderment at the apparently cynical (but possibly fair) treatment of their Mawddach announcement was genuine. The company itself had already given the game away when Sir Val spoke on 'Panorama' six months previously. In terms of the later public relations exercise, his candid and welcome remarks had proved injudicious.

The domestic fortunes of RTZ did not improve in the months of April and May. Partly due to the massive problems faced and caused by their Avonmouth zinc smelter (which was forced to suspend operations because of high lead levels present in the blood of workmen), the company's pre-tax profits for 1971 showed a drop to £68 millions from £85·5 millions the year before. RTZ were under withering fire from anti-apartheid groups at home who were (and are) distressed by company policy in South Africa and Namibia, from workers outraged by conditions at Avonmouth and from critics of their plans for development in Britain's National Parks. The 17 May Annual General Meeting promised to be a stormy one, not least because many of RTZ's most vociferous critics had in the past twelve months also become minor shareholders.

But two more bombshells were to be dropped on RTZ's Snowdonia interests in the weeks before the AGM. Firstly the local Transport and General Workers' Union branch in Merioneth voted to oppose any scheme for opencast copper mining in the area, and by doing so illustrated the serious erosion of local support for the company. The temporary and unstable nature of likely employment opportunities was becoming generally understood; the dismantling of landscape did not seem to offer the enormous benefits previously indicated, and the Dolgellau Rural District Council and Plaid Cymru were increasingly under pressure for supporting RTZ. Secondly it was now that the formerly ardent and influential advocate of mining in Snowdonia, Edwin Arnold – the *Daily Telegraph* mining correspondent – came out strongly against opencast workings in the National Parks.

Mr Arnold's conversion, which he described on 17 April under the heading 'Keep the mines away from our beauty spots', came during a visit to Scotland's Westfield Coal Mine – Britain's largest open-pit mine. In 1971 this mine produced 1·26 million t of coal and shifted 19 million t of waste material. According to Mr Arnold's calculations the smallest conceivable operation in Capel Hermon would shift a comparable volume of material each year and would give an annual output of copper in concentrates (assuming 0·6 per cent grade) of 30 000 t. A larger operation would yield 100 000 t of copper in concentrates and would involve the shifting of 60·3 million t of material each year. Such a mine, were it to have an active life of fourteen years, would require the movement of 844·2 million t of ore and waste, (enough to bury the city of London to a depth of 255 m – nearly 150 m higher than St Paul's). The scale of operations appalled him. Furthermore RTZ would (before commencing operations) have to build concentrating plants, offices, workshops and possibly on-site housing; to bring in electric power lines; to bulldoze adjacent valleys to make slimes dams; dam and pipe a nearby river for all-year-round water supplies; and either install a smelter or realign, resurface and widen the roads to be used for shipment of the concentrate. The purpose of Mr Arnold's article was, he declared, to provide 'the Snowdonia conservationists, whose cause I now espouse' with 'the technical facts (of) just how great the danger is'. The journalist knew and had visited major open-pit copper mines at Palabora (in the Transvaal), Mount Lyell (Tasmania), and Nchanga (Zambia) but the location of these was such as to cause nothing like the damage which Snowdonia would suffer.

I no longer believe, as I once did, that mining in Britain's National Parks is such a good thing. These areas of unique beauty in our tiny, crowded island must, I now feel, be preserved at all costs for the nation and posterity... Given the huge social costs of Snowdonia copper, I feel as a nation we can afford to forgo that much domestic mine output and buy it from the world market.

Mr Arnold had come to agree that Britain was neither rich enough to afford to sell Snowdonia, nor poor enough to need to.

The RTZ Annual General Meeting was indeed a stormy one with well-briefed questioners (largely of RTZ policy abroad) falling into the age-old trap of making impassioned and lengthy speeches rather than putting short, sharp and precise questions to the RTZ Board. An RTZ anti-report in the same format as the official company report was produced by a new-founded and deliberately mysterious organization calling itself Counter Information Services, and this dealt with Avonmouth and Snowdonia, as well as with the politically more volatile issue of RTZ involvement in Namibia. This AGM was the first time (in the author's experience) that a concerted attempt had been made in the UK by people with no former connections with a company to influence its policy by becoming shareholders. (The corporate debate of the Thalidomide–Distillers controversy developed in a different fashion and primarily involved existing shareholders.) The methodology has subsequently been, and increasingly will be, applied elsewhere, since the AGM is the only political forum likely to influence multinational corporations, the budgets of which exceed national budgets and the Boards of which regard themselves as answerable only to their investors.

One week after the Annual General Meeting came the single most effective blow to the chances of RTZ getting permission to mine in Snowdonia. Benefiting from the enormous amount of work which had by then been done by opponents of the mining programme, a BBC 'Horizon' team led by Mike Barnes put together a film entitled 'Do you Dig National Parks ?' In it, Amory Lovins – one of the FOE research team – played a leading role, and both he and the present author participated in a talk-in broadcast afterwards, with Mr Roy Wright, Deputy Chairman of Rio Tinto. The programme was first broadcast on 22 May 1972.

The film itself was of immense value to the anti-mining lobby since it both drew together the many strands of the debate and also goaded the reluctant RTZ into some form of response. It presented not only the views of people outside the Park but also the real worries and desires of proponents and opponents within it, and brought home to everyone the scale of likely operations, and the toxicity problems which might accompany the mining of copper from Capel Hermon. In the subsequent interview Mr Wright was challenged on the question of whether physical and biological restoration were in fact possible for a large opencast copper mine. Mr Wright, Mr Kincead-Weekes of the UK Metal Mining Association, and Professor Lovering, a former President of the Geological Society of America, had to agree that nowhere in the world had this sort of restoration actually been achieved. That was not to say it was impossible, but the fear that part of Snowdonia would become the testing ground for currently theoretical methods of restoration was acutely felt by Mr Wright's questioners. The presenter, Ludovic Kennedy, asked Mr Wright on what criteria he would base a decision to permit or to refuse mining, were he the Secretary of State for Wales, and – in the most interesting exchange of the discussion – Mr Wright immediately resorted to the Zuckerman Commission in an attempt to fend off the question : 'The Zuckerman Commission, which is a very distinguished Commission, will report very soon and it will say "Yes, you can mine" . . . or it will say "We don't think you should." If it says "No, we don't think you should", then we as a company . . . will certainly say "That's the end; we stop." ' The present author maintained that this was not the case, that the question had not in fact been put to the Commission, and that they would not answer it. Events were to prove Mr Wright wrong.

When, three days later, on 25 May, *The Times* printed a letter from Sir Val Duncan in which he challenged the BBC film's assertion that RTZ's drilling was illegal, Friends of the Earth replied suggesting that he make public the source of such advice since it ran directly counter to advice given to them. The correspondence ceased somewhat abruptly at that point, one explanation being that at that time RTZ's solicitors were trying to secure modifications in the texts of two books which dealt with RTZ's operations and interest in Snowdonia.

The first of these was a detailed case study of the Snowdonia National

Park written by Amory Lovins and photographed by another of the FOE team, Philip Evans. It was entitled *Eryri, the Mountains of Longing*. The second was *River of Tears* written by Richard West, which dealt with RTZ's activities around the world. *Eryri* got a particularly rough ride when, three days before its publication date of 22 July, RTZ's solicitors, Goodman Derrick and Co. – the Goodman being the noticeably ubiquitous Lord Goodman of the Arts Council, the Newspaper Publishers' Association etc., etc. – wrote to the publisher, George Allen & Unwin, charging that parts of the book gave 'a seriously distorted picture of our client's activities and intentions in Snowdonia and are plainly defamatory.' The publishers immediately withdrew the book and postponed publication. The ensuing discussion between solicitors for both parties lasted for months and Goodman Derrick's original ten-page memorandum of alleged inaccuracies led to the inclusion in the book of a 650-word statement by RTZ in which they stressed that they felt strongly 'that the book gives the misleading impression that they (RTZ) carry on their activities in a furtive and sometimes illegal manner.' Paradoxically the late intervention of RTZ resulted in the book getting two batches of (glowing) reviews – one immediately before non-publication and one before it was published.

Zuckerman and Stevens

All in all things had not gone too well for RTZ in the early summer of 1972, but interesting developments later in the season seemed to indicate that the company's interest in Capel Hermon was far from dead. In June there appeared press reports that RTZ was investigating potential sites for a copper smelter around Milford Haven. Sir Val Duncan had already stressed that 'should Coed-y-Brenin turn out to be an important producer of copper ore, this would be a key factor in the establishment of a copper-smelting complex at some suitable location in this country.' Could it be that a Milford Haven smelter and an associated sea-link was the method to be employed in handling Snowdonia's copper concentrates?

On 25 June the Government outlined new mining legislation to be introduced in November which would ease the problem many mining companies had in obtaining UK mineral rights. Often these rights were untraceable, having been passed on from owner to owner or retained by one party when another took over land rights. The new enactment would grant access to companies where the mineral-rights owner could not be traced. The Government was clearly determined to do whatever was required to encourage a new British mining boom. But RTZ found itself still unable (or unwilling) to report on results of the Capel Hermon investigations. Drilling had been completed a few months before when on 4 July the company declared that it would take no decision on what to do next until Lord Zuckerman's Commission had reported. Exactly one month later the Government announced the establishment of its own inquiry into planning controls of mineral exploration and working. This exceedingly high-powered Commission, under the chairmanship of Sir Roger Stevens QC, was given a brief which broadly overlapped that given by the mining companies to Lord Zuckerman. The advantage which it had, though, was that it was an official and obviously independent body established by Government to advise Government. It was very much the body the establishment of which was advocated by FOE in their evidence to Zuckerman. The question now became whether RTZ would wait both for Zuckerman and Stevens before making up its mind.

Undoubtedly RTZ's most evocative argument in favour of mining (although somewhat devalued) remained job-provision, and in August they found themselves in the happy position of having one of their directors appointed Chairman of the Welsh Industrial Development Board. It is no reflection on the man concerned to say that this did not give the best public appearance of impartiality, and it promoted a few wry smiles from RTZ-watchers. Like God, the Devil seemed to be everywhere!

On 12 September 1972, the Zuckerman Commission finally reported, and their report advanced the National Parks Mining Debate but little. While some of the material included in their dissertation remains of undoubted value to those who do not know much about the methodology of exploration and mining, their recommendations left much to be desired both by RTZ and by its opponents. Briefly, the Commission's main recommendations were that:

1 A distinction should be made between two stages of exploratory drilling and that the first stage (known as scout drilling) should be deemed a permitted development for which no permission is needed. The second stage (evaluation drilling) should require permission and all such applications made in designated protected areas (such as National Parks) should be called in for decision by the appropriate Minister.

2 Public inquiries into proposals of the latter type should be restricted in their scope and should deal solely with the merits of drilling. It is open, however, to a mining company to apply simultaneously for further drilling and mining, in which case both proposals should be the subject of discussion at the inquiry. All parties to the inquiry should agree to a statement of the main facts pertaining to the case.

3 Mining interests should make available to local people and environmental groups information relevant to their concern and interests 'subject to normal commercial practice'.

4 The Government should invite mining companies to consider volun-

tarily establishing a Renewal Trust which would receive from and disburse to mining concerns (un-taxed) monies to be used in the rehabilitation of non-ferrous mining sites.

5 Toxic substances liberated in the course of mining should be contained on-site. Waste rock disposal areas should be capable of sustaining the required vegetation cover.

6 Various biological surveying, monitoring, pollution-controlling and landscaping standards should be maintained.

These recommendations, were they to be acted upon, would present a number of difficulties to bodies interested in problems likely to be caused by large-scale metal mining operations in the UK. Firstly, the distinction drawn between scout and evaluation drilling (which was made by RTZ at the Dolgellau inquiry) is an arbitrary one. The same equipment and processes are involved in both stages, and together they constitute a single type of operation. It seems inconceivable that an amended Town and Country Planning Act could (unlike A. P. Herbert's Lord Justice Wool) provide a 'subtle distinction between the two halves of an umbrella'. Any distinction in practice would depend upon a mining company's own interpretation of what it was doing, and a company might well prefer to do as much drilling as possible before applying for permission – just as RTZ did in Capel Hermon.

Secondly, that discussion at a public inquiry can be confined solely to a drilling programme and can exclude the possibility of later mining, has been shown to be possible. The question is whether it is desirable. Currently, frustrated debates like that at Dolgellau exploit the only real public forum in which principles underlying this sort of development can be debated before the actual development becomes imminent. While legalistically some may think such debate to be misplaced, it nevertheless flourishes at public inquiries simply because Parliament, the Department of Trade and Industry, the Department of the Environment and the Welsh Office have failed lamentably to debate the issues themselves and to lay down firm guidelines as to what should and should not be permitted in Britain's ten National Parks and many Areas of Outstanding Natural Beauty. Until Parliament decides what protection to give what Zuckerman refers to as 'protected areas', these will remain unprotected.

Thirdly, an agreed body of fact, if it were to deal (as it would have to) with the technicalities of exploration and exploitation processes, could not normally be arrived at in consultation between objectors and proponents of a scheme, since the objector would be entirely dependent upon the proposer telling the whole truth, and would normally not have available to him the means of verifying it. It is precisely because mining companies show a general reluctance to provide opponents with all available information that recommendation three above is meaningless; 'normal commercial practice' means keeping quiet about what you're doing and what you intend to do.

Fourthly, the restoration of biological fertility and control of toxins are what *1066 and All That* would described as good things. The problem however is whether such containment of poisons is possible. The 'disposal area' of no large-scale opencast copper mine has ever been restored to biological fertility, but the only reference to this problem made by the Zuckerman Commission reads: 'The mine waste could be toxic and, in consequence be unsuitable for plant growth. The restoration should produce a soil which provides enough nutrients and retains enough moisture to allow vegetation to become established. We have been informed that techniques have been devised to achieve these ends.' It is a great pity that the Commission did not present the information which they evidently had been given, nor identify its source.

The other recommendations are less contentious and generally fair. The problem of administering some sort of 'renewal trust' which would cater for an enormous range of mining operations is one with which Sir Roger Stevens is currently grappling. But the most important feature of the Zuckerman Report was its refusal to answer the question RTZ had not put: whether large-scale mining should be permitted in a National Park. This refusal left the unwanted baby comfortably ensconced in RTZ's lap. It also gave the press and commentators a field day. Radio and the newspapers interpreted the report either as an exercise in fence-sitting or as veiled approval for mining in the Parks. Edwin Arnold in the *Daily Telegraph* said that the mining industry itself was getting brickbats which would be better directed at the Government: 'Why indeed doesn't the Government commission its own exploration work from Britain's excellent and under-employed geological consultancies? That way the Government would have full responsibility rather than getting it on the cheap from the mining houses.' The attack seemed a reasonable one, and Mr Arnold could have added that, were the Government to do their own research, they might also attempt to devise a rational resource-use policy tying together demand, real need and supply.

Perhaps most important of all, the seemingly increased likelihood of mining in Snowdonia prompted the people of Capel Hermon to form the Cwm Hermon Defence Committee and to launch a fund to stop RTZ levelling their hills. Both national and local opposition had hardened considerably. RTZ's allies in Merioneth seemed more muted in the voicing of their support.

Withdrawal

In November, Amory Lovin's book *Eryri, the Mountains of Longing* was finally published, receiving its second round of favourable reviews as well as journalistic sympathy for the treatment R TZ had given it. The book's publication injected life into a campaign which had never experienced a lack of pressure points to tap from time to time, but the course of which was becoming increasingly difficult to plot. Friends of the Earth, other conservation organizations and the mining companies each prepared evidence for presentation to the Stevens Commission which seemed to be the new focus of attention in the mining debate; and as one-share shareholders FOE prepared for the next R TZ Annual General Meeting. It was crucially important to discover what the company planned to do in Capel Hermon – and when.

Then, on 19 April 1973, the day before Good Friday (when there were no papers to report the news) R TZ announced their abandonment of their Capel Hermon copper prospect. The decision, to which no reference was made in the Chairman's speech, appeared in the Company Report:

Riofinex has completed its preliminary evaluation of the results of its recent drilling in the Coed-y-Brenin area of North Wales. Mining studies indicate that the potential ore availability could be 200 million t at an average grade of around 0·3 per cent copper. Engineering estimates based on normal evaluation procedures including environmental factors show that it is extremely doubtful that a mining operation could be economic in the forseeable future. Accordingly, R TZ has decided that it would not be justified in proceeding further.

Simon Millar calculated that, at the then prices, the copper would be worth £300 millions. Mr Kincead-Weekes of the UK Metal Mining Association is on record as saying that, in an area where physical restoration is inevitably required, it would cost a company about as much money to fill a hole as it would to dig it. Some reporters described the decision as a straightforward economic one, and others ascribed it to the considerable pressure to which R TZ had been subjected. The whole story could only be told by someone privy to the deliberations of the R TZ Board, and presumably it never will be.

But it still remained important to establish that the company had really given up their interest in the prospect. So the FOE research team went back to Capel Hermon to check that the company had in fact not gone ahead with the purchase of buildings which it was thought locally would house their administrative staff. In addition, the present author wrote to Sir Val Duncan. The answers were the same; R TZ had withdrawn from Capel Hermon and had no intentions of returning.

Conclusion

That then, is the end of the story, or seems to be. But, from the conservationist's point of view, every victory won is temporary and every defeat permanent. There is nothing to stop RTZ and other companies returning to Capel Hermon or proposing large-scale mining operations for other areas within Britain's National Parks.

With current regional policies concentrating ever more capital expenditure and job provision in the highly populated South East of England (witness the proposed Maplin airport, seaport, refineries, new towns, etc.) and apparently refusing to devote equal effort to the attraction of service and light manufacturing industries to areas like North Wales, a mining company can expect reluctant support from the local population when it puts forward plans to modify some of Britain's most inspiring landscape. This landscape and the cultural heritage of the people who are part of it are valuable, fragile and worthy of real protection and assistance. It is now possible for them to be exchanged for the formerly unwinnable metals beneath the hills. Society as a whole must ponder the imponderables and decide, via its elected government, what it wants.

In the final analysis, and in the real perspective, there is only enough copper in Capel Hermon to satisfy current world demand for that metal for four weeks ; there are other qualities in Capel Hermon, and places like it, which are more difficult to quantify but of no less value. The choice between them must be made. Is Britain rich enough to sell Snowdonia ? Are we poor enough to need to ?

4 Bedfordshire Brick

Jeremy Bugler

A traveller from London to the city of John Bunyan – Bedford – passes through one of the richest mining areas in Britain, where in huge brick pits clay is worked and turned into bricks. One in every five houses in Britain is made of clay from the brickfields of Bedfordshire and one in every three is of clay from the combined brickfields of Bedfordshire and Huntingdonshire. From these pits have come enough bricks to build perhaps four and a half million houses, schools and other buildings. The bricks produced from the Bedfordshire brickfield over a period of five weeks or so would, placed end to end, encircle the Earth. The field thus produces very many more than 2000 houses a week – a record of production that few small areas of the country can parallel; yet it takes up little more than one per cent of the area of the county.

But these bricks, though such a valuable social contribution, are produced at a social cost. The area has been described by the Chief Planning Officer of Bedfordshire County Council, Mr Geoffrey Cowley, in these terms:

In land-use terms the area is still basically rural in character, but the activities associated with brickmaking dominate the landscape; the batteries of tall chimneys, the gaping holes of active and derelict clay workings, the constant flow of brick-laden lorries, the sight and smell of effluent from the chimneys; all in all a depressing experience. As the brick industry has developed, the rural scene has been changing also. Trees have died, trees are dying and the hedgerows are being removed. The treescape is declining due to a variety of factors ... the brick industry, farm husbandry and old age have all contributed. The poorness of the overall scene is aggravated by the flat terrain so that in the absence of trees the features alien to the countryside dominate the picture. These conditions may be unattractive enough to the traveller but it is not an uninhabited area and some 7000 people are living with these problems all the time.

Brickmaking

Those remarks were written in 1967 in the Bedfordshire County Council publication *The Bedfordshire Brickfield*: and many people would maintain they remain precisely as true today as they did then. The Bedfordshire brickfield is situated in a valley in central Bedfordshire known variously as Marston Valley, the Vale of Bedford, and perhaps most realistically as 'The Brickworks Valley'. The field exploits the land on which it lies – the Oxford clay formation which lies diagonally across England from Dorset

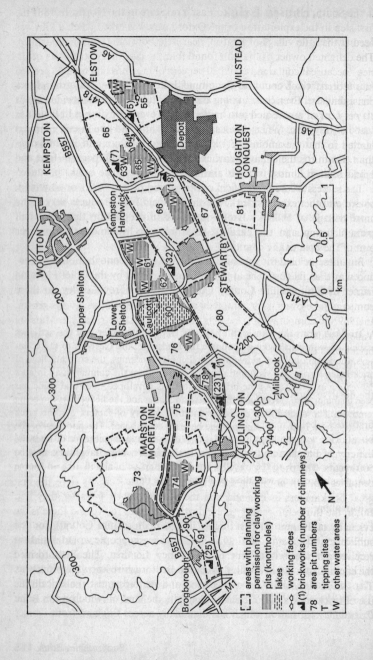

ELSTOW

WILSTEAD

A418

A6

Depot

KEMPSTON

B557

HOUGHTON
CONQUEST

55

(5)

65

64

(7)

63 W

65

65 W

18 W

66

67

81

WOOTTON

Kempston
Hardwick

W

W

61

62

32

STEWARTBY

A418

Upper Shelton

W

Lower Shelton

60 W

Caulcott

80

W

76

200'

Milbrook

300'

(1)

78

23 T

LIDLINGTON

300'

400'

MARSTON
MORETAINE

75

77

73

74 W

Brogborough

90

91

(25)

M1

B557

200

300

200'

300'

0   0.5   1
|___|___|
km

N

areas with planning
permission for clay working

pits (knottholes)

lakes

working faces

78   area pit numbers

(1)   brickworks (number of chimneys)

T   tipping sites

W   other water areas

in the South, north-eastwards to East Yorkshire in the North. In 1881 the first step in the exploitation of the Oxford clay was taken when a kiln was fired at the little village of Fletton, near Peterborough (Huntingdonshire). The delighted owner of the kiln found that the clay had marvellous qualities – because it contained about 20 per cent of moisture, it could be pressed into a brick which could be fired immediately if the clay was ground to a consistent size. Even better, it was discovered that the clay contained about 10 per cent of a carbonaceous material which acted as a kind of built-in fuel in the brick. When the kiln was fired, the carbonaceous material ignited so that the amount of fuel required to produce the bricks was le s than two-thirds the quantity required for other types of clay. In short, the bricks seemed almost to make themselves.

The success of the brickworks at Fletton led other brick manufacturers to exploit other exposures of Oxford clay. In 1897 the Forder works at the small village of Pillinge, Bedfordshire, adopted the Fletton process of manufacturing and the Bedfordshire brickfield really dates from this event. The original Forder brickworks grew successfully, absorbed other companies, particularly those finding the going difficult in the 1920s slump, and was then itself absorbed into a much larger company which in 1936 named itself the London Brick Company Limited. Over the years the brick company take-overs have continued and London Brick has always grown. In 1969 the company took over its chief Bedfordshire rival, the Marston Valley Brick Company; and then in 1971 it absorbed the last Fletton brickworks owned by Redland, the brick and tile corporation. Today the Bedfordshire brickfield *is* London Brick, and vice versa. It has about 12×10^6 m^2 of clay in Bedfordshire yet to work; and in a field further to the north around Peterborough it has about 7×10^6 m^2.

Brickmaking is one of the oldest activities of semi-civilized man, the first bricks being made of sun-dried clay. It is uncertain when the first burnt brick was produced; but bricks produced in a kiln were used to build the city of Babylon and bricks have been found which date back at least 5000 years. The use of bricks flourished in England in the third and fourth centuries AD, but not in the later Dark Ages. The Romans were the first great brickmakers in England and the craft lay dormant after they left. But in the thirteenth century the industry started to revive and there is the evidence of Hampton Court built in the reign of Henry VIII for the sufficiency of the craft of English brickmaking at the time. Brickmaking received a further boost after the Great Fire of London, which transformed the capital from a wooden, inflammable city to a more durable brick city. The Queen Anne and Georgian period of architecture 'set the seal on the use of brickwork as a material of dignity and charm' as the London Brick Company itself has written.

Until the middle of the nineteenth century, the process of manufacturing bricks was slow and tedious and mostly carried out on or near the site where the actual bricks were required. The clay was dug in the autumn and allowed to weather through the winter; in spring it was spread, watered and tempered by being trodden into a pliable lump. After this the bricks were moulded by hand and were then fired. In the nineteenth century, instead of the hand-and-foot operation, mixing mills were powered by steam which also drove machines from which a continuous column of clay emerged to be cut off by wire into the appropriate size of a brick.

The valuable Oxford clay is known as 'knotts' in the industry. Tradition has it that the knotts owe their name to their hardness; workmen in the early days at Fletton cut downwards through the overlying clay – brown clay known as callow – until a change in consistency stopped them, rather as a knot in a piece of wood will jar a saw. To get at the knotts the brown callow clay, which varies in thickness from 3 to 6 m, has to be stripped off for it is too plastic to be used in brickmaking. After the callow clay has been rejected and moved separately by the huge drag line excavators the brickmakers employ, the valuable knott clay is laid bare. It occurs in depths varying from a metre or so to over 30 m, and typically a layer will be 14 m thick. Sometimes what is known as a blue clay is found between the callow and the knotts, and this also has to be stripped off and dumped. These waste clays are fed on to conveyor belts and shifted round to a part of the brick pit that has already been worked out, or they are fed on to a mobile 'gantry stacker' which drops the waste into rows of conical mounds well clear of the face. This form of waste disposal creates huge pimples in a worked-out pit, and has led to the Bedfordshire brick pits being called 'moonscapes'. (Indeed they have been used by film companies to simulate those desolate lunar landscapes.)

Once smaller drag-line excavators have stripped off the reject blue or callow clay, much larger 'walking drag-lines' having buckets with a capacity of over 4.5 m^3 move in to tackle the knott clay. These massive drag-lines feed hoppers, which in turn feed either ropeways or conveyor belts or a railway, which take the clay back to the brickworks for processing. But before leaving the pit the conveyor belt drops the worked clay onto vibrating metal bars, known in the trade as a 'grizzly'. The smaller pieces of clay fall through on to a belt which takes them straight to the brickworks. The larger lumps are carried to what is called a 'kibbler' for breaking down. At the same time any pieces of rock or fossil are segregated and thrown out. At the brickworks further grinding and grading takes place before the clay passes on to the brick presses which operate with two pistons, one from above and one from below. The brick is then subjected to four squeezes or pressures. This process, a feature of the London Brick

Company, is described in a pun of a trade mark 'Phorpres', which is actually used to describe the company's bricks. After pressing, the bricks, known as 'greens', are left to dry out and are then fired.

The construction industry uses mainly three kinds of bricks – facings, commons and engineering bricks. Facing bricks are used on external walls and in positions where appearance is important. Engineering bricks are bricks of exceptional strength and low porosity. Commons are used elsewhere in buildings. In the Fletton brick industry, both facings and commons are produced.

The dereliction of success

Over the years the London Brick Company has been doing very well with its flettons, facings or commons. 1973 was a very good year indeed for London Brick and at the company's annual general meeting the chairman told shareholders that during the last two and a half years London Brick had increased its annual production by 619 million bricks – a rise of twenty-nine per cent. Production exceeded 3000 million bricks for the first time – a total the chairman termed 'staggering'. Many of the bricks which contributed to it came from fields outside Bedfordshire but the Bedfordshire brickfield made a notable contribution.

The slump in 1974, particularly in house building, however, set back London Brick's fortunes. At the 1974 annual general meeting, Sir Ronald said that five works had already had to be closed down because of the decline in house building and that more works were threatened. He reported that London Brick barely operated at a profit in the first half of 1974 and the first half year results would be 'extremely poor'. However, this slump only conforms to the pattern of boom – slump – boom which the company has lived with over the years and which has, nonetheless, over the years made it a very profitable company.

The headquarters of London Brick in the Bedfordshire field is an industrial village called Stewartby. Once it was Wotton Pillinge, a small insanitary agricultural village ; but, as the original Forder works prospered, the brick makers, Sir Harry and Sir Malcolm Stewart (the founder of the company), decided to plan and develop a model village which they immodestly named after themselves. It is an example of industrial patronage that must go along with the housing developments of the Cadburys at Bourneville. Stewartby village is cheek by jowl with the massive Stewartby brickworks and has a population of about 1100 people living mainly in company houses. Families of the men who work in the brick kilns live in these houses, each fairly similar to the next, and set out amid lawns and company-built communal dwellings like the United Church, the Club and the substantial Memorial Hall built in the style of a New England church.

Inside the Memorial Hall you can read inscriptions that bear witness to the families who have served faithfully both London Brick and its companies : A. Cox, J. Cox, R. Cox ; A. C. Goodman, J. Goodman, W. Goodman ; A. S. Caves, A. W. Caves, E. J. Caves, H. J. Caves. Stewartby also has large playing fields, a swimming pool and two general stores. Some of the village inhabitants are elderly people living in seventy-eight bungalows provided by a trust formed by the late Malcolm Stewart. To this day the company refers to these people as 'old servants' of the company. All the bungalows are occupied rent free and the occupants can be reminded of their patrons just by looking out of the window and watching a working drag-line excavator hauling up clay in the great Stewartby pit.

All around the Stewartby village is London Brick country. Some of the land is the desolate worked-out pits ; other land is mostly farmland owned and leased to tenant farmers by London Brick or farmed by London Brick itself. The proximity of the barrenness of the pits to the reasonably fertile agricultural land is curious. Worked-out pits, after a passage of time, are by any stretch of the imagination a depressing scene. They are steep sided, usually fenced off to prevent people from falling into them, and J. P. Bristow, then deputy chairman of London Brick, told a conference organized on the brickfield in 1968 that 'it is most unlikely that anything can be made to grow' in the pits. All that would grow 'on the cold, wet, yellow clay is what grows there now – coltsfoot, weeds, teasels, coarse grasses and the odd bush'. These vast soured pits are what the brick companies are left with after the digging – a massive land-pollution problem, possibly outdone in terms of scale only by the problems faced by the National Coal Board with its tips for colliery slag and waste. The cubic capacity of the existing pits in Bedfordshire is more than 60×10^6 m³. To fill them would require as much material as would fill St Paul's Cathedral more than 200 times. The Stewartby brickworks alone, according to the company, receives clay at the rate of 500–600 t an hour, or about 45 000 t a week. Approximately it can be calculated that the brickfields at Stewartby thereby consume 38 000 m³ of clay a week, with the company as a whole consuming at least 114 000 m³ a week and very probably more with the boom in brickmaking in 1972 and 1973. In the Bedfordshire brickfield an area of over 6×10^6 m² has been dug for clay, but there is still an area of almost 12×10^6 m² for which planning permission to extract clay exists.

It is thus possible to say that the land pollution, the problem of derelict land in Bedfordshire, is today only one-third of what it may be when all the area is stripped and dug. It is extraordinary but nonetheless true that the government does not recognize that there is any such thing as derelict land in the Bedfordshire brickfield. Successive governments have used a definition of derelict land that is administratively convenient but somewhat at odds with the physical facts. Derelict land is defined as 'land so damaged by industrial or other development that it is incapable of beneficial use without treatment'. Only such land is open to grant aid from the central government for restoration. This definition therefore excludes land that has become 'naturally' derelict. It ignores land that has been neglected or land ravaged by the Armed Forces. The most debatable aspect of all is that it ignores land that is still part of an active industrial site. Thus the derelict slag heaps surrounding a still-working colliery do not qualify as derelict land as far as Whitehall is concerned. For County Councils in different parts of the country, the definition is a hindrance since the county is always being given huge new areas of derelict land when a colliery closes. Thus it is that the total amount of derelict land in Britain is growing, not shrinking, despite the vigorous reclamation programmes being run by the government. Government figures show that between 1964 and 1969 in England and Wales 200×10^6 m² more was added to make a final derelict total of 460×10^6 m². But taking a realistic definition of derelict, the figure swells still further. The Civic Trust has estimated that the amount of derelict land is growing at about 14×10^6 m² annually. Professor Gerald Wibberley has calculated that mineral workings add derelict land at the growth rate of 48×10^6 m² a year. John Barr, in 1969, estimated in his book *Derelict Britain* (Penguin) that the total true area of derelict land was a figure of 1000×10^6 m², which he compared to the size of the county of Huntingdonshire. The official government definition of 'derelict land' also excludes land which is spoiled by natural causes and also a number of specific categories amongst which is 'land damaged by development but which is subject to conditions attached to planning or other statutory arrangements providing for after-treatment'.

Value-added restoration

This is important for the Bedfordshire brickfield, for it is the case that all the brickpits were given the permission necessary for their working with specific conditions attached for their full restoration after they have been worked out. For example, in 1972 the London Brick Company received permission to excavate clay from further areas in the brickfield, but the Minister of Housing and Local Government set out some conditions in a letter dated 17 July 1952. It is a crucial brickfield document and therefore worth reprinting in full :*

*Non-metric units have been left in this letter as quoted. For conversion: 1 acre ≃ 4×10^3 m², 1 foot ≃ 0.3 m.

The Estate Manager
The London Brick Company Limited
Stewartby
Bedford
1913/9/1;   1882/9/2
FWW/MET/11

17th July 1952

Sir

Town and Country Planning Act, 1947
(Tenth Schedule)

I am directed by the Minister of Housing and Local Government to refer to the applications made by you on behalf of the London Brick Company Limited, for permission to develop for the excavation of brick clay land situated near Stewartby and Marston Moreteine, submitted to the Bedford and Ampthill Rural District Councils on the 10th December, 1946, and referred to the Minister for a decision in accordance with his Directions to those Councils dated 9th January, 1947. By virtue of the provisions of the Tenth Schedule to the Town and Country Planning Act, 1947, the applications fall to be dealt with under the Act.

2. The land which forms the subject of the applications covers a total unworked area of approximately 1800 acres and comprises eight separate sites shown hatched black on the accompanying plan. It is understood that the sites numbered 1, 2, 4, 5, 6, 7 and 8 are intended to feed the works at Stewartby.

3. The Minister has fully considered your Company's proposals particularly in the light of the discussions which took place at Stewartby on 2nd June, 1948, between representatives of your Company and other interested parties. He is advised that the concentration and continuance of the workings in this area is dictated by the presence of abundant reserves of a clay particularly suitable for large-scale brick production, which has led to the establishment of a group of works with a very large aggregate brickmaking capacity.

4. The importance of the proposals from the national aspect both as regards land use generally and the maintenance of brick supplies over a long-term period has been carefully considered by the Minister. In the light of the information supplied to him, he has come to the conclusion that the proposed extension of the workings in this area, with the facilities for brick production that are available, is in the national interest and that it should therefore be allowed, provided that the order of working is regulated to minimize disturbance to agriculture, and provided also that appropriate measures are taken for the after-treatment of the sites, as discussed in the following paragraph. He observes that under these circumstances the Local Authorities will raise no general objections to the proposals.

5. In reviewing the factors to be taken into account in deciding what conditions should be imposed, the Minister considers that the main planning problems presented by these large scale excavations concern the appearance of the sites, both during and after working, and their ultimate use. As long as working proceeds, the effect on the amenity of the area can be mitigated only by appropriate measures of screening. On abandonment, even when all overburden has been

respread on the pit floor, the resultant surface may be 50 feet or more below ground level and, as in the present case, the pits can normally be expected to flood with water to a substantial depth. The ultimate aim of restoration must in general be to fill in these pits completely and so provide a surface, at approximately the original ground level, which can be put to some further use. In pursuance of this aim, the Minister proposes to require your Company not only to return all surplus waste and overburden arising from the working, but also to fill the excavations with whatever further material may be available. He recognizes that the supply of suitable filling material is likely to be inadequate for a considerable time to come and that in the meantime the pits must remain incompletely restored. Without abandoning the ultimate aim, it is, therefore, necessary to consider what measures of treatment can be adopted in the interim period. The Minister considers that, so long as these pits remain unfilled, they are less unsightly if they become flooded, particularly if they are properly screened by trees or shrubs or by intermittent ridges of callow suitably vegetated and that in certain circumstances pits so flooded may be capable of being put to some use. He proposes in this case to require your Company to screen the workings. The existence of these deep flooded pits, however, raises certain problems of their own. Though the question was not considered at the meeting with your Company, the Minister invites your Company and the local planning authority to consider whether it would be economically and technically practicable so to dispose of part of the overburden as to form a shelving bank around the edges of the flooded pits, not only in order to reduce the danger inherent in any deep flooded pit with steeply sloped sides, but also with the object, if necessary, of providing additional support for any margins selected for tree planting.

6. At the meeting on 2nd June, 1948, the local authorities urged that steps should be taken to improve the appearance of a cutting into which a stream previously crossing the site had been diverted, and particularly of the associated mounds of overburden. The Minister welcomes the undertaking your Company gave to take appropriate action in this matter; and he would also draw your Company's attention to the importance of consulting the Drainage Authority (in this case the Bedford First Internal Drainage Board) on such matters as the further stopping or diverting of any other watercourses on the sites.

7. In connection with the areas associated with the Stewartby works, your Company have explained that in certain circumstances it may be necessary to vary the order of working mentioned at the meeting on 2nd June, 1948. The Minister has therefore decided not to impose any stated order of working in regard to the areas numbered 4, 5, 6 and 7: but he wishes to draw attention to the desirability, for reasons of agricultural production, of leaving area 7 untouched for as long as practicable.

8. In the exercise of his powers under the above-mentioned Act the Minister accordingly hereby grants permission for the winning and working of brick clay on the areas shown hatched black on the enclosed plan subject to the following conditions:

(1) The winning and working of minerals shall take place in accordance with

the following programme –

(a) On the three north-eastern areas which are to provide materials for the Coronation Works, operations shall proceed progressively in the sequence indicated by the numbers 1, 2, 3 on the accompanying plan.

(b) On the five areas to the south-west which are to provide material for the Stewartby Works, area 8 shall not be worked until the working of the remaining areas (4, 5, 6 and 7) has been sensibly completed.

(2) Trees and shrubs shall be planted to screen the workings in accordance with a scheme to be agreed with the Local Planning Authority or in the event of disagreement as shall be determined by the Minister.

(3) All waste arising from the working or processing of the clay shall be deposited in the workings in such a manner, and the excavated areas shall be further restored by such filling and levelling as may be agreed with the Local Planning Authority, *having regard in the latter respect to the availability of suitable filling materials at suitable times on reasonable terms* [italics added], or to any representations that such materials are not available, or in the event of disagreement as shall be determined by the Minister.

(4) All plant and machinery installed in connection with the working or restoration of the land shall be removed at such time or times as is agreed with the Local Planning Authority that they are no longer required for those purposes, or in default of agreement as the Minister shall determine.

9. This letter is issued by the Minister as his formal decision and does not purport to convey any approval or consent which may be required under bye-laws or Acts other than the Town and Country Planning Act 1947.

10. Copies of this letter and the accompanying plan are being sent to Bedfordshire County Council, Ampthill Rural District Council, and Bedford Rural District Council.

> I am, Sir,
> Your obedient Servant,
> J. B. PROPER
> Authorized by the Minister
> to sign in that behalf.

The crucial wording, for the economics of restoration, are those in italics. Similar ministerial permissions date back to 1947 (Marston Valley Brick Company), 1949 (Redland – Flettons – then called Eastwoods) and in 1952 (Redland and the London Brick Company). A 1949 planning permission, for example, says

... overburden with any other suitable filling materials available at reasonable times on reasonable terms shall be deposited within the excavated areas and shall be thereafter consolidated and levelled in agreement with the local planning authority, or in default of such agreement to the satisfaction of the Minister.

The interpretation of this planning permission has been a matter of disagreement between the brick companies and the local planning authority,

Bedfordshire County Council. The local authority believes that the crucial phrase 'on reasonable terms' means that brick companies should not have to pay an inordinate price for filling materials so that restoration would be hopelessly uneconomic.

J. P. Bristow, at the brickfield conference of 1968, told the audience (which included Neill Macdermot, then Minister of State at the Ministry of Housing) that the company's policy of making a charge for any use of the pits

... fulfils the ministerial conditions as to back-filling the pits with suitable filling materials available at reasonable times and reasonable terms. The planning authority has been aware for the past fifteen years that we do make such charges and have never challenged them.

In short, London Brick considers that the planning permission means that the company must fill the pits, provided that they can get suitable materials at a suitable time that would ensure the company a reasonable economic gain. The local authority has not been able to convince London Brick that its own definition of the planning permission should be adhered to, so we must now look at the problem of what is to be done with these massive pits, which have a cubic capacity of perhaps more than 75×10^6 m^3 of material.

Because of the eccentricity of the Whitehall definition of what constitutes derelict land, Bedfordshire can look to little help from central government to solve the problem. Instead it depends on the initiative of the London Brick Company and whatever encouragement and provocation is to be obtained from the local authority. Up to the mid 1960s, the restoration of these massive worked-out pits was more or less in abeyance and proceeded, if at all, through small-scale and fairly random filling of pits with refuse. Thus the brick companies (there were several at this time) did some back-filling using reject bricks, a private operator tipped railway waste into pit No. 78, domestic rubbish was tipped into pit No. 55 by Bedford Municipal Borough, and in pit 90 by Ampthill Rural District Council and Urban District Council. The operators and local authorities who did this tipping were charged a small fee for doing so; the amount of waste they actually put into the pits was totally insignificant in comparison with the Bedfordshire problem of derelict land. At the end of the 1960s another reclamation scheme was initiated when the company started negotiating the handing over of pit No. 60 – 10^6 m^2 of water-filled pit known as Stewartby lake – to the County Council, charging a peppercorn rent of £50 a year. Now the lake is managed by Stewartby Water Sports Club which has a membership of over 900 and which in its first season used the water for angling, sailing, water-skiing and skin-diving. It is expected that the lake will be expanded as a country park to include a sailing club with mooring space for 750 boats, parking for 1000 cars, childrens' play facilities, paddling pools, picnic areas, and so on.

But in the 1960s the company was unable to find any form of waste that would fill the pits at a reasonable rate to ensure a gradual restoration of the pits to a state of health and use to the community. It can be argued that a solution was deterred by the insistence of London Brick that its pits, though empty, were assets that had to yield more income in the process of being restored. Thus the Deputy Chairman of London Brick, Jeremy Rowe, told me in November 1970: 'We have always had in mind that we have had assets in our pits.' He said again: 'Restorations and schemes in the past have always failed because no one was prepared to pay.' And at the 1968 brickfield conference J. P. Bristow said: 'We regard these pits as one of our assets and as such have always made a charge, a very reasonable one, for their commercial use in any shape or form.' Jeremy Rowe also told me: 'There's money in reclamation, just as in the old days there was money in dereliction.'

Several possible restoration schemes ran into both technical and financial snags. One idea was to use the pits as reservoirs, but they have one major problem to overcome if adapted as reservoirs – when a brick pit is dug its sides are exceedingly steep and the almost-vertical sides would be highly unstable as a reservoir because the water levels in reservoirs fluctuate with water demand. So, in order to turn the pits into reservoirs, the sides would have to slope to an angle of about one in five and the side face would have to be lined, possibly with hardcore. Such a process of adaptation requires massive amounts of both money and land. In order to stabilize the sides, the size of the pits is greatly enlarged. The Great Ouse River Authority gave London Brick a figure of £1·3 million as the cost of converting into a reservoir one pit near Peterborough having a potential storage volume of nearly $1·8 \times 10^6$ m³. So it is cheaper to dig a new reservoir than to adapt an old brickpit. The River Authority estimated the unit cost of the Peterborough pit would work out at £740 per 10^3 m³ compared to £165 per 10^3 m³ for an orthodox reservoir newly dug. London Brick has made various suggestions for adapting the pits for water use, such as asking the River Authority to only half-fill a pit, making it much cheaper to stabilize. These schemes seem to have come to nothing, partly because the River Authority was not enamoured by the pits as 'instant reservoirs', and partly because the London Brick Company was not itself prepared to pay large sums of money to convert the pits and thus restore them for a different purpose – holding water for the local populations.

Another restoration scheme that has come to nothing would actually have greatly minimized the derelict-land problems in two counties – the problem of massive mounds of colliery waste in Nottinghamshire and that of the empty claypits in Bedfordshire. There was a plan for running a kind of merry-go-round of trains with spoil to fill the pits. Since Nottingham has about 12×10^6 m^2 buried under tips of colliery waste, it has a considerable problem. The Bedfordshire scheme was put forward to take care of it ; it was suggested that 3–4 million t a year dumped in the pits, sometimes even over the pits so that small hills could be built, might turn the flat dull brickfield valley into something more attractive. The scheme foundered, to the frustration of Nottinghamshire's county planner, J. H. Lowe. The crucial reason was initially the reticence of anyone to come forward to pay the bill. British Rail calculate that an annual average charge of 72·5p per t would be needed to shift the spoil the 150 km to the south. But no help was forthcoming from central government, which anyway did not consider the land derelict. And London Brick itself was not prepared to pay out considerable sums for this problem.

It is very unlikely that London Brick would be voluntarily converted to the principles of restoration, whether or not the company can gain thereby. The reason is that in 1963 the company signed an agreement with the Central Electricity Generating Board that has meant a considerable restoration programme for the brickpits around Peterborough. In the early 1960s the CEGB felt that, with the demand for electricity doubling every ten years and new power stations being built, it was facing a formidable problem of what to do with the pulverized fuel ash (PFA) left after the coal has been burnt at these power stations. It was thought that the worst surplus would occur at the generating stations on the River Trent, stations such as Drakelow (1450 MW), Westburton (2000 MW) and Ratcliffe (2000 MW). So the CEGB was pleased to agree with London Brick to supply about 50 million t of fuel ash from the generating stations to fill the brickpits. More than 4×10^6 m^2 of pit, about a third of London Brick's present total excavated area, is to be filled with this fuel ash. This scheme has brought in a regular merry-go-round of trains from the power stations to the brickpits. The CEGB spent £3·5 million on building a railway terminal and equipment to pump the pulverized ash, mixed with water to form a slurry, into the pits. In 1966 the first PFA trains came in and ash started to be pumped into the pits, to dry out later and harden, to be restored as material for housing or farms or factories. About 80×10^3 m^2 a year of derelict pit are now being filled. By a stroke of good luck, close to the brickfield is an excellent source of top-soil – washings of sugarbeet from a huge British Sugar Corporation processing plant nearby. The top-soil is stock-piled and in time spread over the ash in a 15 cm layer.

What will happen to the restored land in the fullness of time has yet to be agreed between London Brick and the Huntingdonshire County

Council. The CEGB exhibits symptoms of having regrets at having committed itself so deeply to the plan. More and more industrial uses are found for PFA every year – it is used in a vast range of building products and even as a base for motorways. It also makes an excellent finish for some types of facing concretes. Initially the CEGB planned to dispose of 30 million t of PFA over a time scale at least up to the year 2000, but in 1971 the CEGB wrote:

The Peterborough scheme is 'a long-stop' for the disposal of ash from several of our new big power stations in the Midlands when no more economic methods of disposal can be made. Increasingly we have been able to find nearer and cheaper sites for disposal and consequently the Peterborough project will take rather longer to complete than we envisaged.

The CEGB's sadness over the scheme may be due to the fact that it pays the whole bill, not only for all the terminals and buildings, but for all the transportation and even a small sum to London Brick for each t of ash dumped. London Brick also secures a small rental for these terminal buildings that the CEGB built. It can be taken as a fact that London Brick themselves are very pleased with the Peterborough scheme, for it accords with their principle of restoring while earning. Indeed in 1968 J. P. Bristow told the brickfield conference:

It may be said, it will be said, that London Brick Company wins always. Account should be taken of dislocations to our workings in the area which were inevitably caused by the Electricity Board. New roads have to be constructed, haulage roads moved, waterways diverted, pumps resited, and whilst the Electricity Board paid for most of that, the whole scheme has to be watched carefully so there is no interruption of production.

However, in the early 1970s, the company turned its mind actively towards the problem of trying to reproduce a CEGB-type scheme for its Bedfordshire brickfield, a larger problem than the Peterborough pits. Two strategies are being pursued. The first involves the disposal of refuse, the second some rather transatlantic ideas. In 1970 the company formed a subsidiary called London Brick Land Development with a few offices at Stewartby. The new company planned to offer a solution to local authorities with a rubbish problem. In May 1973 it was announced by the Greater London Council that special trains are to carry about 1200 t of London's refuse daily to the worked-out Bedfordshire brickpits. This new method of disposal for a massive amount of refuse from the capital was expected to start in the spring of 1975 and to cost the GLC about £1 million a year. The scheme was unveiled to the public by Arthur Edwards, chairman of the GLC Public Services Committee, who said that one environmental advantage is that the use of rail facilities will take off the roads of London something like 100 lorry-loads of refuse a day. Another environmental advantage is clearly what is going to happen in Bedfordshire. Subject to planning permission, London Brick expect to build an enclosed refuse-transfer station beside the main London Midland railway line at Brent Terrace, Cricklewood. The refuse from an area with a population of about a million will arrive at the transfer station in local authority collection vehicles and will then be compacted into enclosed containers to be loaded on railway wagons. The transfer station is expected to handle about 320 000 t a year and plans to operate for about twenty years.

This scheme in itself will not be enough to solve the derelict-land problem of the Bedfordshire brickfield. Even if one takes it that the GLC scheme will contribute 10 000 t of rubbish or 30×10^3 m³ compacted per week, clay will still be taken out of the Bedfordshire brickfield at a faster rate than that at which rubbish will be put back, for the brick kilns at Stewartby alone consume 38×10^3 m³ of clay a week. However, London Brick hopes to sign up other local authorities for this rubbish-disposal method. London Brick Land Development is offering local authorities a package deal. Council rubbish trucks deliver the refuse to the transfer stations (built by London Brick), the rubbish is compacted, taken by rail or road to the pit side, and tipped. The tippings will be compressed and spread in two-metre layers with soil between each layer. When the pit is full, it will be covered with soil and returned either to agricultural or industrial use. London Brick will, of course, retain the freehold of the restored land. The GLC contract is only one that London Brick Land Development has been seeking. A third of the country's population lies within an 80 km radius of the Bedfordshire pits, and these people generate some 7 million t or 21×10^6 m³ of refuse a year. But London Brick has not yet (March 1974) been able to get all its contracts with local authorities signed, as firm decisions have been delayed by the changes in the local government structure (which in many cases alter the responsibility for waste disposal) coming into effect in April 1974. Rubbish disposal is an unappealing and irksome problem in modern life. The Greater London Council itself has spent huge sums disposing of rubbish. In 1971 it opened a massive incinerator at Edmonton, costing £10 million, with a treatment cost running to the order of £2 per t of rubbish. Even a smaller town such as Luton generates 250 t of rubbish a day. The huge area around London, however, is experiencing very severe problems of refuse disposal, and, at least in theory, the idea of solving them by using the Bedfordshire pits is excellent from an environmental point of view.

The second and 'transatlantic' idea that London Brick entertains for the brickpits involves a partnership with the Duke of Bedford, whose property at Woburn Abbey is not very far away. In 1972 London Brick announced that it had joined forces with the Duke of Bedford to build 'a Disneyland-style family fun centre' in mid-Bedfordshire. A report in the London *Evening Standard* said that the centre would cover 2.4×10^6 m^2 of worked-out brickfields and could later spill over to take in an extra 1.6×10^6 m^2 of the Duke's nearby safari park at Woburn. London Brick was reported to have taken a 50 per cent shareholding in City Fantasia (Holdings), a private company formed to carry out the project. Apart from the Duke of Bedford, other shareholders include the Chipperfield family who run safari parks throughout the country, and also a small group of business-men who apparently thought up the idea over a year ago. The initial cost of the scheme is likely to be around £1.5 million with London Brick supply-ing the major part of the money. The *Evening Standard* report said that the development is likely to split in due course into various parks, each with its own characteristics: 'There will be, for instance, African and Indian villages and a mock up of a Wild-West town. Another big idea being con-sidered is the possibility of setting up a dinosaur-land, and prehistoric fossils are frequently unearthed during excavations.' (The most spectacular of these finds occurred in August 1963 when a workman at the company's Coronation pit noticed some large bones sticking out of the overburden at the end of the pit. Staff from the British Museum travelled to the pit and identified the skeleton (which was much damaged by excavation) as a pliosaur, one of the *Plesiosauria* family, a group of carnivorous aquatic animals with massive paddles to propel them through the water. The 'Stewartby pliosaur' (as the company calls it) is claimed to be the largest pliosaur known from the Jurassic rocks. A reconstruction and scale model exists in the British Museum (Natural History) in South Kensington, London.) By March 1974 no planning permission had been given by Bedfordshire County Council for such a Disneyland scheme, nor had the scheme been worked out in detail. However it is clearly another adaptation of London Brick's principle that the pits should be restored in a manner that produces earnings for the company.

It is this principle of London Brick that has caused perhaps the greatest controversy in its attitude towards restoration. Critics argue that London Brick enjoys three stages of profits from the land – profits from digging out the clay, profits again from charging a fee to customers, and profits a third time from using or selling the restored land. Since agricultural land is now being sold for sums two or even three times greater than those of 1970, the profits could be considerable. One critic at the brickfield conference of 1968 described this principle as 'like a pickpocket selling back the wallet after he has emptied it'. The question becomes critical if it should prove to be the case that London Brick's schemes for refuse disposal and/or Disneyland type schemes do not restore the pits at the rate at which some had hoped.

With the brickfield working at record pace in 1972 and 1973, it was more than ever the case that land was becoming derelict at a faster rate than it was being restored, or could be restored with the new GLC scheme in progress. If other local authority schemes were under way, a different state of affairs might hold. At the time of writing, restoration has never remotely approached the rate of despoliation. If this should continue, the queston arises as to what should be done about it.

Some sections of the population might say that it is simply a matter of enforcing the planning conditions. Certainly the planning permission has not been enforced. A factor in the attitude of central government is perhaps that nothing should be done to seriously inconvenience the flow of bricks at a time when the country has been continuously in a period of housing crisis. Following this line of thought there have been suggestions that the restoration of the brickpits should be partly a matter of government subsidy. In particular, this has been suggested for a revival of the scheme to transport colliery slag from the Nottinghamshire coalfield to Bedfordshire. In 1967 it was calculated that the spoil from four of these collieries in particular, producing a total of about 3·2 million t a year would be sufficient to fill pit No. 74 ($7·7 \times 10^6$ m³), for example, in four years only. The factor that always ensured that the colliery-slag scheme would be stillborn was the reluctance of anyone to pay the bill. But there is a precedent for a contribution from the government in the contributions made by the government towards the Ironstone Restoration Fund set up under the Minerals Working Act 1951. Under this scheme the government does pay a share towards the cost of reclamation in addition to payment from the landowner and the mineral operator. Of course, such a payment for restoring the Bedfordshire brickpits would be a subsidy to the London Brick Company or to the National Coal Board or to both together. Indeed, it is quite possible to entertain arguments that government should subsidize the dumping of refuse in the Bedfordshire pits or the adaptation of the Bedfordshire pits to reservoir use. In all these cases the government would be paying a sum of money which could be variously seen as a subsidy to the London Brick Company to solve its own derelict-land problem or a subsidy to ensure that the people of Bedfordshire live again in an attractive and productive landscape.

It may be that additional factors come into play because the London Brick Company is a private company (though a public company in the sense of being quoted on the Stock Exchange and having many shareholders amongst the public). The recent profit record of London Brick has been badly affected by the depression in the private house building industry, where activity in 1974 was thought to have been 50% below that in 1973. London Brick made a record and thumping profit of £8·93 million in 1973, but 1974 looked to be a much leaner year. In the year ended 31 December 1972 London Brick's profit was £7 573 808. This was an increase of almost exactly £1 million on the previous year's net profit before tax of £6 578 234. In 1970 the company's profit was considerably lower at £3 661 427. The healthiness of the 1972, and indeed the 1971, profit figure can be seen from its relation to turnover. In 1971 the turnover of the company was some £36 million and in 1972 the turnover was a little more than £41 million. These are very good profit figures as a proportion of turnover. The payment of dividends to shareholders has also been satisfactory. It is, of course, grossly simplistic to look upon profit as that portion of the balance sheet that lines the pocket of those connected with the company. For example, London Brick intends to spend, through its subsidiary London Brick Land Development Limited, more than £1 million in the project with the GLC for the disposing of refuse in the clay-pits. By June 1974 London Brick's shares had reached a low of 34½p which was a dramatic contrast with the vertigo of the previous year when they reached a high of 95p. Once again, boom – slump – boom. In 1973 these shares reached a high of 95p and a low of 62p up to the date of 21 May. Several of the directors of the company are shown by company records to have shareholdings in the company, by far the largest being that of Sir Ronald Stewart who on 31 December 1972 owned 56 445 ordinary shares and 2500 preference shares. His non-beneficial interests also meant that he had an additional 28 845 ordinary shares and 7700 preference shares. Mr Jeremy Rowe, the Deputy Chairman, is shown as owning 8941 ordinary shares. Many of the other shareholdings of directors are small, the smallest being that of 600 ordinary shares in the name of Sir Stanley Morton, who is also Chairman of the Building Societies Association, of the Abbey National Building Society and of the National Housebuilders Registration Council. He joined the board of London Brick in June 1972.

The pollution of brickmaking

It is possible that clay working in Bedfordshire has had other costs. At the turn of the century the brickfield area was well clothed with trees. Bedfordshire's county planner, Geoffrey Cowley, wrote in his report *The Bedfordshire Brickfield* in 1967 that

Today some reasonably well-treed areas remain, but large stretches of countryside are practically devoid of trees. For instance, there is scarcely a tree to interrupt the view from the lower slopes of the green sand ridge near Ampthill across to the brickworks chimneys at Stewartby. The trees that formerly existed were mainly hedgerow oak and elm with a good proportion of ash, whilst on the green sand ridge and the hilly boulder clay country areas of parkland contributed to the sylvan character of the district ... Since the last War grazing land has progressively been converted to arable, so that the need for hedgerows has been reduced and trees have lost their economic functions. In parkland areas, too, trees have been removed and over the whole area there has been little, if any, replacement of dead trees. The situation has been aggravated by the ravages of Dutch Elm disease . . . The existing picture is one sparse in hedgerows and trees, but in addition many of the trees that do still stand are dead or dying and stag-headed, so that there is visible decay to stand testimony to the decline in the quality of the landscape.

London Brick's enthusiasm for the tree has improved during the 1970s. Up to 1970 the company had planted 50 000 trees in the period since the last War, not a considerable total and, on at least one expert's reckoning, only the work of a single forester. Many of the trees planted died, perhaps because of alterations in the water table, perhaps because of air pollution. But in late 1970 London Brick seemed to experience a new enthusiasm and it agreed with the County Council to provide 2×10^5 m² in the brick-field for the experimental planting of 50 000 trees over a five-year period. These trees will be used partly as screens round the pits to reduce eyesores. The idea of the County Council and London Brick is to find what types of tree grow best in the brickfield and whether they can grow them as eco-nomic plantation crops. There is little chance of the trees ever actually being planted in the bottom of the pits, which is cold and dead soil, but there is some indication that the brickfield may once again be a pleasantly wooded area. The cost of this experiment is being split three ways: between London Brick (fifty per cent), The Countryside Commission (37·5 per cent) and the County Council (the remainder).

Several theories have been advanced as to why the original trees have suffered. One possibility is that a lowering of the watertable has occurred due to the digging of the clay pits and that the actual change from stock farming to arable farming has again affected the watertable. However, Mr Cowley also says that it is interesting that certain air-pollution-resistant species of trees, such as poplars, willows and elms, have done reasonably well in the brickfield country. This has led to some theorizing that the tree problems in the brickfield are at least partly caused by sulphur dioxide pollution from the 110-odd chimneys in the brickfield. These chimneys emit large volumes of sulphur dioxide and also smaller amounts of fluorine and other gases. The charge is that the sulphur dioxide from the chimneys can in certain circumstances (particularly a temperature in-version in which a layer of cold air prevents the dispersal of pollutants) damage the local vegetation. According to Mr Cowley:

Evidence from this country does suggest that where the degree of wind exposure is high the effects of industrial air pollution, including sulphur and fluorine compounds, are intensified. These result in the browning of foliage leading to the subsequent loss of vigour and ultimate die-back of the tree completely, giving a stag-headed appearance.

The exact reason for the lack of vigour of the Bedfordshire trees in the brickfield area cannot be identified with certainty. However, the brick-field chimneys are more clearly the cause of another air-pollution problem – the result of the emission of the fluorine compounds. The Oxford clay described by one writer as 'the answer to the brickmaker's prayer' because of its quality of containing 'fuel', also contains a number of impurities, the most troublesome of which is fluorine. When the clay is burnt and the bricks are fired, fluorine is released from the brickfield chimneys. The danger lies in the effect it can have on livestock. In certain conditions when the fluorine compounds fall on the grass, cattle which eat heavily contaminated fodder go down with fluorosis, defined as a condition which develops as a result of the prolonged ingestion of excessive quantities of fluorine compounds. Symptoms of fluorosis in cattle are damage to the teeth, lameness due to damage to the joints and bones, and sometimes loss in milk yield and bodily condition. The lameness particularly is caused by changes in the structure of the bone so that fractures of the pedal bone occur.

Fluorosis as such occurs in various parts of Britain, and in 1964 a report from the Ministry of Agriculture, Fisheries and Food was published entitled *The Occurrence and Effects in Industrial Areas of England and Wales between the years 1954 and 1957 of Fluorosis in Cattle*. The report was written by K. N. Burns and Ruth Allcroft of the Central Veterinary Laboratory, Weybridge, Surrey. The survey examined a number of industrial areas of Britain such as the vicinity of Sheffield, Scunthorpe and Stoke-on-Trent. It also looked at the Buckinghamshire and Bedfordshire brickmaking areas. It reported:

Fluorosis has occurred previously in this area and was investigated in the late 1930s when the source of fluorosis was shown to be the local clay . . . On three of the badly affected farms, a change to an arable system was made and this has remained. Districts visited during the present survey included Stewartby, Houghton Conquest, Lidlington, Marston Moretaine, Ridgmont, Wootton, Elstow and Wilshamstead. In contrast to the West Riding of Yorkshire and Stoke-on-Trent there is almost no industry other than brickmaking and some of the farms are immediately adjacent to the brickworks. The farmland around the brickworks is flat, the southern part of the area is bounded by a range of low hills which deflect the smoke carried by the prevailing south west wind and concentrate the drift particularly towards the districts of Lidlington, Marston Moretaine, Stewartby and Houghton Conquest.

Investigators examined forty-three farms and found that, in addition to the three farms that had abandoned grazing, there were eight that had been severely affected by fluorosis and a further eight that had been slightly affected, so that nineteen out of the forty-three farms had been damaged by fluorosis. They reported that most of the farms with the damaging fluorosis were between and among the brickworks or within about 3 km to the north and east, which is the area over which most of the smoke is deposited. There were affected farms on the slopes of the range of hills at the southern end of the brickfield, but on top of and beyond these hills only slight dental fluorosis was found. The clinical effect most noticed was lameness, acute and severe, but generalized stiffness also occurred. The investigators thought that the clay soil baked very hard in early summer and may have contributed to the incidence of lameness. As far as loss of production was concerned, in non-lame animals such loss was noticeably less severe than in the West Riding or Stoke-on-Trent and was at present only in two of the seven herds classified as severely affected with lameness. There was no loss of production in slightly or not affected herds and the quality of grassland available to the cattle of the Bedfordshire brickfield was noticeably better than in the other two areas. However, of those animals that actually were lame, loss of production had occurred.

The whole 1956 to 1957 investigations covered 832 farms throughout the country in twenty-one industrial districts; damaging fluorosis, severe enough to cause economic loss, was found on 170 farms in seventeen districts. The investigators stated that control is difficult and that the best strategy was to prevent the pollution at source or alternatively to take up a system of husbandry that would eliminate or reduce the risk of fluorosis. A number of farmers in the brickfield area have taken the hint; hence the switch from dairy and stock-farming to arable farming where there is no risk of fluorosis. This approach has the sanction of the Chief Alkali Inspector, who heads the Alkali and Clean Air Inspectorate, the body in Britain that is concerned with the control of air pollution in many of the most troublesome industrial processes. The Alkali Inspector records in his report for 1965 that 'there is a farming hazard ... ' and says that this can be obviated by good farming practice. Some of the farmers that do continue to practise dairy farming use a substantial amount of brought-in food. They do not repeatedly graze the same meadow.

The London Brick Company itself practises successful dairy farming at the Stewartby farm, very near the brickworks. The 1972 annual report of the London Brick Company records with pride:

Our own estate provides evidence, if such was needed, of how successfully you can farm in the immediate environment of the brickworks ... 1972 was a particularly good year. A substantial acreage of cereals was grown with satisfactory yields and, for the fifth year in succession, our Stewartby farming unit won the Bedfordshire Farmers' Day Cup for the highest total points in the grain and root crop classes. The grasslands also yielded sufficient grazing and hay for the feeding of our two pedigree dairy shorthorn herds. These cattle, reared on our farms, at Peterborough and Bedford, and numbering some 450 head, had a spectacular year in the show rings, gaining some 26 prizes, including 12 firsts. One of our home-reared cows – 'Phorpres Wild Maid the Thirteenth' – was champion Interbreed Dairy Cow at the Royal Norfolk Show. She also made a clean sweep by winning both the female Dairy Shorthorn and Breed Championships at this show and the East of England Show.

The company's results for 1972 show that farm products and farm cottage and other rents made a profit of £93 981 compared to the profit of £43 331 in 1971. However, this figure does not indicate the profit and loss of specific farms as distinct from rent, etc. It must also be recorded that at least one farmer, George Patrick, who farms 68×10^4 m^2 at Bury Farm, Houghton Conquest, which is some 3 km from the nearest brickworks, has had incidences of fluorosis in his cattle recently. A report in the London *Evening Standard* of 29 November 1972 records that he claims that over the years more than 200 cows of his have had to be destroyed because of deformities caused by fluorosis.

A third troublesome pollutant is issued by the brickfield chimneys – gas probably containing what are called 'mercaptans' that give a strong smell or 'rubbery' odour. The Alkali Inspectorate has received a number of complaints over the years from members of the public, and many of them concern this unpleasant smell. In addition, complaints have been made about the release of sulphur dioxide, apart from its possible effects on the landscape. The County Medical Officer, Dr McLeod, told me in 1971 that he would not advise a person with bronchial difficulties to live in the brickfield, though the exact effects on human health were hard to quantify.

An attempt to measure this public-health aspect was made by a previous County Medical Officer who in 1960 produced *A Report on Atmospheric Pollution in the Brickworks Valley*. The report comprised the findings of two separate studies, one a clinical investigation into the respiratory condition of people who lived in the district and the other on the measurement of atmospheric pollution. The report showed that, as far as pollution by sulphur gases was concerned, the situation was like that of a small industrial town, but in the case of smoke (including soot ash and gritty particles) it was little different from any other rural area. The clinical study showed a greater evidence of chest symptoms in a sample of people from the brickworks valley living at Lidlington than in a comparable sample from a control area at Risely. However, because differences in some other actors, such as cigarette smoking, in the two populations were not properly evaluated, this finding does not give us conclusive evidence as to the effect of atmospheric pollution. But the air pollution does, of course, worry the country planners. Geoffrey Cowley, for example, says that it restricts his planning freedom: 'The smell is such that I couldn't place an old people's home there or a hospital.' Local people who have lived in the brickfield for years have grown accustomed to the smell, and really only notice it when they return from a holiday. This may happen because of the fact that certain odours actually atrophy the ability to continue sensing them.

The problem is not receding. The 1971 report of the Alkali Inspectorate, published in November 1972, records that 'there has been a noticeable revival of public concern about emissions from Fletton brickworks, and several general area complaints against the industry have been received. In these cases it has not been possible to do more than assure complainants that the problem is still being actively studied, though no early solution is in sight.' An earlier report of the Chief Alkali Inspector, that of 1965, sets out why it is difficult for the brick companies to eliminate their air-pollution problems. The kilns used for firing Fletton bricks are practically all 'continuous kilns'; the bricks are set, dried, fired and cooled in a series of individual chambers. It has been established that most of the trouble-some pollutants, the fluorine and the mercaptons, are released during a stage preliminary to proper baking, a combustion stage when the bricks are heated to between 100 °C and 700 °C. This is called the 'coming-hot' stage.

The possibility has occurred to people that if, at this 'coming-hot' stage, the troublesome pollutants could be separated from the rest of the brick-works gases, which make up a huge volume, they could then be treated. By the time all the gases are mixed up in the chimney, the concentrations of fluorine and sulphur dioxide are really too weak to be removed. The problems of separation of the 'coming-hot' gases are not technically difficult. London Brick's researchers have found on an experimental basis that they can separate these gases, but they have not yet found how they can treat them – in other words, prevent them from being released as pollutants. In 1971 the researchers were examining a process referred to them by the Alkali Inspectorate – a process which had been applied on a small pilot basis in the United States. It is really designed for sulphur dioxide removal not for the smell constituents or fluorine. Under it a magnesium oxide 'cake' is used as an absorber of the sulphur dioxide; the theory is that the used 'cake', by now magnesium sulphide, could be taken to a nearby acid works and there regenerated again into magnesium oxide, so that the 'cake' could then be returned to the brickworks. The 1971 Chief

Alkali Inspector's report also records that a new kiln has gone into production, served by a 90 m chimney, and this is provided with the means, by steam and flues, to enable the 'coming-hot' stage gases to be withdrawn into a separate ring or flue. Currently, then, it seems that research is still primarily being directed into preliminary investigation and that there is no immediate chance of the London Brick Company installing in all its brickworks efficient methods of removing the pollutants.

This is particularly so for sulphur dioxide. The Alkali Inspectorate's principal method is to require London Brick to build higher chimneys on its new brick kilns so that the pollutants are spread more widely. Where new brick kilns are being built the chimney stacks are now above 90 m. But many of the older brick kilns cannot take the weight of taller stacks, and such is the longevity of the kilns that the brick companies are reluctant to phase them out purely on the grounds that their chimney stacks are too short. As a result a very high level of dispersion is not being attained, although the Chief Alkali Inspector concludes in almost every one of his annual reports that levels of sulphur dioxide and indeed the fluorine concentrations 'continue to be satisfactorily low . . . '.

This strategy of requiring the companies to build taller chimneys is known as the 'tall-stack policy' in Britain. It is the most favoured tactic of the Alkali Inspectorate when faced with a troublesome sulphur pollution problem. The CEGB, for example, is constantly being required to build higher and higher stacks on its new power stations and indeed the Alkali Inspectorate has a complicated formula for calculating the necessary height of the chimney stacks. This policy has a number of defenders amongst the clean air policy establishment in Britain, but there are indications that it may create as many problems as it cures. Evidence for this was produced by researchers at Harwell Atomic Research Station when in 1971 they found that photochemical smog had been present in the South of England at the time of an experiment. The photochemical smog is caused from the unburnt emissions from cars uniting with small droplets of water to create a mist. If the atmosphere is in any way acidic because of the higher level of sulphur dioxide emission from tall chimneys in the vicinity, the small droplets of water contain sulphuric acid, which aggravates the photochemical problem.

However, there are ways of removing sulphur dioxide as well as simply dispersing it. A power station on the Wood River in Illinois uses a process to 'wash the fumes'. This process is known as the Moncanto Cat-Ox, and it recovers sulphuric acid which, in theory anyway, can be sold. The cat-ox process has been investigated for adaption for the brickfields but regrettably it is not suitable. Such is the massive amount of gases emitted from the forest of chimney stacks in the brickfield that it has been calculated that it would need the entire 10 million ton capacity of Stewartby Lake near the London Brick headquarters to wash less than one week's emission of pollution. This would have the unwelcome effect of creating a water pollution problem.

The attitude of London Brick towards air pollution has led it into controversy. In 1971, its chief research officer, Dicky Richards, told Jon Tinker, Environment Consultant of *New Scientist*: 'The problem is to find a method of treatment. If someone had a process which showed some promise, we would be prepared to have a go at it. We look into any new idea that turns up. It is not that there are things to be done and we are refusing to spend the money.' Mr Tinker attacked the company for this type of attitude and asked if it was satisfactory for a company with a £25 million turnover to wait for ideas to turn up. In 1971, Mr Richards also told me: 'The company has not done any work removing fluorine apart from a scheme putting lime in the process to remove it. That didn't work. The company's work has been to see the effects of the fluorine after it has left the chimney.' He added: 'Up to the moment, no practical method for removing sulphur or fluorine has been found.' The charge against London Brick is that it has not done sufficient work in developing treatment processes of its own. After all, it is, as it says in its own publicity, 'the world's largest brickmaker'. It has been suggested that the company should spend large sums of money to find a method of treating, as well as simply separating, the 'coming-hot' gases containing the pollutants.

A considerable degree of controversy has also been created by the role of the Alkali Inspectorate in the Fletton brick industry. As is its practice in dealing with all industries, the Inspectorate leaves the monitoring of ground level concentrations to the London Brick Company, taking samples only on the intermittent visits of its inspectors. In 1971 the Inspectorate took a total of fifty-five samples from fifty-three chimneys in the Fletton brick industry. These gave average acidity of 0·127 grammes per cubic metre expressed in terms of sulphur dioxide. However, the Inspectorate took no samples whatever of fluorine or fluorides. The report records that the industry 'continued to monitor the local environment and submitted to the Inspector the results of the tests. Ground-level concentrations of sulphur and fluorine compound continued to be low.' The charge is not being made here that London Brick is in any way falsifying the data; the charge is only being made that this work should properly be done by the Alkali Inspectorate and it is being remiss in not doing so.

Over the years, research into the problems of the Fletton brick industry has been done not only by the laboratories of the brick companies but perhaps even more elaborately by government laboratories, such as the Warren Spring Laboratory. Thus the report of the Chief Alkali Inspector for 1970 tells us that two secret reports have been prepared by the Laboratory, entitled *Laboratory Investigation on the Production, Evaluation and Removal of Brickwork Odours* and *A Review of the Possible Processes for the Removal of Sulphur Oxide from Fletton Brickworks' Gases*. The attitude of both the government and the government laboratories to date has been that the air-pollution problems in the brickfields are an irritating inconvenience that should not be allowed to interfere with the business of producing bricks for the nation's houses.

But whatever the attitude of the government might be, the air-pollution problem is undoubtedly a cost, or diseconomy, that has to be taken into account when looking at the 'politics of the brickfield'. A solution to these problems almost certainly requires a change in the nature of the controlling body, the Alkali Inspectorate. The principle on which the Alkali Inspectorate practises is that 'the best practicable means' should be used by industry to reduce and eliminate pollution. The phrase is nowhere in the Alkali Acts precisely defined, but one can gather its drift by definitions in the Public Health Act 1956 and the Clean Air Act 1956. In these Acts, 'practicable' is taken to mean reasonably practicable having regard to local conditions and circumstances, to the current state of technology, to the financial implications and to compatibility with any duty imposed by law. 'Means' is taken to include the design, installation, maintenance and manner and periods of operation of plant and machinery, and the design, construction, and maintenance of buildings. Thus in practice the phrase 'best practicable means' tends to have the result that, where a process for removing a pollutant is well known, the Alkali Inspectorate operates efficiently enough to see that it is used and taken advantage of. But if the means for efficient pollution prevention is not known, the Alkali Inspectorate is poorly placed because 'best practicable means' is a blunt-edged weapon for provoking a company to start research to discover a method of removing the pollution. The phrase 'best practicable means' would be more relevant to the twentieth century if it could be redrafted so that in certain circumstances an industry could be required to search for a solution to its pollution problem, in its own laboratories and by spending its own money, rather than rest its case on the fact that no one else has come across a solution that could be applied to it.

The Alkali Inspectorate also embodies, in its attempts to make sure that pollution standards are adhered to, a view about industry and the environment. This is best expressed by a statement in a paper written by a former deputy inspector, E. A. J. Mahler, in an appendix to the 1966 report. He said:

Emissions in terms of both concentrations and mass rate of emission must be reduced to the lowest practicable amount. The determination of what is practicable demands striking a balance between technical possibilities on the one hand and costs on the other. But the technically possible would be impracticable if the costs were so high that the manufacturing operation was thereby rendered unprofitable or nearly so.

The question to direct to the Bedfordshire brickfield problem is whether the London Brick Company might have been rendered 'unprofitable or nearly so' if it had been required to spend larger sums searching for a solution to its fluorine, smell and sulphur dioxide problems. Given the company's profit, particularly in proportion to turnover, it may be hard to think so. Making bricks is a good and sound business and not an industry on the breadline or nearly so. For particular brickworks, however, there are problems. The brick industry is a peculiar one subject both to seasonal fluctuations and demand and to cyclical fluctuations dependent on the rate of house building. According to the report (No. 150) by the National Board for Prices and Incomes on 'pay and other terms and conditions of employment in the Fletton brick industry and the prices charged by the London Brick Company published on July 1970': 'The brickworks have learnt by experience to cope with seasonal fluctuations by adjusting production and laying down stocks of bricks when necessary. Cyclical fluctuations are more serious in their impact and present the industry with severe problems because of their unforeseeable nature.' The report goes on to set out how the Fletton brick production expanded very considerably from 1958 when 1·5 million bricks were produced to 1965 when a peak was reached. But there were serious setbacks in 1966 when production slumped to less than 3 million, and in 1969 when it was 2·9 million. At the end of 1969 stocks reached a record level of over 10 per cent of annual production. More recently the brick industry has been booming and London Brick has reopened works that were closed down during a slump in the early 1970s. London Brick has a number of rather elderly works creaking somewhat at the joints. Many of them are among the worst polluting brickworks because of the relative shortness of their chimney height. It is at least very possible that some of these works might be closed permanently if decent and rigorous pollution standards were enforced. However, the government is unlikely to take such drastic action or try to force the pace. The latest initiative on the air-pollution front has been a suggestion made by Eldon Griffiths, Parliamentary Under Secretary of State at the Department of Environment, in 1972, that the brick industry cooperate in setting up a liaison committee for the Fletton brick industry. This committee, on which the Alkali Inspector, the local authorities and the brick companies are represented, will examine ways of improving air-pollution control. It is another example of the British preference in pollution control for voluntary consultation.

On the other hand, almost every industry brings benefits as well as costs. One of the benefits of the London Brick Company in the Bedfordshire brickfield that has to be estimated is its bringing of employment. This also tends to be somewhat cyclical and fluctuating. When a brickworks is closed down a fair number of men are released from work. Thus in 1968 we found that the London Brick Company employed 10 398 people, with an average pay of some £1200 a year. In 1970 the number of people employed had dropped to 8332 (on average). In 1972 the average employment figure was 9557, and the remuneration of this payroll was £1 8612 207. Thus the 'average' London Brick employee earned in 1972 a sum approaching £1800 a year, although one should perhaps be somewhat suspicious of averages. In 1973, 9364 employees earned £21 315 538 and although this figure, both in terms of employees and in terms of money paid out, will have dropped with the slump in 1974, nevertheless this is clearly a significant amount of cash input to what would in other respects be a purely rural area. It has been a feature of the brick industry, however, that the basic hourly rate for labourers, which is the key rate in the industry, is fairly low, although the industry does provide a high level of overtime upon which wages are made up. The 1970 National Board for Prices and Incomes report found that the level of overtime was accounted for largely by time-workers as opposed to piece-rate workers, and the time-workers worked on average 49·1 hours a week. The piece-workers were better paid than the time-workers. But the workers are divided into many occupations, some of them with colourful names such as smudgers, blockers, banders, drawers, wicket-erectors, and kiln burners.

Solutions

How to clean up the brickfield? We have seen that the approach embodied by London Brick towards the problem of derelict land is classic of a private company in a free-enterprise economic climate. The company looks upon the pits primarily as assets and the rate of restoration is clearly geared to the rate at which profitable waste can be found or customers with severe enough waste problems to pay good money to dump the waste in the brickpits. We have seen that because of the eccentricity of the government's definition of derelict land, there are no grants available to the Bedfordshire County Council, for example, to take some of the derelict pits in hand and restore them themselves.

If the brickpits were part of a defunct company and a totally derelict working, then they would be within the civil servants' definition of derelict land. Since 1970, a fairly vigorous government programme has been pursued on official derelict land, and in counties like Durham and Lancashire large and radical crash programmes are under way to attack the problem. But none of this is any use to Bedfordshire. Bedfordshire has a private-enterprise derelict-land problem. We have seen how under this system it is likely that the process of extracting clay in the Bedfordshire brickfield will proceed even faster than the process of restoration. And we should remember that, of the 18×10^6 m^2 of clay over which the London Brick Company has planning permission to dig, there are nearly 12×10^6 m^2 still to go. Although in terms of the percentage of land in Bedfordshire such an area may be less than 1 per cent, it is still a formidable scar on the landscape. The London Brick approach may be successful, but it depends upon the vagaries of the market. The prospect of a 'Disneyland' in one of the pits must depend on the sponsors' ability to satisfy planners that they will not create an even worse scar on the landscape. In short, and obviously enough, restoration under this type of approach is not something that will happen *regardless*. It will happen only if the price is right.

We are thus forced back to reading again the words of the planning permission upon which London Brick works its land. The crucial words in the planning permission were 'the availability of suitable filling materials, at suitable times on reasonable terms'. London Brick has always interpreted this as 'availability at a reasonable profit'. The County Council disputes that this is the intention of the planning permission. However, the County Council has done little to try to enforce adherence to its interpretations of the planning permission, and it is not open to members of the general public to take action in the courts to see that the terms are enforced. The result is a kind of sterile academic bickering over the semantics of a planning permission consent while all the time the drag-line excavators gobble up more clay and the brickpits of Bedfordshire get bigger and bigger.

There may be some environmentalists who would be willing to try to ensure that clay was no longer won in this manner; that bricks were produced from other materials, especially waste materials from which American companies have shown that perfectly sound building bricks can be produced. Indeed, sound building bricks can be produced from the pulverized fuel ash from the CEGB power stations that is dumped in London Brick's pits near Peterborough. The argument of such environmentalists is based partly upon a conviction that the brick itself is an outdated building unit. They point to the fact that bricks have been subject to increasing competition from alternative building materials in recent years. This is especially true of internal brickwork, for the standard Fletton product – namely the commons brick – is today often replaced by plaster board, concrete blocks, plastic units or hollow clay blocks. In 1960 twice as many commons bricks as facing bricks (used on external walls and therefore valued for their attractive appearance) were delivered to the brick industry as a whole. However, in 1969 commons bricks only exceeded facings by some 40 per cent. The brick industry generally would counter such arguments by saying that the excellent qualities of the brick of sound-proofing, thermal insulation, load bearing and ease of construction ensures the product's survival, and they would point out that their market in facing bricks is also booming.

Another factor has to be taken into account: more modern types of building material can also be produced from the Oxford Clay dug out of the brickpits. The Redland Brick Company made at their Fletton brickworks a small quantity of brick known as 'Calculon'. These bricks are described by London Brick as being similar in height and length to the standard brick but nearly double the width. Although Calculon was originally developed for the requirements of structural load-bearing brickwork they are very suitable to replace the ordinary bricks in a traditional 9 inch (22·9 cm) thick wall – the kind of standard load-bearing wall in many houses today. London Brick claims that in this way the productivity of the bricklayer is increased and the cost of the brickwork reduced. Since taking over the Fletton brickworks at Redland, the London Brick marketing organization has sought to further the sale of these Calculon units and claims that, so successful has the exercise been, it has been possible to double the production of Calculon and extend its manufacture to other works. In addition, London Brick produces from the Bedfordshire brickfield other items such as field-drain pipes, clay pipes and hollow clay blocks.

In my view it is simply unrealistic to expect new building materials to 'drive out the brick' so that the brickfields will cease to present a problem and it will be possible for even a civil servant to class them as derelict land. A different approach, to try to ensure that in future any company that gets permission to dig land for some mining purpose does in fact get round to restoring it in the end, has been advanced by Lord Kennet, at one time Under Secretary of State to Anthony Crosland in the 1966–70 Labour government. For a period after Labour lost office, Lord Kennet was chairman of the Council for the Protection of Rural England, and in one speech he suggested that a condition of planning permission should be that the company concerned 'posts a bond'; in other words that the company should pay a considerable sum of money, which would grow according to the amount of land worked, into a trust fund. The trust could be activated in certain circumstances. It could be used to ensure that restoration continued while the process of working was going on; it could be used in the event of the reluctance or bankruptcy of a company. In these cases the County Council would simply be empowered to invoke the trust fund and to use its money to clean up the landscape.

The advantage of such an approach is that it gets round the real moral difficulty of whether the taxpayer should actually be asked to contribute sums of money to help a private company clear up a problem of its own making. In the case of a public company, such a position is more tolerable, even if it is still unpleasant to pay the taxes. But a company such as London Brick is a successful and usually expanding enterprise able to disperse considerable funds to its shareholders. Is it right that these shareholders should also benefit from sums given to their company by the general public? It is surely arguable that only when companies realize from the outset of a mining endeavour that they must calculate fully for immediate restoration costs, that such restoration is likely to occur. The cost of restoration should feature in the price of the product; the people buying bricks, should be paying a few pence with each thousand bricks as a contribution towards tidying up the landscape of Bedfordshire. For landscape is transparently a public property. Even for a travelling salesman hurrying through the area, it is a not unimportant matter that he drives through a soured and unpleasant landscape. Within the roughly six parishes that make up the brickfield population there are some 10 000 people living. The labour force of London Brick in the Bedfordshire brickfield is approximately 5–6000 workers, many of whom come into the area and a number of whom are immigrants. But for all these people it is a matter of concern that they have to live and work in a disfigured landscape.

This remains true even if it is understandable that someone who works for London Brick can see things differently. Thus James Bristow, the former deputy chairman of the company and a current member of the Board, could say at that brickfield conference back in 1968: 'We think it [the brickfield] is a scene of intense industrial activity in a country which lives by industry. We don't find it depressing.'

5 The Cow Green Reservoir

Roy Gregory

Upper Teesdale is one of the wildest and loneliest parts of England. Extending over about 200×10^6 m², it stretches from the town of Middleton-in-Teesdale up into the Pennines, to the source of the Tees high on Cross Fell. In the upper reaches of the valley there are few signs of human life, far less of modern civilization. It rains a good deal, and the clouds sit like mist on the bleak, peat-covered fells. A few kilometres upstream from the boiling torrent of Cauldron Snout, where the river runs deeper and quieter, there is Cow Green. The name refers to an area of land on the western flank of Widdybank Fell, above the abandoned workings of the old Cow Green lead mine, and about one km from the river itself. Although it appears on maps, until recently 'Cow Green' conveyed little even to those who knew the area well, for it is not a name that local people, or anyone else, commonly use to describe this particular patch of Widdybank Fell.

Remote though they are, the hills and valleys of Upper Teesdale have never been entirely empty. The area has long been prized by climbers and walkers, country-lovers and naturalists. And for more than a hundred years the rare plants that survive in Upper Teesdale have made it an area of great interest to botanists. In the unusual combination of sugar lime-stone and acid peat soils found on Widdybank Fell, climate and geology between them have nurtured what some eminent botanists consider to be assemblages, or 'communities', of rare plants that are unique in the United Kingdom. These communities may well have been there undisturbed since the period immediately after the last ice age, more than 10 000 years ago. When the Cow Green mine closed in 1954, it seemed that no one but naturalists and country-lovers would ever again come to this out-of-the-way and inhospitable corner of Upper Teesdale.

A breakthrough at Billingham

About 110 km downstream, the river reaches industrial Teesside. In the depression between the wars, few areas suffered worse from unemployment and, more than thirty years later, the region still has an air of conva-lescence. Not surprisingly, Teesside has always been intensely preoccupied with the problems of getting and keeping industry. In recent years it has been reasonably successful in attracting new firms, and in encouraging those already there to expand. Even so, in the harsh winter of 1962–3 the unemployment figures for Teesside were among the highest in the country.

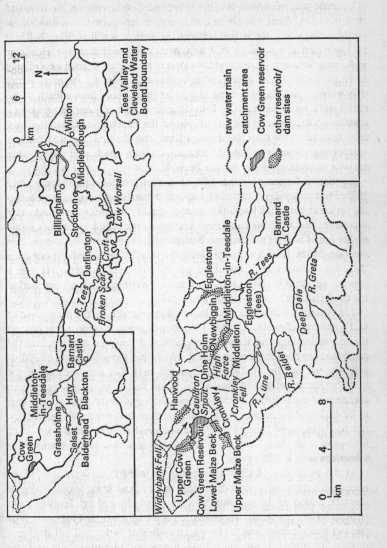

Tees Valley and Cleveland Water Board boundary

raw water main
······ catchment area
▨ Cow Green reservoir
⸭ other reservoir/
  dam sites

N

0   6   12
km

R. Tees
Wilton
Middlesbrough
Billingham
Stockton
Darlington
Croft
Low Worsall
Broken Scar

Cow Green
Grassholme
Selset
Balderhead
Blackton
Middleton-in-Teesdale
Hury
Barnard
Castle

Widdybank Fell
Upper Cow Green
Cow Green Reservoir
Lower Maize Beck
Upper Maize Beck
Harwood
Cauldron
Spout
Cronkley
Dine Holm
High Force
Cronkley Fell
Newbiggin
Middleton-in-Teesdale
Middleton
Eggleston
Eggleston (Tees)
R. Tees
R. Lune
R. Baldet
R. Greta
Deep Dale
Barnard Castle

0   4   8
km

It was a painful reminder of the past : full employment was not something that could ever be taken for granted in the North-East.

Teesside was vulnerable because it depended so heavily on the iron and steel industry. What was needed, as everyone recognized, was diversification. Consequently, the arrival between the wars of new firms like Shell and ICI was seen as a godsend. ICI were particularly welcome, for with their wide range of activities, even at the worst of times they seemed never likely to be in trouble on all their products simultaneously. By the early sixties they were employing something like 30 000 men, more than a tenth of the entire work force on Teesside. Providing thousands of jobs, and making a massive contribution to the rate income of the local authorities in the area, they were far more than just another firm ; they had become a stable and comforting presence, a valued institution whose needs and wishes were matters of great consequence on Teesside.

At their Billingham works, ICI have been producing ammonia since 1925. For many years coal was an important constituent in the manufacturing process ; but in the late fifties, as high-quality coking coal became more expensive, and as other countries developed production techniques based on the use of natural gas that was both plentiful and cheap, the competitive position of the British ammonia industry steadily worsened. At one time there were fears that it might go out of business altogether. It was a depressing outlook, not least because there is a considerable export market for the fertilizers produced from ammonia.

The situation was saved, and the industry rescued, by the persistence of ICI's research chemists. Early in 1960 they began to develop a new process for converting naphtha, a readily available and cheap oil fraction, into the gases that are needed for ammonia synthesis and the production of hydrogen. By the middle of 1963 it appeared that this new technique, the 'naphtha steam reforming process' as it was called, might have extensive commercial possibilities. Technical breakthroughs of this importance have to be exploited as quickly as possible, for once lost, overseas markets are not easily regained ; the pace of technological change being what it is, hesitation and delay can easily fritter away a hard-won competitive advantage.

At the beginning of 1964, two questions faced ICI. Were they to go ahead with the new process on a large scale ? And if so, should the new plant be added to the company's existing installations on Teesside ? On technical and commercial grounds, they were satisfied that full-scale production was feasible. And so far as Teesside was concerned, all the signs seemed favourable. It was known that a new port was to be built at Teesmouth ; road and rail communications in the area were good enough ; oil was available at the Teesside refineries ; there was plenty of skilled labour ;

and from the Ministry of Housing and Local Government's Hydrological Survey of 1961 the potential supply of water in the area appeared to be adequate. Moreover, it was at about this time that the Government was beginning to take an interest in the North-East and its economic problems. In February 1963 Teesside had been declared a Development District, and soon afterwards Lord Hailsham made a highly publicized visit to the North-East. In November 1963 there followed a White Paper – the 'Hailsham Report' – announcing that new financial incentives were to be given to industrialists prepared to set up or expand in the region.

Against this background, in January 1964 I C I decided to build two of the largest ammonia plants in the world, each capable of producing 1000 t of ammonia a day. In September 1964 it was decided to add a third plant of the same size. At their Wilton works the production of hydrogen was also to be increased to permit a large expansion of the output of nylon and similar petrochemicals. It is a fact about expansion in the chemical industry that new products and new techniques often require water in very substantial quantities.

The authority responsible for providing Teesside with water is the Tees Valley and Cleveland Water Board. As constituted in 1964, the Water Board had been in existence for only six years, though various forerunners trace their history back to the establishment of the Stockton, Middlesbrough and Redcar Water Company in 1851. The chairman of the Board was Alderman Charles Allison, a member of the Stockton Borough Council for almost fifty years and a powerful and well-known public figure on Teesside. Like a good many other trade unionists of his generation, Allison had never forgotten the misery of the thirties; the dole queue, the means test, victimization and the soup kitchens, were among his sharpest memories. As he was later to observe, 'all these things have happened in our lifetime, and those of us who have grown old in administration feel that we should do everything we possibly can to avoid a repetition'. There were other veterans of the depression on the Tees Valley and Cleveland Water Board who shared Allison's memories and attitudes : when it was a question of jobs, men of their age and background were rarely in doubt about what was important. The Water Board supplied a large rural area covering more than 130×10^4 m^2, and served about 450 000 people, the bulk of them in Middlesbrough, Stockton-on-Tees, Thornaby-on-Tees and Redcar. In one respect, however, their clientèle was unusual ; considerably more than half their water went not to domestic consumers but to industry. By far the largest customer was I C I. By the late fifties this preponderance of industrial users was making long-term planning increasingly difficult for as we shall now see, technological innovation can drastically change an industry's water requirements with very little warning.

As late as August 1963 ICI had assured the Water Board, at officer level, that in the immediate future they would need no extra water beyond their existing allocation. Within twelve months, in July 1964, the Water Board were told that, as a result of the new ammonia plants which were planned, ICI would, after all, require additional water quite soon. Those in ICI responsible for organizing the supply of water were as much taken by surprise as the Water Board. Since it takes only about two years to build a fertilizer plant, but usually between five and seven years to plan and build a reservoir, the makings of a problem were built into the situation from the very beginning. Later on, ICI were to be accused of not making their requirements known early enough, and of not starting the search for extra water sufficiently far in advance of their need. The truth of the matter is that, if water is to be available as soon as it is required, the search must be started and the supply organized long before there can be any guarantee that it will ever be needed. Looking for water that may never be required is not a task that anyone in private industry undertakes with enthusiasm.

By August 1964 ICI were in a position to state their requirements more specifically. They would need an additional 50×10^3 m³ a day by 1966 for the installations already under construction; for the new nylon and fertilizer plant to be built between 1965 and 1970 a further 63×10^3 m³ a day would be required. The Water Board now made inquiries of other large industrial users on Teesside, such as Shell and Dorman Long. Their replies indicated that a further 45×10^3 m³ a day would be needed, over and above ICI's 113×10^3 m³ a day. It was, of course, the responsibility of the Water Board to provide the water; but since ICI were guaranteeing most of the capital for what was clearly going to be a major project, and one in which they had a vital interest, from now onwards the company and their advisers were to work closely with the Board and their consultant engineers.

Thus, in the summer of 1964, the problem confronting ICI and the Tees Valley and Cleveland Water Board was that of finding an extra 158×10^3 m³ a day, a formidable task considering that at this stage the entire output envisaged by the Board from their Teesdale sources amounted only to 292×10^3 m³ a day. In August 1964 the Water Board instructed their consulting engineers to prepare a report and make recommendations for increasing their safe reliable yield – the volume of water that can be supplied from reservoirs under drought conditions – from 292 to 450×10^3 m³ a day.

There were several possibilities. One was a large impounding reservoir, well upstream on the Tees, from which the water could be piped to the consumer. This was rejected because of its relatively low reliable yield and because of the expense of pipeworks. Another possibility was an artificial storage reservoir, near the consumers, into which water could be pumped from the river and stored until it was needed. This, too, was rejected, chiefly because a lowland reservoir of this kind would have been very expensive in terms of the agricultural land flooded. A borehole scheme, for the abstraction of water from underground sources in the area between Darlington and Hartlepool, was also briefly considered. But the consultants decided that only a carefully designed pilot scheme, phased over a number of years, would show conclusively whether or not sufficient water could be provided in this way. The remaining possibility, and the one favoured by the Water Board's consulting engineers, was to build a river-regulating reservoir on the upper reaches of the Tees, or on one of its tributaries.

The principle of river-regulating reservoirs is simply to store surplus water in the winter, releasing it into the river for abstraction at a suitable point on the lower reaches when it is needed during the drier summer months. Reservoirs of this kind have many advantages. The only construction work required is the dam, behind which water from the higher reaches of the river collects. The channel of the river, itself serves as a natural aqueduct, carrying water from the upland gathering grounds to the point of abstraction downstream. This technique avoids the expense of a pipeline, secures a higher reliable yield from the river's tributaries, and improves the regime of the river. For these reasons, river-regulating reservoirs were coming very much into favour with River Boards and water engineers in the early sixties. In the circumstances, the Water Board's consultants had no hesitation in opting for this type of reservoir, particularly as in 1959, on the last occasion when the Board had needed to increase their supply, they had been strongly pressed by the then Wear and Tees River Board and by the Ministry of Housing and Local Government to install a regulating reservoir.

There were many possible sites for a river-regulating reservoir in Upper Teesdale. But in their search for the most suitable, the consulting engineers had to take account of a number of important constraints limiting their freedom of choice. The site had to be large enough to yield sufficient water, and it had to be geologically sound, in the sense that water would not leak away through the floor or sides of the valley. It had to be reasonably accessible, otherwise there would be difficulties during construction. Obviously, the Water Board and I C I wanted the reservoir built as cheaply as possible. It was also a point of some importance that the reservoir should not provoke serious opposition, for it had to be ready by 1970. Battles over reservoirs can consume a great deal of time, and whilst money can buy most things, it cannot buy the time taken up by determined objectors, intent on using all available means to fight a project they dislike. And this brings us to the botanists.

Official conservation policies in this country really go back to 1947. In that year, the Ministry of Town and Country Planning recognized the importance of conserving wild life for scientific purposes when they adopted a special report from the Wild Life Conservation Committee calling for the establishment of National Parks and National Nature Reserves. This report actually singled out the rare flora and fauna and the bogs and grassland of Upper Teesdale for particular attention, and recommended that the whole of Upper Teesdale should be made a Conservation Area. In 1949 the Nature Conservancy was set up, and one of its earliest decisions, three years later, was to establish the Moor House Nature Reserve, on the south side of the very highest reaches of the Tees. In 1957 it proposed another reserve – the Upper Teesdale Nature Reserve – to cover a large area on the Yorkshire side of the Tees, to the south of the river between the Cauldron Snout and High Force waterfalls. The Conservancy opened negotiations with the local landowners in 1959, and the area was eventually declared a Nature Reserve in 1963. Though it was planned to extend the reserve to take in Widdybank Fell, this had not been done in 1964. And oddly enough, even as late as 1966 the map of the proposed Nature Reserve still did not include a stream named Slapestone Sike. It was later to be said that the section of Cow Green on either side of this stream was of the very greatest scientific importance. Whether the omission of Slapestone Sike – described by one prominent botanist as a 'staggering oversight' – was due simply to a clerical error (as the Natural Environment Research Council was to allege) or whether it indicated that very little scientific research of any significance had been carried out there (as ICI and the Water Board were to suggest), must remain part of the argument. Though it did not fall within a Nature Reserve, in 1950 Widdybank Fell had nevertheless been notified to the Durham and Westmorland County Councils by the Nature Conservancy as a Site of Special Scientific Interest, a status it shared with a further 200×10^6 m² of Upper Teesdale. Clearly, finding a reservoir site acceptable to the scientists in an area like this was not going to be easy.

As it happened, ICI and the Tees Valley and Cleveland Water Board had crossed swords once before with the scientists over a reservoir in Upper Teesdale. In 1956, as a result of an earlier expansion programme, ICI had asked the Water Board to find them additional water. The Board had examined several possible sites for a reservoir, including one at Cow Green. At that time they were still thinking in terms of a piped supply reservoir, and when Edgar Morton, the geologist retained to advise the Board, reported in September 1956 that a reservoir here might leak, the Cow Green site was abandoned. There were two other possibilities, at Dine Holm and Balderhead. Eventually, the Board chose Dine Holm, some little distance upstream from High Force. The news of this decision had immediately provoked an outcry from the scientists, and in February 1957 a letter appeared in *The Times*, signed by fourteen eminent botanists, deploring this incursion into an internationally acclaimed area of scientific interest. The area below Cauldron Snout was described by Professor D. H. Valentine of the University of Durham as probably the worst possible site for a reservoir in the Tees Valley from the scientific point of view. In due course, the Nature Conservancy too came out against Dine Holm, and in the autumn of 1957, when it was learned that the Water Board intended to promote a Private Bill seeking permission for a reservoir here, the Conservancy informed ICI, the Water Board, and the Durham County Council that it would strongly oppose the project.

The widespread scientific opposition to Dine Holm made a powerful impression at the very highest level within ICI. The company spent about £6 million a year on scientific research, and was anxious not to appear an unenlightened and philistine juggernaut. It seemed that the botanists had a case, and it was clear that Dine Holm was by no means the only practicable site. In the circumstances, ICI decided that they ought not to be associated with this scheme, and withdrew their support for the Bill. As a result, in December 1957 the Water Board gave up the Dine Holm project, and instructed their consulting engineers to re-examine the other possibilities. Finally a site on the river Balder, a tributary of the Tees, was selected, and in 1959 a Private Act empowered the Board to proceed with a new reservoir at Balderhead.[1]

Well aware that Upper Teesdale was a highly sensitive area, and having run into trouble with the conservationists once before, this time ICI decided to feel their way carefully. In fact, they set out with the deliberate intention of making this new reservoir project a classic illustration of the virtues and rewards of prior consultation with those affected. But, of course, there were many scientists and scientific bodies interested in various aspects of Upper Teesdale. Who precisely was to be consulted? To ICI it seemed that the organization best placed to speak authoritatively for the scientists and conservationists must obviously be their official voice, the Nature Conservancy.

'The best laid schemes . . . '

Intent on avoiding a repetition of the Dine Holm affair, in August 1964 Julius Kennard, the Board's consultant engineer, approached the Nature Conservancy to sound out its views. On 1 September, at the Conservancy's offices in Belgrave Square, he met Max Nicholson, the Director General, for what was to be the first of several informal talks between the two men. Kennard brought with him a map showing the location of no less than seventeen sites in Upper Teesdale that looked possible on the basis of the Hydrological Survey of 1961. Among them was Cow Green. When he examined the list, Nicholson apparently said that on botanical grounds the Conservancy would object very strongly to some of the sites that were included. Kennard, however, formed the impression that Cow Green was not likely to be among those that would be most objectionable. Other members of the Conservancy's staff were present at this meeting, but it was left to Nicholson to do most of the talking. According to Kennard, nobody threw up his hands in horror at the mention of Cow Green, which of course was hardly surprising, because the name meant nothing in scientific circles.

Together with Dr J. L. Knill, an expert on reservoir geology, Kennard then visited Upper Teesdale to inspect the seventeen possible sites. In October Kennard received Knill's geological appraisal. In Knill's opinion none of the possibilities was wholly free from geological problems, but Cow Green, Lower Maize Beck, and Harwood seemed to be the safest. Knill was aware of the earlier adverse report on the geology of Cow Green, but disagreed with Morton's findings.

On 20 October, Kennard returned to London for a second meeting with Nicholson. This time he had with him R. Hetherington, ICI's technical adviser on water supplies. They were now in a position to eliminate a good many of the initial possibilities. Seven had to be ruled out at once because they would not have provided enough water. To four others – at Cronkley, Cronkley Bridge, Holm Wath, and Dine Holm – Nicholson expressed strong opposition. The six sites left in the running were at Upper Maize Beck, Harwood, Langdon, Eggleston Burn, Middleton and Cow Green. Two of these, however, were not acceptable to Kennard. Eggleston Burn was a very doubtful proposition on geological grounds. And from what he had seen of the Middleton site, Kennard realized that a reservoir there would flood several hundred acres of agricultural land, besides probably submerging part of the village of Newbiggin. As he well knew, ICI and the Water Board were as anxious to steer clear of a fight with the farmers as they were to avoid a battle with the conservationists. It would indeed have been ironic had ICI outraged the agricultural interests in order to increase their output of fertilizers. So, there remained four sites. Arranged in Nicholson's order of preference they were at Langdon, Harwood, Upper Maize Beck and Cow Green.

From Kennard's point of view, the first three sites were certainly feasible. But by comparison with Cow Green, they all had serious disadvantages. The catchment area for Langdon was smaller, and the geology less sound. A reservoir at Harwood would have flooded a good deal of farmland, and would have required a much higher dam than at Cow Green.

Upper Maize Beck was a very remote and inaccessible site, and the dam would have been even higher. As Kennard saw it, therefore, Cow Green looked very much the best proposition, and before leaving he told Nicholson that he intended to recommend the Water Board to carry out a detailed site exploration there. For his part, Nicholson was non-committal. The Nature Conservancy would have to arrange an on-site investigation, he said, in order to assess the degree of objection. The late autumn was hardly the right time to begin a survey of this kind, and in any case, he added, it would be for one of their committees to make the final decision as to the Conservancy's attitude.

ICI, the Water Board and their advisers were well pleased by Nicholson's attitude. He appeared to appreciate their problems, and he seemed to be concerned to strike a balance between the needs of industry and the claims of conservation. Even so, Kennard was agreeably surprised when on 23 October, only two days after their meeting, he received a letter from Nicholson which seemed to put Cow Green in the clear so far as the Conservancy was concerned. Nicholson wrote that he too believed in quiet negotiations. This was a far more civilized way of settling problems than what he called 'an open fight in the chaotic conditions of a public inquiry'. He had been trying to gauge the probable reaction of the Conservancy to Cow Green, and what he had discovered he set out in his letter to Kennard. As this letter was to assume some significance, part of it must be quoted in full:

Since your call here, I have been able to find an opportunity which I had not expected so soon for sounding out the opinion of our members who will be responsible for determining the Conservancy's attitude, and as a result of this I think that you could safely go a little further and inform the Board that you now have reason to believe that if the difficulties on your side of the Cow Green site could be overcome [a reference apparently to the possible geological problems] it would be most unlikely to be objected to by the Nature Conservancy. Indeed, if the Board felt able to put up proposals for this site embodying a similar approach to that adopted at Diddington so that it would form a point of attraction for visitors who would otherwise be straying on the more scientifically vulnerable areas of Upper Teesdale, then the Conservancy might feel justified in actively supporting such a project in face of the opposition from certain quarters which would be inevitable for any reservoir above Middleton.[2]

Kennard and Hetherington could not believe that Nicholson would have written in these terms had he not been sure of his ground. He was saying, so it seemed, that not only would the Conservancy not oppose Cow Green, they might even support it. As Kennard was to remark, when he and Hetherington discussed the letter they both thought that they had achieved a remarkable success. It now appeared that the Water Board had been given the green light for Cow Green. Had they known what lay behind Nicholson's letter they might have been less sanguine. The SSSI in Upper Teesdale covers a very wide area, and the Conservancy possessed only the sketchiest scientific maps of parts of it. In a general way, the importance of Widdybank Fell was well understood, though how far the rare flora on the fell impinged upon Cow Green was by no means clear. In any case, if (as seemed possible) Kennard was proposing to build the dam at Cow Green, the reservoir itself would be upstream from Widdybank Fell and the vegetation there would not be much affected. Nicholson also had at the back of his mind the recollection that Cow Green had been passed over in 1956 on geological grounds; the geology of the site had not changed since then. And, as luck would have it, none of the three members of the Conservancy consulted by Nicholson had reacted strongly against Cow Green, either because they themselves were not specially interested in the particular type of vegetation found there, or because from what they could understand of it, the Water Board's scheme seemed to be reasonably acceptable from a botanical point of view.

However, it quickly became apparent that in his efforts to be helpful, Nicholson had been over-confident. Immediately after the meeting with Kennard he instructed Dr Derek Ratcliffe, then a Nature Conservancy botanist concerned with vegetation surveys, to carry out a systematic investigation of the Cow Green site on behalf of the Conservancy. But as the weather during the winter of 1964–5 was unsuitable for survey work, it was not until well into 1965 that Ratcliffe was able to produce his report. In the meantime, Nicholson asked the Conservancy's Northern Regional Officer to make contact with scientists known to have first-hand experience of Upper Teesdale, to assess their reaction to the alternative sites mentioned by Kennard. One of the botanists consulted was Professor Valentine of Durham University. From this and other quarters Nicholson was soon made aware that he had seriously underestimated the hostility that a reservoir at Cow Green would provoke.

On 2 November 1964 the Tees Valley and Cleveland Water Board officially informed the Nature Conservancy that they had been advised to undertake further explorations at Cow Green. If the site proved to be geologically feasible, they said, discussions with the Conservancy would be reopened. When Nicholson wrote back on 3 November he was a good deal more cautious. The Conservancy, he replied, could not commit itself until a definite scheme came forward. The helpfulness and candour of the Board's consulting engineers had been much appreciated, and further talks about Cow Green would be welcome. Nevertheless, the Conservancy was disappointed that none of the less objectionable sites had proved technically feasible, for there could be no doubt that any site in Upper Teesdale,

Cow Green included, would inevitably give rise to a considerable amount of opposition in various quarters. If the geological report on Cow Green should be favourable, the Conservancy would not be able to give its view on the site at short notice, though it would approach the problem with a desire to be as helpful as possible.

Just over a month later, on 8 December, the Water Board announced that they intended to build a new reservoir in Upper Teesdale. Nothing was said about a specific site. By this stage, however, the Nature Conservancy's attitude had become much more distant, and on 11 December its Northern Regional Officer wrote to the Water Board pointing out that 'beyond reasonable investigation of certain sites' the Conservancy was 'entirely uncommitted about reservoir proposals in Teesdale'. The green light was now at amber.

If Cow Green was no longer certain of as smooth a passage as had seemed possible in October, the Water Board still had no inkling of the storm that was soon to break about them. Speaking at the Board's meeting in January 1965, for example, Alderman Allison could scarcely credit that anyone would be perverse and misguided enough to impede a project so vital to the prosperity of Teesside. 'Are we going to have the position arise', he asked, 'where people who think more of flowers and plant life than of industry can impose their will ?' Another member of the Board aevised his colleagues not to panic. He was satisfied that public opinion would not permit idealistically minded people, or cranks, to hinder such an important development. Opposition was irritating, he admitted. But then, so was a flea, and that could be quickly settled with a puff of insecticide.

By February 1965 the consulting engineers had completed the first stage of their exploratory work on the Cow Green site. The geological survey had been considerably more thorough than the 1956 investigation, and they were satisfied that a reservoir at Cow Green definitely would not leak. It was known that of the $3 \cdot 1 \times 10^6$ m² needed for the reservoir less than $0 \cdot 1 \times 10^6$ m² were part of the SSSI. But since so much of Upper Teesdale also had this status – if indeed it was not part of an even more sacrosanct National Nature Reserve – ICI and the Water Board concluded that on this score Cow Green would probably be no worse than anywhere else, for the chances were that there would be protests from the conservationists, whichever site was chosen. In any case, ICI had by now made their own inquiries about the scientific importance of Cow Green and about the value of the work in progress there. A company like ICI has well-informed scientists of its own, with their own contacts in the research world ; from them it learned that there were many botanists who knew nothing of Cow Green or of any significant field work in this particular area. And when they found out more about the nature of the research that *was* in progress in Upper Teesdale, ICI's scientists were not impressed. Accustomed as they were to systematic experimentation, under rigorously controlled laboratory conditions, they saw the Upper Teesdale botanists as being engaged upon the somewhat dilettante Victorian pursuit of labelling and categorizing rare flora. There were scientists in the universities who shared this view; but as ICI were to discover, when some of the doyens of the academic world took their stand on the unique value of Cow Green, other botanists were not easily persuaded to come forward to contradict these eminent men in public.

In May the consulting engineers handed over their final report to ICI and the Water Board. They recommended, as a temporary measure, that the Board should apply to the Northumbrian River Authority for a licence to abstract more water from the Tees to meet any immediate deficit in the next few years. More important, they also recommended that the Water Board should build a river-regulating reservoir at Cow Green. So far as ICI and the Board were concerned, the die was now cast.

The next move was up to the Nature Conservancy. In fact, it had little choice but to oppose Cow Green, because by this point Ratcliffe had reported on the results of his survey of the area threatened by the reservoir. According to Ratcliffe, the western slopes of Widdybank Fell were of very special scientific interest, and in his view the loss of even 0.1×10^6 m^2 would be a very serious matter, for each part of this highly diversified complex of species was almost totally dissimilar from the rest. On 22 July, therefore, the Nature Conservancy told the Water Board that it intended to object to the choice of the Cow Green site. At the same time it asked the Board to investigate another possibility on the confluence of the Tees and Mattergill Sike, further upstream. This site, which fell within the Moor House Nature Reserve, was to be known as Upper Cow Green. Presented with a new alternative, the Board's consulting engineers did ask for a geological report; but they refused to consider it seriously, partly because they felt sure it would not provide enough water, and partly because they calculated that it would cost about twice as much and would take something like two years longer to build.

At this stage in the proceedings, everyone concerned with the case was under the impression that the final decision on Cow Green would lie in the hands of the Minister of Housing and Local Government under Section 23 of the 1945 Water Act, possibly after a public local inquiry if there was substantial opposition to the project. In accordance with the usual procedure, on 27 July the Board submitted to the Minister for his informal comments a Draft Order empowering them to go ahead with the reservoir at Cow Green. For their part, the Ministry evidently knew enough about the situation to sense that there was a controversy in the air, and it seemed to them that this was just the kind of scheme that the newly created Water Resources Board might be asked to advise upon. Set up under the 1963 Water Resources Act to advise the Government on the conservation and provision of water in England and Wales, the Board looked to be the ideal body to produce an impartial and authoritative report on the range of possibilities. Accordingly, on 3 August, the Water Resources Board and the Tees Valley and Cleveland Water Board were asked to collaborate in an urgent examination of the problem of how best to provide Teesside with additional water.

The need for this water was too pressing for the Water Resources Board to carry out an exhaustive survey of all the possible sources in the Tees catchment area. Nor was there enough time for it to assemble its own data. Consequently, it had to rely on the Tees Valley and Cleveland Water Board and their consulting engineers for most of the factual information that was needed to make a recommendation. As it appeared to the Water Resources Board, the problem was this. On existing policies, and with existing sources, there would be a deficiency of 103×10^3 m³ a day by 1971, of 225×10^3 m³ a day by 1982, and of 495×10^3 m³ a day by 2000.[3] The Water Resources Board could see no possibility of finding the additional supplies outside the Tees catchment area in time to meet the extra demand in 1971. Nor was there any chance that desalination would come to the rescue in time. In the short run, it might be possible to fill part of the gap between demand and supply by pumping about 27×10^3 m³ a day from the magnesium limestone area north of Darlington.

As a solution to the Water Board's problems, the Water Resources Board considered both river-regulating reservoirs and the idea of a pumped, storage reservoir downstream from Darlington. A regulating reservoir, it thought, was much to be preferred, chiefly because the river would benefit from increased flows during dry weather.

If the answer was a river-regulating reservoir, where should it be built? On the available information, seven of the sites previously investigated by the Water Board seemed to be worth a second look. These were at Eggleston, Harwood, Middleton, Lower Maize Beck, Upper Maize Beck, Cronkley and Cow Green. In addition, the Water Resources Board also examined the Upper Cow Green site, the possibility now being advocated by the Nature Conservancy. The significant variables taken into account in each case were: the probable date of completion, the cost, disturbance – such as the extent and nature of any damage that would be inflicted on scientific interest, farming, houses, and roads – and technical factors, that is, the yield and capacity of the reservoir, the size of the area to be flooded, and the length and height of the dam. The Water Resources Board's findings for each of the possible sites can be conveniently set out in tabular form (see Table 1).

When it reported to the Ministry of Housing and Local Government on 20 October the Water Resources Board thought that three of these sites warranted further discussion. Upper Cow Green would produce a significantly smaller yield than Cow Green; it would require a much longer and higher dam; it was estimated to cost £3 million more than Cow Green; and it would probably not be ready until 1971. If the geology proved to be sound, Middleton would provide a larger yield than any of the other sites investigated, and in relation to the very large quantity of water that it would supply, the cost would be quite reasonable. (It was later revealed by Kennard that owing to a typing error in the consulting engineers' office the Water Resources Board had accidentally been led to believe that Middleton would cost £1 million less than the true figure.) On the other hand, Middleton would mean flooding $4 \cdot 0 \times 10^6$ m^2 of agricultural land, including two complete farms and parts of twelve others. About ninety other properties of various kinds would also disappear beneath the water, and a reservoir here would take three years longer than at Cow Green to construct. And if the Water Board were to commit themselves to a large reservoir at Middleton in the 1960s, they would be saddled with an inflexible pattern of supply in the 1980s and 1990s, by which time sources outside the Tees catchment area might have become available.

This left Cow Green. On the debit side, it was strongly opposed by the Nature Conservancy. However, it would cost £2–2·5 million (a reservoir at least £1·5 million more),[4] and it seemed to be the next logical step in the development of the water resources of the Tees Valley. But the decisive factor, as the Water Resources Board saw it, was that of all the sites under review, Cow Green alone could be completed by 1969; if either Upper Cow Green or Middleton were chosen, industrial developments already under construction might go short of water, with a consequent threat to output and employment.

By this stage, an important new fact about Cow Green had come to light. About $1 \cdot 2 \times 10^6$ m^2 of the site, it turned out, were common land. This discovery gave rise to legal complications that were now to change the whole character of the case.

In the normal way, the Water Board would have sought to acquire the land by means of an Order, authorizing compulsory purchase, under the Water Acts of 1945 and 1948. But because common land was involved, the Acquisition of Land (Authorization Procedure) Act of 1946 would have applied, and the Order would have been subject to special Parliamentary procedure, unless the Minister of Land and Natural Resources gave his certificate that an equivalent area would be given in exchange for use as

Table 1 Water Resources Board Report: river-regulating sites

Site	Capacity 10^6 m³	Yield 10^3 m³ a day	Length m	Height m	Cost £ million	Water area 10^6 m²	Disturbance	Intended completion date
Cow Green	40·5	157·5	525	22·0	2·0–2·5	3·3	area of SSSI	1969
Upper Cow Green	35·1	130·5–135·0	1550	46·4	6·0	3·4	nature reserve	1971
Cronkley	36·0	135·0–144·0	518	53·4	4·0	2·0	nature reserve	1971
Upper Maize Beck	24·8	85·5– 90·0	952	48·5	4·0	2·7	nature reserve	1971
Lower Maize Beck	24·8	81·0– 90·0	1180	56·1	4·5	1·2	nature reserve	1971
Middleton	81·0	337·5	1180	54·0	6·0	4·0	farmland, roads, houses	1972
Harwood	36·0	135·0–144·0	1310	43·6	5·0	1·4	area of SSSI agricultural land, houses, roads	1971
Eggleston	36·0	135·0–144·0	1010	58·6	5·3	1·7	road diversion	1971

common land. Moreover, the Minister had been advised that his consent under Section 22 of the Commons Act of 1899 was necessary for the grant or enclosure of common land, even when the Order authorizing the compulsory purchase was subject to special Parliamentary procedure. In giving or withholding his consent under the Act of 1899, the Minister was required to have regard to the same considerations, and if necessary hold the same inquiries, as were directed by an earlier Commons Act of 1876. This meant that, before determining the application, the Minister had to be satisfied that the grant or enclosure was expedient, having regard to the 'benefit of the neighbourhood' and to 'private interests', as these expressions were defined in the Preamble to the Act of 1876.

Normally, the Minister would have ascertained the views of people in the neighbourhood by means of an advertisement in the local press and, probably, by means of a public local inquiry. As neither of these steps had been taken, the Minister of Land and Natural Resources was in no position to say what his view would have been had the Water Board applied to him for consent to the grant and enclosure of this common land.

Anyone who has followed this argument closely will see that nothing in it absolutely ruled out the administrative procedure. But clearly, the interaction of nineteenth-century and modern legislation has produced a situation of some complexity. No one could guarantee that hidden legal traps would not be sprung; and with common land involved, it was clearly going to take the Ministry of Housing and Local Government even longer than usual to reach a decision on the Order. In the circumstances, the Ministry apparently took the view that the Water Board would be well advised to adopt an alternative procedure, and promote a Private Bill.

The situation was explained to representatives of ICI and the Water Board at a meeting in London on 27 October 1965. Not all the arguments favoured going by way of a Private Bill. With the administrative process, the Minister has to be convinced; but this is the only hurdle to clear. It is true that there is often a long delay, of uncertain duration, while the Minister makes up his mind on the Order after a public local inquiry. But at least a water authority can be sure that the Minister's decision will be based upon a rational and well-informed appraisal of all the relevant considerations. A Private Bill, on the other hand, certainly has the virtue of a fixed timetable: if successful, it is bound to be through Parliament by the end of the current session. At the same time, an opposed Bill may have not one but several critical hurdles to clear in its passage through the Commons and Lords. And in the last resort, particularly if it achieves some notoriety, its fate may be settled by the outcome of a vote that owes less to reason than to assiduous lobbying, skilful oratory, and relatively ill-informed sentiment. However, since they attached so much importance to the time factor, ICI and the Water Board decided, not without misgivings, that the wisest course was to promote a Private Bill. The Bill was laid before the House of Commons on 27 November 1965.

The friends of Cow Green

While the water engineers, administrators and lawyers were at work on their inquiries and calculations, the opponents of the Cow Green reservoir had also been busy. As we have seen, it was not until July 1965 that the Nature Conservancy, the 'official' voice of conservation, came out against Cow Green. When the Water Board had announced on 8 December 1964 that they intended to build a large new reservoir in Upper Teesdale, the Conservancy's response, more than six weeks later, was to issue a statement saying that it had agreed 'without prejudice' to test borings at Cow Green to determine whether or not a reservoir on this site was technically feasible. Since the Conservancy's own survey had not yet started, this was perhaps as far as a statutory body could properly go at this stage. But it was not exactly a clarion call to arms, and to a number of botanists it seemed that the Conservancy might not altogether appreciate the importance of the area. As they saw it, a far more vigorous campaign was needed.

The unofficial resistance movement began to take shape early in 1965. Alarmed by the Nature Conservancy's statement published that morning, on 26 January four members of the Botanical Society of the British Isles – J. E. Lousley, J. C. Gardiner, S. M. Walters and E. Milne-Redhead – met in London to discuss the situation. This quartet made a formidable combination. Neither Lousley nor Gardiner were professional botanists, though Lousley was one of the best-known amateurs in the country. But in their working lives both had considerable experience of the business world, Gardiner being financial adviser to Charles Clore and Lousley an investment manager by occupation. For them, ICI's reservoir scheme came to assume something of the character of a City take-over bid that had to be beaten off. Walters was a Cambridge botanist, with a wide range of contacts in the universities, while Milne-Redhead, as Deputy Keeper of the Herbarium at Kew, provided a link with the non-academic professional botanists. They were all familiar with Upper Teesdale – like many others, Lousley's interest in botany had been first aroused as a result of a visit to this area many years earlier – and they were all deeply concerned about the fate of the rare flora there. At this initial meeting they decided to organize a letter to The Times and to ask the Council of the Botanical Society of the British Isles to set up a special committee which would launch an appeal for funds and mobilize support for an objection to the reservoir on scientific grounds.

A similar nucleus of objectors had formed in the North-East. Here the leading figure was Dr Margaret Bradshaw, a Staff Tutor in botany in the Extra-mural Department of the University of Durham. As the controversy developed, she was to play an increasingly important part in stimulating and extending the opposition to the Cow Green reservoir. Bradshaw was dedicated to Upper Teesdale and its botanical treasures. She had taken an academic post in the North so as to be able to botanize in Teesdale and had worked in the area for the previous fifteen years. This was her world, and she was a determined woman.

To begin with, the tactics of the successful Dine Holm campaign were repeated. On 4 February a letter appeared in *The Times*, signed by fourteen eminent botanists. Among scientists, they wrote, there was grave anxiety about the Tees Valley and Cleveland Water Board's plans for a reservoir in Upper Teesdale. The Tees Valley above High Force was of unique scientific value in Britain. The scientific research already carried out in this area, embodied in more than a hundred publications, had given the Teesdale vegetation, with its extraordinary assemblages of rare species, an outstanding international reputation. Upper Teesdale was an irreplaceable open-air laboratory and ought to be protected from the gross interference and destruction that would inevitably result from the construction of a reservoir and the impounding of the headwaters of the river Tees. 'Whilst we are not unmindful of the claim of industry in an expanding economy', the letter concluded, 'we cannot believe that the values of our society are so crudely materialistic that we shall consciously permit the destruction of such a splendid heritage, for what can be, at best, only a short-term solution of the problem of industrial water.'

The letter had the desired effect. Public interest was aroused, and letters began to flow into the accommodation address used by the Botanical Society of the British Isles at the Natural History Museum. A spokesman for the Society declared that if the Cow Green scheme was not modified they would join forces with the Northumberland and Durham Naturalists' Trust in an appeal for financial support from the public, so that the scientific case could be adequately represented at the expected public inquiry. On 25 February, by resolution of the Council of the Society, the Teesdale Defence Committee was formally established. It was agreed that the Durham and Northumberland Naturalists' Trust should be represented on it, and the Defence Committee met for the first time in the following month. Whatever line the Conservancy might decide to take, the irregulars were now organized and clearly determined to make a fight of it.

Indeed, in the North-East the Northumberland and Durham Naturalists' Trust had already gone into action, distributing a polemical leaflet, appealing for donations, and urging people in the area to protest to their

MPs about the proposed reservoir. This initiative in turn triggered off the hoped-for response, and very soon letters and feature articles were appearing in the local press speculating on the probable effects of the reservoir. It was suggested, for example, that once it was built, never again would the great waterfall of High Force be seen in full spate.

In the North-East there was never any popular ground-swell of opposition to the Cow Green reservoir, and outside of scientific and amenity circles, the objectors' efforts to enlist support were not particularly successful. When it came before Parliament, the Water Board's Bill was to be supported by the North-East Development Council, the Northumbrian River Authority, and the North Riding and South Durham branch of the National Farmers' Union, whilst the Durham, Westmorland and North Riding County Councils, the three Rural District Councils and the three Parish Councils involved had no objection to the reservoir. Nor had any of the landowners or tenants in the vicinity. Not even the Darlington Corporation, an ancient foe which had opposed almost every scheme ever proposed by the Water Board and their predecessors, objected to the Cow Green site.

In the scientific world, however, the Teesdale Defence Committee were making much better progress. Among those approached and asked to help were Professor H. Godwin of Cambridge University (a Fellow of the Royal Society and a member of the Nature Conservancy) and Professor C. D. Pigott of the University of Lancaster (formerly one of Godwin's students). Godwin was an authority on plant ecology, and Pigott had carried out a great deal of research in Upper Teesdale. Both were men whose views carried considerable weight in botanical circles, and both were to throw themselves wholeheartedly into the fight against the reservoir. Godwin, in fact, undertook to circularize botanists all over the world, and dispatched a round-robin to elicit help for the Defence Committee on an international scale.

At this stage they were apparently hoping that a forceful demonstration of hostility would persuade the Water Board and ICI to think again, as they had over Dine Holm in 1957. However, when Gardiner and Lousley met representatives of ICI in July 1965, it was evident that this time the company had no intention of backing down. ICI said that they were prepared to make available a sum of £100 000 for an intensive programme of research, to be supervised by the Nature Conservancy, before the valley was flooded. They were also prepared to make special arrangements to ensure that as little damage as possible was done in the area round the reservoir during construction. But on one thing they were quite insistent: the reservoir had to be at Cow Green.

The botanists acknowledged that the financial offer was a well-meant gesture; but in their view, a temporary reprieve was not enough. Clearly, there was going to be a battle over Cow Green, and now, they decided, was the time to launch their campaign in earnest. Organized by Pigott, an Upper Teesdale Defence Fund was set up with a target of £5000, and before long no less than 3500 donations had been received, Samuel Silkin, QC, MP, was retained to represent the Committee at the expected public inquiry, and 40 000 copies of a well-produced illustrated booklet entitled *The Threat to Upper Teesdale* were sent out urging people all over Britain to oppose the scheme. The coverage was thorough, not to say lavish. One distinguished scientist who received no less than three copies of the booklet was James Newman, the head of the Biology section at ICI's Jealott's Hill Agricultural Research Station at Bracknell, and the company's principal scientific adviser on the botanical issues raised by the Cow Green case.

By the end of 1965 a formidable range of scientific societies had been mobilized in opposition to the Cow Green reservoir. They included the British Ecological Society, the Council for Nature, the Lake District Naturalists' Trust, the Linnean Society, the Northumberland and Durham Naturalists' Trust, the Society for the Promotion of Nature Reserves, and the Yorkshire Naturalists' Trust. In January 1966, in association with the Botanical Society of the British Isles, these bodies jointly petitioned against the Water Board's Bill, claiming that it would damage the rights and interests of their members, because they visited the area in question for research and study. The reservoir, they pointed out, would fall within a Site of Special Scientific Interest. Because of its special geographical formations and climatological history, the area supported a vegetation that was unique in this country. This had been recognized by the Nature Conservancy, which had declared that much of Upper Teesdale, including the reservoir site, should be managed as a Nature Reserve. The reservoir would destroy a remarkable complex of plant communities, and (they maintained) would severely damage other plant communities on the riverside slopes downstream from the site itself.

Had it not outraged the botanists, the proposed Cow Green reservoir would never have become the international *cause célèbre* that it did. But the scientists were not alone in their opposition, for the prospect of a reservoir had also aroused the wrath of the amenity interest and of all the many organizations that concern themselves with the preservation of the countryside. Upper Teesdale is unquestionably an area of very considerable natural beauty, and for years walkers and climbers have enjoyed this wild and rugged stretch of the Pennines. When they realized what was afoot, the amenity societies and leisure organizations – the Council for the Preservation of Rural England, the Commons, Open Spaces and Footpaths Preservation Society, the Countrywide Holidays Association, the

Cyclists' Touring Club, the Holiday Fellowship, the Ramblers' Association, and the Youth Hostels Association – all took their stand with the scientific objectors, and they too presented a joint petition against the Bill.

Their petition maintained that the reservoir would probably be included within an Area of Outstanding Natural Beauty by the National Parks Commission. They pointed out that already the County Development Plan showed it as an Area of Great Landscape Value. High Force and Cauldron Snout, they contended, were by common consent among the finest waterfalls in England. A dam of the type proposed, just upstream from Cauldron Snout, would be an incongruous and unwarranted intrusion at a scenically high point in the dale. It would be visible not only in the immediate vicinity of Cauldron Snout, but also from a wide area of high ground to the south and south-west. A reservoir at Cow Green would mean diverting the Pennine Way, the long-distance hikers' route that runs from the Peak District to the Cheviots. In addition, the amenity objectors alleged that when the water level in the reservoir fell during the summer, or at times of low rainfall, a wide and ugly expanse of shore would be exposed, much of it littered with mud and bare peat. In dry weather, the reservoir would be a blot on the landscape.

Like the Nature Conservancy, the two sets of petitioners were prepared to argue that if there had to be a reservoir in Upper Teesdale (and this they doubted), it should be built at Upper Cow Green. Botanically, this was not such an important site as that chosen by the Water Board. The area was very little visited, the scenery was not so dramatic, and a dam here could be blended into the landscape.

It is always sound tactics for objectors not simply to oppose, but also to try to undermine the developer's case. They can do this by suggesting that his scheme has intrinsic weaknesses, even on his own criteria and in terms of his own objectives. If they can bring forward a credible and workable scheme of their own, their chances of success are even better. Early in 1966 the petitioners approached P. R. Jeffcoate, a well-known water engineer. Julius Kennard, the Water Board's consultant, was one of the foremost experts on reservoirs in the country: Jeffcoate was an authority on borehole schemes, and he was asked to look into the possibility of alternative arrangements that would avoid the need for any reservoir at all in Upper Teesdale.

As we have seen, there was now a formidable list of organizations petitioning against the Bill. Almost every naturalist and amenity society of any standing was in the field against the reservoir. To judge from appearances, the prospect of a reservoir at Cow Green had provoked a spontaneous, independent, and horrified reaction within more than a dozen specialist and well-informed societies and associations, all familiar with the scientific riches of Upper Teesdale and all capable of seeing at once (or of working out for themselves) what exactly the effects of the reservoir would be.

The reality was perhaps less dramatic but more interesting. It is unlikely that the resistance movement was quite the unprompted and spontaneous expression of consternation that its leaders and organizers claimed. Societies and associations are dignified by impressive titles; but in the last resort they are only structured collections of individuals, temporarily or permanently united in the pursuit of a particular interest or objective. There are certain interests that go naturally together; individuals who are members of one society are likely to belong to other organizations concerned with similar or related activities. Through their multiple and interlocking memberships and affiliations, a small but dedicated group of energetic people may be able to activate centres of opposition across a whole range of institutions. Bearing in mind the inventory of bodies that petitioned against the Bill, the affiliations of a few of the leading objectors are of some interest. The following lists are no doubt far from comprehensive.

Dr Bradshaw's role in the controversy has already been mentioned. She was a member of the Council of the Botanical Society of the British Isles and of the Northumberland and Durham Naturalists' Trust, the British Ecological Society, the Society for the Promotion of Nature Reserves, the Yorkshire Naturalists' Trust and the CPRE; she was also an Associate of the Council for Nature. Professor Godwin was not only Treasurer of the Botanical Society of the British Isles, but also a member of the Northumberland and Durham Naturalists' Trust and the Society for the Promotion of Nature Reserves. The President of the Ramblers' Association, Dr A. Raistrick, was Vice-President of the Yorkshire Area of the YHA, and a member of the CPRE, the Commons, Open Spaces and Footpaths Preservation Society and the Yorkshire Dales (West Riding) National Parks Planning Committee. And among others who took a prominent part in the fight against the reservoir, Dr K. R. Ashby was a member of the Northumberland and Durham Naturalists' Trust, the CPRE and the Ramblers' Association, and Tom Stephenson, the Secretary of the Ramblers' Association, was a member of the CPRE and of the executive of the Commons, Open Spaces and Footpaths Preservation Society.

The objectors were to claim that seldom had a proposal of this kind aroused such unanimous opposition from so many scientific societies and bodies concerned with protecting the countryside. This was certainly true. Yet as the exchanges before the Select Committees of the House of Commons and the House of Lords were to demonstrate beyond doubt, in the early days, before the battle was joined, there were only a handful of people in the whole country who knew enough about Cow Green and its rare flora to appreciate precisely what was at stake. It was not until the Cow Green case was well under way that most of the naturalists and botanists who had at once rallied to the support of the Defence Committee knew exactly what floristic assemblages were to be found on the western slopes of this part of Widdybank Fell, or how precisely the reservoir would affect them.

Why was it then, that so many learned societies could become so excited and embittered about a project when they possessed so little first-hand knowledge of its implications ? How was it that so many responsible and well-known figures were prepared to vouch for the tremendous value of the Cow Green flora in letters to the press and at public meetings ? And even if they appreciated the enormous value of these plant communities, how could they be sure that the reservoir would do so much damage ?

In part, it was because of the snowball effect created by respect for the word of colleagues and fellow professionals, men whose reputation and position seems to guarantee their integrity, knowledge and sound judgement. Once the resistance movement had started, once two or three eminent authorities had given a lead, and lent their names to the cause, others were soon convinced that something vital must be at stake at Cow Green and were quickly drawn into the pool of opposition. To give but one example, on 6 July 1966 the world-famous naturalist Peter Scott was to write to The Times, declaring that the area in danger contained unique scientific material. Later, before the House of Lords Select Committee, he was asked how he knew that this was so. How did he know ? Because, among others, Professors Godwin and Pigott and members of the Botanical Society of the British Isles had told him. Godwin himself, it should be said, had visited Cow Green only three or four times in his life. None of this is intended in the slightest to detract from the sincerity of those who led the opposition to the reservoir. They had a cause that was dear to their hearts, and some of them evidently believed in it with a passion and conviction more often associated with religion or politics than botany and conservation. Their campaign was skilfully organized, they worked hard, and they were prepared to give freely of their time and money.

But the influential 'amenity network' of personal contacts only partly accounts for the widespread opposition that was now building up against the Cow Green reservoir, and it certainly does not entirely explain why the petitioners were so successful at the national level in recruiting well-wishers, raising money, and engaging public sympathy. The fact was that the objectors had caught a favourable tide just when it began to run steadily in their favour. By the middle sixties the importance of conservation and ecology was becoming far more widely understood and acknowledged than a decade earlier; and by now, industrial development that threatened amenity was more likely than in earlier years to attract the attention of the mass media. Many of those drawn into the Cow Green controversy neither knew nor cared about the minutiae of the dispute. It was the principle that mattered. Upper Teesdale was undoubtedly an area of exceptional scientific interest and of great natural beauty. As a matter of principle, it was wrong to despoil or disturb areas like this. A stand had to be made somewhere, and if industry were permitted to build a reservoir at Cow Green, if this case was lost by default, nowhere else would be safe. The Water Board and ICI, it is true, could count on the support of local trade union leaders and of MPs for industrial constituencies in the North-East. But there are naturalists and country-lovers all over the country, and many of them are articulate people who will take the trouble to write to their MPs – and they all have MPs. There was, too, an element of David and Goliath in the situation. To be smaller and weaker than the giant is no doubt a genuine handicap; on the other hand, in Britain, it is never a disadvantage to be regarded as the gallant underdog.

Nevertheless, in many respects the dice still seemed to be loaded against them. In ICI they were taking on not just a rich and powerful industrial giant, but an institution that enjoys a considerable public reputation for enlightened and responsible behaviour. And in this instance, ICI were themselves about to embark upon what everyone agreed were good deeds. If their plans went ahead, they would be expanding industrial output, increasing exports, and providing employment in an area where jobs are valued above almost everything else. They had also offered the Nature Conservancy no less than £100 000 for scientific research at Cow Green. In all the circumstances the botanists could easily be represented as selfish eccentrics, jeopardizing the economic prosperity of Teesside, callously endangering men's jobs in the process, and all for the sake of a few obscure plants on some remote and inaccessible hillside high on the Pennines. On the face of things, it was not a promising hand.

The Tees Valley and Cleveland Water Bill was given its First Reading in the House of Commons on 26 January 1966. An unopposed Second Reading followed on 1 February, and the Bill was then referred to a Select Committee for consideration in detail. It was a curious situation, for whereas conflicts between the needs of industry and the claims of conservation are very much a contemporary phenomenon, the Private Bill arena harks back to a Parliamentary process that enjoyed its heyday in the eighteenth and early nineteenth centuries. At all events, the lines were now drawn and the scene set for one of the most extraordinary conflicts of interest and value in recent years.

Whitehall takes a view

Private Bills are initiated by local authorities, statutory undertakers or business corporations seeking powers that they need, but do not possess, under existing public law. The Government is not directly involved. But the intentions and objectives of those who promote Private Bills may be of considerable interest to individual Government departments, and these departments will ask, or be asked, to make known their views to Parliament. At least five departments – the Ministry of Housing and Local Government, the Board of Trade, the Ministry of Land and Natural Resources, the Department of Education and Science, and the Department of Economic Affairs – were concerned in varying degrees with the fate of the Cow Green scheme. The convention is that the Government is one and speaks with one voice: consequently in the early months of 1966 there was a good deal of inter-departmental consultation designed to hammer out an agreed governmental view on the principle of the Bill. In the end, however, only three departments – Housing and Local Government, Land and Natural Resources, and Education and Science – were to submit reports to the Select Committee of the House of Commons.

There are situations in which Government departments become the 'representatives' of interests and interest groups; when conflicts of interest occur in the outside world, these disputes are inevitably projected into the central administration. The Board of Trade and the Ministry of Housing and Local Government had known about the problems of ICI and the Water Board for well over a year. At one time, of course, it had been thought that the Minister of Housing and Local Government would decide the issue. The Ministry had by now digested the Water Resources Board's favourable report on Cow Green, and in December 1965 one of the Ministry's own Engineering Inspectors had visited the area. His assessment of the situation reached the Ministry on 13 January 1966; as he saw it, there was an urgent need for a new source, a reservoir at Cow Green was the most economic scheme, and it could be developed more quickly than any alternative source to meet the demands of large industrial consumers in the area. The Minister had been left in no doubt about the feelings of MPs representing Teesside constituencies and about the views of trade unions and industrialists in the North-East. And on 7 January 1966 the Executive Committee of the North-East Development Council, a body made up of representatives of local authorities, industry, trade unions and other public bodies, announced that the Bill had their full support. There was also Government policy for the distribution of industry to be taken into account: it was a cardinal feature of this policy to encourage all forms of industrial development in the North-East. Without an adequate and secure supply of water, there would be no expansion.

The Ministry of Housing and Local Government, however, had a responsibility not only for the supply of water, but also for the countryside and the preservation of amenities. On 4 April 1966 they received the observations of the National Parks Commission on the Bill. The Commission, not surprisingly, was flatly opposed to the Cow Green site, pointing out that for some years it had had in mind the possibility of designating Upper Teesdale as a National Park, or as part of one. The Commission told the Ministry that a reservoir at Cow Green would introduce civilization and artificiality into an essentially wild area that ought to be kept in its existing state as part of the diminishing reserve of wild country still available to the public for recreation and scientific research.

However, in the Ministry of Housing and Local Government, one important decision had already been taken: amenity objections could not weigh heavily against the need for adequate supplies of water. The National Parks Commission's memorandum, therefore, made little impact on the Department.[5] For their part, the Ministry of Land and Natural Resources shared Housing and Local Government's favourable attitude towards the Bill, and were happy enough with the choice of the Cow Green site. Both departments agreed that it was the botanical objection which was important, and neither rated this difficulty significant enough to justify building the reservoir elsewhere.

By contrast, the Department of Education and Science were by no means convinced that a reservoir had to be built at Cow Green. Within the machinery of Government, the Department naturally felt themselves to be the guardians of scientific research, and their initial hostility to the Cow Green scheme was confirmed and reinforced as a result of the stand taken by the Natural Environment Research Council (NERC), which by now had become responsible for the work of the Nature Conservancy.[6] In a formal submission to the Secretary of State for Education and Science it explained why Upper Teesdale was of such great scientific interest, and why it believed that the Cow Green scheme should be opposed.

The NERC argued that the scientific value of Upper Teesdale was determined by a combination of unusual physical conditions. The rare plants in the area formed unique communities of great genetic and evolutionary interest. For the elucidation of late glacial conditions in Great Britain, and for the study of plant migration to this country, Upper Teesdale was nowhere equalled. It was true that research on the soil and vegetation was still only in the early stages; but if continued, it might well lead to knowledge that would have an important bearing on upland use in the United Kingdom. According to the NERC, a reservoir at Cow Green would destroy about 0.1×10^6 m^2 of the special vegetational complex there. As a result of damage that might occur during construction it would endanger up to 0.4×10^6 m^2 of land of the highest scientific interest. And it would cause changes in the vegetation near the margins of the reservoir by reason of wave erosion, spray and slight localized alterations in the climatic conditions. The reservoir would also create 'visitor pressure', which could interfere with much that was of value, through picnicking, flower-picking, plant collection, pollution and fire. In the NERC's view, if there had to be a reservoir in Upper Teesdale, the Upper Cow Green alternative would be acceptable, and this site ought to be thoroughly investigated before there was any question of approving Cow Green.

Now that a specific alternative to Cow Green was in the running, backed by a responsible body like the NERC, the essential nature of the dilemma began to emerge. It was a problem that was later to tease two Select Committees. But for the moment it was Whitehall that had to come to grips with the intractable questions of value that lay at the heart of the case.

The difficulty was succinctly and clearly analysed in an inter-departmental memorandum of 28 February 1966. There was now support for Upper Cow Green. As opposed to Cow Green, however, it would take longer to build, the capital cost was estimated to be more than twice as much, and 1.0×10^6 m^2 of the reservoir site would fall within the Moor House Nature Reserve. On the other hand, to flood the Cow Green site might be to deprive the nation of a unique scientific area, with great research and educational potential, the value of which could not be quantified. But, whilst it was true that nobody could put a money value on this potential, the cost of preserving it could be measured. The cost of preservation would be the additional construction charges incurred at Upper Cow Green (estimated to be an extra £12 million in loan charges spread over a sixty-year period), together with the risk of lost industrial output in the event of a dry or drought year between 1970 and 1972. The value of the output that might be lost could be anything from £8·5 million to £35 million, depending on the level of rainfall. Up to 25 per cent of this lost output might have been earmarked for export.

Whilst the NERC's plea for the preservation of Cow Green made no impression on the Ministry of Housing and Local Government, the Department of Education and Science was more receptive, and the Secretary of State took the view that the Bill ought not to be supported unless the alternative site at Upper Cow Green proved on further investigation not to be feasible at all. He agreed that Upper Cow Green would indeed be more costly; and it would mean taking a chance on the possibility of drought conditions for a year or two before it was built. As against this, however, there was the irrefutable argument that the scientific damage arising out of the Bill was absolutely certain and irreversible for all time.

There was thus a clear difference of opinion between the two Government departments chiefly concerned with the Bill. If there was to be a common governmental line, it had to be decided whether the scientific objections to Cow Green were to carry the day, or whether the Bill should be given the Government's blessing. This was a crucial point in the case for, whereas Government support could not ensure a safe passage for the Bill, Government hostility would almost certainly have killed it. Precisely how, or at what level, the difference was resolved is not known outside Government circles. But eventually it was the view of the Ministry of Housing and Local Government, backed by the Board of Trade and the DEA, that prevailed. Towards the end of April 1966 the Minister of Housing and Local Government and the Minister of Land and Natural Resources were able to report on the Bill, and both supported it without reservation. The Secretary of State for Education and Science also supported it, though he made it quite clear that only the compelling economic and social arguments had forced his hand, and that he had reached his decision with great regret and reluctance.[7]

Parliament decides: The House of Commons

In the meantime, the Select Committee had been set up under the chairmanship of Clifford Kenyon (Labour, Chorley). The three other members were Lieut. Cmdr. S. L. C. Maydon (Conservative, Wells), Paul Hawkins (Conservative, SE Norfolk), and George Perry (Labour, Nottingham South). Kenyon and Hawkins both had strong links with the agricultural world, Perry was chairman of the South Derbyshire Water Board, and all except Maydon had considerable experience of local government. When they assembled for the first time on 4 May 1966 they can hardly have foreseen what a gruelling course lay ahead. Over the next three weeks they were to sit for twelve full days, much of the time listening to highly technical arguments on subjects as diverse as industrial chemistry, water engineering, water finance, geology, botany and ecology. Even studied at leisure and at the reader's own pace, a good deal of the verbatim transcript is difficult enough to follow; what the committee were able to make of some of the more recondite exchanges between counsel and specialist witnesses must be left to the imagination.

The Tees Valley and Cleveland Water Board were represented by P. Boydell, QC, and F. H. B. Layfield (who, it will be recalled, had appeared for one of the local authorities objecting to the CEGB's proposed Holme Pierrepont power station). Counsel for the petitioners were H. Marnham, QC, and M. Fitzgerald. On the promoters' side, the principal witnesses were Kennard, Knill, Hetherington, Allison and Newman, together with G. M. Thompson, the Water Board's engineer, Dr J. Newberry, an engineering geologist, Dr P. G. Harvey of ICI, N. A. F. Rowntree, the Director of the Water Resources Board, S. F. Jones, the secretary of the North Riding and South Durham branch of the NFU, Dr S. Gregory, a climatologist at the University of Liverpool, B. S. Furneaux, a soil surveyor, Dr A. S. Thomas, a botanical consultant, F. Gibberd, the architect, E. A. Morris, the Water Board's Chief Executive Officer and S. W. Hill, an expert on water finance. For the petitioners the chief witnesses were Gardiner, Bradshaw, Godwin, Pigott, Stephenson, and Jeffcoate, together with Dr M. W. Holdgate of the Nature Conservancy, Dr G. A. L. Johnson, Lecturer in Geology, and Dr A. Raistrick, Reader in Applied Geology, both of the University of Durham.

In essence, the case made out by ICI and the Water Board was this. The extra water to be provided by the reservoir was needed, it was needed urgently, and there was no reasonable alternative to Cow Green. It was true that other sites in Upper Teesdale were technically feasible. But some of them would not yield enough water, some of them would cause a great deal of disturbance to agriculture and amenity, and all of them would be considerably more expensive than Cow Green. None of them, moreover, could be brought into service as quickly as Cow Green. This was a consideration of great importance because until the reservoir became operational, a drought year of anything like the severity of 1949 or 1959 would seriously interfere with production at the ICI works, with a consequent loss of output, much of which would have been exported.

They conceded that if the Bill went through, a small area containing flora of some scientific interest would be flooded. The reservoir might also detract somewhat from the natural beauty of this part of Upper Teesdale. But, as ICI and the Water Board saw it, both the naturalists and the amenity societies had wildly exaggerated the extent of the damage to their interests. This was particularly true of the botanists. All the rare flora on Cow Green could be found above as well as below the proposed top water level of the reservoir. In fact, they claimed, only three of the plant species on the proposed site could be described as genuinely rare. They were the Yorkshire milkwort, the Teesdale violet, and the Teesdale sandwort. The Yorkshire milkwort could be disregarded, for it also grew on nearby Cronkley Fell, where it could not possibly be affected by the reservoir. There was no point in becoming excited about the Teesdale violet, they said, because it was quite widespread in other parts of the world; indeed, if the botanists would look carefully enough it might also be found on limestone elsewhere in England, for it could easily be mistaken for the common dog violet. Only the Teesdale sandwort seemed to be seriously at risk, and even that would probably survive, given reasonable care while the reservoir was being built.

Some of the Water Board's witnesses were even to suggest that the Cow Green vegetation was not made up of relict ice-age flora at all, but had arrived in relatively recent times. This particular part of Upper Teesdale, it was implied, had become unique rather suddenly, just when the reservoir was proposed. No doubt some botanists were deeply interested in Cow Green; but they had been carried away by their enthusiasm, and were trying to give an altogether misleading impression of the scientific significance of the site. Anyone who looked carefully at the scientific literature on Upper Teesdale would find that very little of it bore directly on Cow Green, or even on the wider area of Widdybank Fell. The botanists and the Nature Conservancy were arguing that pure research, unrelated to any specific objective, had often produced applications of great practical importance in the past, and might well do so again here. But this was a specious argument that could be used in support of virtually any piece of academic research, however improbable the chances of any useful application. Experience does indeed show that unforeseen results of practical value frequently do come out of pure research; but the likelihood of such an occurrence in respect of one particular piece of pure research is very slight. And the fact was, they said, that the rare flora on Widdybank Fell were not even remotely related to crop plants of any economic importance.

In short, the case for the Water Board rested upon three propositions. First, Cow Green was the best site in terms of the Board's obligations and objectives. Second, the petitioners had exaggerated the scientific importance of what would be lost if Cow Green were flooded. And third, by comparison with all the alternatives, the quantifiable value of Cow Green's advantages was so substantial that it easily outweighed the unquantifiable scientific and aesthetic value of anything that would be destroyed.

On the other side, the petitioners were at pains to emphasize that this was no case of a handful of botanists whipping up synthetic indignation in a desperate campaign to preserve a stretch of countryside that happened to be of passionate interest to themselves and to themselves alone. What happened at Cow Green, they said, was of great concern to scientists all over the country, and indeed all over the world. The Water Board and ICI, moreover, had either misunderstood or deliberately misrepresented the scientific issues involved, for when the Bill's promoters went to such lengths to show that this or that rare plant on Cow Green was also to be found elsewhere, they were very largely missing the point.

It was perfectly true – the petitioners would be the last to deny it – that some of these rare flora were of great interest in themselves. So far as some of them were concerned, the proposed reservoir would destroy a significant proportion of the total population known to exist in the United Kingdom. And, despite what ICI's witnesses had said, a study of these plants might well yield results of great genetic and evolutionary interest. Professor Pigott, for example, argued that experiments on wild plants of this kind, surviving as they did at the limits of their tolerance, in an extremely harsh environment, could in time help mankind understand why the properties of crop plants permitted them to live only within specific environments. Yet it was not so much the presence of individual rare plants on Cow Green that fascinated the botanists. Rather, it was the unique *communities*, or assemblages, of these ancient relict species that made the western slopes of Widdybank Fell an area of such outstanding scientific interest. As Professor Godwin and Dr Bradshaw pointed out, species that were only to be found separately in the arctic, or in alpine regions, or in widely scattered parts of Europe, were here growing together. To study the ecology of these extraordinary communities the botanists needed to be able to examine the *whole* of each complex or series of plants, and they needed to be able to compare one assemblage with another. About 0.1×10^6 m^2 might not sound much. But to flood this area would be to slice off the lower end of several natural series. This would very much reduce the range of varying conditions that made these slopes an area of such enormous scientific potential. On Widdybank Fell, botany students were able to test ideas and hypotheses of fundamental importance. Once destroyed, this valuable stock of scientific capital could never be replaced. It certainly ought not to be sacrificed for the kind of short-term economic advantage that would be conferred by the Cow Green site.

How much of an impact the botanists and their arguments made on the Select Committee must remain a matter for conjecture. In their own line of country they were professionals and specialists, and they doubtless genuinely believed Cow Green to be of first-rate importance. But few experts relish the unfamiliar hazards and trials of the witness stand at a public inquiry or before a Private Bill committee, and university professors are in some ways worse off than most. They are accustomed to lecturing *ex cathedra*; their professional pronouncements are rarely challenged or contradicted, at least not by laymen. Nothing in their training fits them to undergo with equanimity a sustained and hostile cross-examination at the hands of a skilful barrister, adept at leading them on, provoking their anger, occasionally catching them out, and extracting the apparently damaging admission. Theirs was a voluntary effort, and they had their own jobs to attend to. When they were first drawn into the controversy some of them may not have realized how much time and work would be entailed. Both Professor Godwin and Professor Pigott were criticized by Clifford Kenyon, the chairman of the Select Committee, for not spending more time at the hearings, and for rushing away after giving their evidence. If Cow Green really was of such vital importance to botanists, Kenyon observed, then

Pigott ought to have been prepared to spend as much time at Westminster as the members of the committee. Pigott apologized, but pointed out that he was paid to teach and could not neglect his students. The chairman was not impressed. A week's teaching, he said, was not much when the petitioners were arguing that the outcome of this case would affect generation after generation of students in the years ahead.

It has already been suggested that very few botanists were well enough acquainted with Cow Green to know for certain exactly what was there, or precisely what would be lost if the reservoir were built. The Teesdale Defence Committee's skill lay in attracting support from a considerably wider circle, some of whom were by no means experts on this particular corner of Upper Teesdale. Under pressure, this sometimes became uncomfortably apparent. Here, for example, is Boydell drawing together the threads of cross-examination, and suggesting that even Professor Godwin, one of the petitioners' principal botanical witnesses, was not as knowledgeable about the flora on Cow Green as he might have been :

Q First, you have not been able to tell us, have you, what plants as individual plants are in the area which will be inundated ? You have not been able to tell me, have you ?

A I have been unwilling to commit myself here and now to doing so, knowing that it is within the Committee to find this directly from Dr Pigott.

Q I understand you to say you were unable to supply them ?

A Very well.

Q Secondly, you are unable to give me any congregation or grouping of plants in the inundated area : this is right is it not ?

A The same applies as before. I am unwilling to do this.

Q Last time you said 'unable'.

A Yes, very well.

Q Are you both unable and unwilling ?

A I am afraid I am unable to do a great many things.

Q Thirdly, since you are unable to give me the details under those two heads you cannot possibly say how plants as individual plants, or with others, in the seventeen areas (on Cow Green) compare with other areas in Upper Teesdale. It must follow, must it not ?

A Not entirely; partially that is true.

The petitioners, however, had another string to their bow. One of their objectives was to demonstrate the loss of scientific and amenity value that the reservoir would entail. The other was to show that, even in terms of the Water Board's own obligations and objectives, Cow Green was in many ways an unsuitable site, and inferior to at least two alternative possibilities. When they see an opening, objectors often adopt this strategy of attacking developers on their own ground: but it is always a difficult and ambitious tack, for to succeed the objectors have to show that they and their expert witnesses know the developers' business at least as well as the developers themselves.

Initially, the objectors attacked the Cow Green site on geological grounds. Whatever the Bill's promoters might say, there was no escaping the fact that the geological survey carried out in 1956 had suggested that a reservoir on the cavernous limestone at Cow Green would not be water-tight. ICI and the Water Board maintained that subsequent investigations had cleared the site on this score; but, the petitioners argued, there must still remain an element of doubt. If these fears were realized, 'grouting' would be required on an extensive scale; that is, liquid cement would have to be injected into the floor and sides of the valley in order to seal it. And if grouting did prove necessary, the cost of the reservoir would be increased, the completion date would be pushed further forward, and even more damage would be inflicted on the vegetation in the vicinity of the reservoir.

As a more suitable alternative, the petitioners began by urging the merits of Upper Cow Green, about 3 km upstream from Cow Green. This was the site, it will be remembered, that was favoured by the Nature Conservancy. Although it fell within the Moor House Nature Reserve, the botanists were prepared, or said they were prepared, to see it flooded if Cow Green would thereby be spared.[8]

The Water Board and ICI had rejected Upper Cow Green at a very early stage. Nor did it ever appear a strong contender once the hearings opened. For one thing, the case for Upper Cow Green was hardly developed in a way calculated to impress the Select Committee with the thoroughness of the petitioners' preparatory studies. According to Kennard, the petitioners had at first proposed a reservoir there with a top water level of 525 m. On this assumption, the reservoir would have cost £6 million (Cow Green: £2·0–2·5 million); it would have required a dam 1550 m long (Cow Green: 525 m) and 46·4 m high (Cow Green: 22·0 m); and it would have been completed in 1971 (Cow Green: 1969). Shortly before the Select Committee proceedings began, however, it was discovered that a reservoir with these dimensions would yield only $130·5–135·0 \times 10^3$ m^3 a day, as opposed to the $157·5 \times 10^3$ m^3 a day that were needed. The specifications were hastily altered, and the top water level raised to 534 m. The effect of this modifica-tion would have been to increase the capacity of the reservoir, bringing the yield up to 171·0–180·0. Unfortunately, in solving the problem of yield, the cost of the reservoir would have risen to £9 million, the length and height of the dam would have increased still further, and (according to the Water Board's experts) the completion date would have receded to 1974.

As the proceedings continued, the petitioners realized that they had a much more promising alternative in the Middleton site. To understand the case for Middleton we must digress for a moment in order to explain the water industry's arrangements for raising capital for major works. Under Section 27 of the 1945 Water Act, the Tees Valley and Cleveland Water Board, like other water undertakings, had a statutory obligation to supply water for industrial purposes 'on reasonable terms and conditions'. On Teeside, the arrangement was that industrial consumers should make a reasonable offer to bear, or to contribute to, the cost of any new works needed to meet their requirements. And so far as the Tees Valley and Cleveland Water Board were concerned, this obligation had been reinforced as a result of being written into several Private Acts. In practice, the industrialists would make their contribution by helping to pay off the loan charges over a period of forty or sixty years. So long as it is ready to pay its share of the capital cost, industry is entitled to demand more water. But there is a corollary: so far as industrial consumption is concerned, the effect of this arrangement is to restrict water undertakings to whatever level of capital expenditure industry is prepared to guarantee.

Consequently, even if a Water Board believes that local industrialists may be underestimating their future requirements, they cannot plan to provide more water than industry says is needed, for then the firms concerned could and would refuse to contribute towards the necessary capital expenditure. And in this event, the money could be raised only by placing the whole burden on the domestic consumer, something the Minister of Housing and Local Government would not permit even if a Water Board were minded to launch a capital project on this basis. In any case, before giving his consent for the development of new sources, the Minister requires proof that there is a real need; and proof is established by the willingness of the firms involved to make a financial contribution, or provide an appropriate guarantee. No other policy makes sense, for the country's water resources are limited, and if one water authority builds reservoirs that are not really necessary, someone else, with a genuine need, may have to go without.

With such a high proportion of their output committed to industrial consumers, this system of capital financing had on several occasions placed the Tees Valley and Cleveland Water Board in difficult and embarrassing situations. The Board had never been able to spend money on new sources until their industrial clients were prepared to guarantee their share of the capital expenditure required. And the industrialists, naturally, always erred on the side of caution, because they were anxious to avoid saddling themselves, for years ahead, with loan charges incurred in providing more water than they needed. By the time they were certain enough of their future needs to give firm guarantees, the unfortunate Water Board was likely to be faced with the problem of providing a great deal more water at very short notice.

In 1966 ICI were prepared to forecast (for guarantee purposes) only a small and gradual annual increase of $9 \cdot 0 \times 10^3$ m³ of water a day after 1970, that is, after the proposed Cow Green reservoir had solved their immediate problem. The petitioners argued that this projection, as usual, would turn out to be a gross underestimate of the demands that would eventually be made on the Tees Valley and Cleveland Water Board. If the Cow Green reservoir were built, then within three or four years of its completion the search would be on again for another major source. At that stage, inevitably, Middleton would be the choice. It was perfectly true that with a yield of 338×10^3 m³ a day a reservoir at Middleton would provide far more water than was needed in the immediate future. It was also true that it would cost more than twice as much as Cow Green, besides taking a good deal of agricultural land and displacing a number of farmers. Nor could it be completed until 1972. But if the Middleton site was bound to be flooded anyway at some future date, how much more sensible to build a reservoir there to begin with, rather than come back to it after the botanical treasures of Cow Green had disappeared beyond recall. It was not a question of *either* Cow Green *or* Middleton. Rather, the alternatives were either Middleton only now, or Cow Green now *and* (inevitably) Middleton later. Either way, a reservoir would eventually be built at Middleton. But whereas Middleton could save Cow Green, Cow Green could not save Middleton, at least not for more than a few years. It would be nothing short of a tragedy if Cow Green were flooded partly because of the arguments against developing the Middleton site, and then Middleton had to be submerged too.[9]

As the petitioners acknowledged, finding enough water to meet ICI's needs before Middleton could be brought into service in 1972 would be something of a problem. The solution here, they argued, was for the Water Board to follow up a suggestion made by the Water Resources Board and abstract water from the magnesian limestone and bunter sandstone area between Middlesbrough and Darlington. Agreed, the Water Resources Board had put a figure of only $27 \cdot 0 \times 10^3$ m³ a day on the reliable yield from this source. But this figure apparently related to a daily rate over the *whole* year. The borehole scheme now put before the Select Committee by Jeffcoate, the petitioners' water consultant, envisaged the abstraction of much larger quantities of water, but over short periods of time. In Jeffcoate's opinion, far more than $27 \cdot 0 \times 10^3$ m³ a day could be abstracted from the magnesian limestone and bunter sandstone if intensive pumping were confined to three or four months during the summer when the extra water was really needed. If a start were made quickly on a scheme of this kind, it would certainly meet the urgent short-term need, and it would also provide a breathing-space, so that a careful and considered view of alternative sources could be undertaken.

The case for the petitioners, then, also rested upon three propositions. First, the Cow Green site was of outstanding scientific importance. Second, by comparison with the petitioners' counter-proposals, the advantages claimed for the Cow Green reservoir were largely illusory. And third, even if there was some short-term advantage in developing the Cow Green site, this advantage was easily outweighed by the enormous, thought unquantifiable, value of what would be destroyed if the reservoir was built. The Water Board and ICI, they implied, were taking altogether too blinkered and jaundiced a view of the alternative possibilities, and altogether too rosy a view of the Cow Green site.

Naturally, the Water Board would have none of this. So far as the technical suitability of Cow Green was concerned, they pointed out that the recent geological survey had been much more thorough than in 1956, and this time the report was favourable. Would ICI really be prepared to spend several million pounds on a reservoir, they asked, if there was a serious possibility of it leaking ? As for the petitioners' alternatives, Upper Cow Green would take too long to build, and the extra expense could not be justified. In any case, Upper Cow Green itself was open to some of the same botanical objections as Cow Green. As the botanists admitted, any site upstream from Cauldron Snout would even out the river flow and put at risk the riverside communities of rare flora below the torrent. If the Middleton site was developed, there would be a justifiable outcry from the farmers. According to the National Farmers' Union, neither Cow Green nor Upper Cow Green was of any agricultural value, whereas on their reckoning a reservoir at Middleton would flood $5 \cdot 2 \times 10^6$ m^2 of farmland, and would affect thirty-nine smallholdings which currently supported about 250 dairy cows, 700 other cattle, 1000 sheep, 100 pigs, and about 2500 head of poultry.[10] Moreover, to build a reservoir at Middleton that could provide far more water than would be needed for years ahead was to tie up capital unnecessarily. And, taking the long view, the Middleton scheme would irrevocably commit the Northumbrian River Authority to this method of supplying water to Teesside, even if less objectionable means of providing it were to become feasible in the future.

On 27 May 1966 the hearings before the Select Committee came to an end. The four MPs had a great deal to ponder, for the verbatim record of the complex and conflicting evidence for and against Cow Green fills 700 pages of typescript. Usually, it is not known how MPs vote on Select Committees, or what arguments weighed with them. In this case, we know a little of what occurred, for one of the four, Paul Hawkins, took the somewhat unusual step of explaining how he had made up his mind, at the same time disclosing how the voting went. Apparently, Kenyon, Maydon and Perry voted to report favourably on the Bill, whilst Hawkins was against.

Hawkins had evidently been impressed with the scientific case for preserving the rare flora at Cow Green. But his main concern had been with the threat to Middleton and the rest of the Tees Valley. He believed that the Bill ought to be rejected, and the Water Board told that they could take no more land in Teesdale for reservoirs. Instead, they should look for underground sources, and investigate the possibility of desalination. In fact, Hawkins seems to have accepted the argument that if Cow Green fell, Middleton would not be far behind. As we have seen, others who sympathized with the agricultural interest were taking the view that if ICI's thirst could be quenched at Cow Green, something would turn up to save Middleton.

Although the Select Committee had approved the Bill in principle, they decided that they wanted more time to consider two of the issues that had arisen during the hearings. They wanted to know more about the possible need for grouting, and they wished to consider further the question of removing from the Water Board their power to reach agreement with large consumers for the payment of contributions towards the capital cost of new works. At their final meeting on 21 June, however, the Committee decided to take no further action. On the financial question, they received a supplementary report from the Ministry of Housing and Local Government, pointing out that the power to enter into these arrangements had proved to be of great value to water undertakers, and that there was no intention of removing it from the public general legislation covering such statutory bodies. On the matter of grouting, the Bill's promoters let it be known that they intended to sink experimental boreholes on the site so as to establish, once and for all, whether or not grouting would be necessary. If the Bill were opposed in the House of Lords, they said, the results of these tests would be available in time to be considered there.

As amended, the Bill now came downstairs from the Committee for its Report stage. Over the next four weeks there was a good deal of lobbying from both sides. The Botanical Society of the British Isles sent out a memorandum to all M Ps reiterating the case against the reservoir, and the promoters countered this with their own document, explaining why it was vital that the Bill should be enacted.

The motion that the Bill should be further considered eventually came before the House on the evening of 28 July 1966, though the actual debate took place on a blocking amendment moved by Marcus Kimball (Conservative, Gainsborough), which read:

That this House declines to consider a Bill which would involve irreparable harm to a unique area of international scientific importance, fails to have regard to the proper long-term planning for the water requirements of the area, and is contrary to the declared advice of the Nature Conservancy and the National Parks Commission.[11]

The Cow Green controversy, Kimball declared, was the most important conservation issue ever to come before Parliament. The Select Committee had done a thorough job of work on the Bill; but they had to remember that the Committee had not been unanimous. If the House failed to take a stand over Cow Green, no other area in the country would be safe. The complex community of rare plants at Cow Green was irreplaceable, and every botanist in the United Kingdom and in Europe subscribed to this view. If the Bill was approved, he said, they would be setting the worst possible example to the underdeveloped countries, where properly planned conservation and the proper use of natural resources were desperately important. The House might ask why, if it was so important, Cow Green had not been included in a National Nature Reserve. The answer was that in 1959 the Water Board had said that they did not expect to come back for more water until 1983. The Nature Conservancy was therefore justified in thinking that there was no urgent need to give the site further protection by bringing it into a Nature Reserve. Scientists, he said, were notoriously bad at giving evidence to Parliamentary committees, for they are reluctant to speculate and say what they *think* will happen. Consequently, their words may carry less conviction than they feel. He had the greatest admiration for the Botanical Society of the British Isles in taking on 'the Goliath of ICI' on this important issue. Had there been proper long-term planning for the needs of the area, the problem facing the House would not have arisen. If the Bill was not rejected, they would be setting an appalling precedent.

Kimball was supported by Arthur Blenkinsop (Labour, South Shields), a former member of the Nature Conservancy. He argued that, if the House approved the Bill, it would in effect be saying, as so often in the past, that nothing else mattered in the North-East except industrial development. It was time that they grew out of this attitude. He was not satisfied that the promoters had made their case adequately, and he doubted whether all the alternatives to Cow Green had been thoroughly examined. Much the same position was taken by Sir David Renton (Conservative, Huntingdon-shire) and Sir John Eden (Conservative, Bournemouth West), who objected to the Bill chiefly on the grounds that Cow Green was only a short-term solution to the Water Board's problem. Perhaps the most spirited attack came from Eldon Griffiths (Conservative, Bury St Edmunds). He conceded that they were choosing not between right and wrong but between right and right. But he had come down against the Bill because he believed that ICI would suffer only inconvenience if the Bill were rejected, whereas if Cow Green were flooded its unique and invaluable vegetation was quite irreplaceable. 'In effect', he declared, 'it is a choice between a dip in ICI's profits, which they would have to accept [Hon. Members : 'No'], or it is the destruction of ten thousand years of unique natural history.' Coming from a Conservative MP this was certainly a surprising interpretation of the problem, though a number of Labour Members probably shared this attitude. Warming to his theme, Griffiths remarked that he had the impression that if a mighty company like ICI wanted water it tended to assume that no power in England could stop it. Why else had ICI gone ahead with their new developments at Billingham without bothering about Parliament? In his view the greater right lay with those who wished to retain a precious portion of our national heritage rather than with those who admittedly needed more water, but who, with a little more expense and a good deal more ingenuity, could obtain their supplies from elsewhere.

As the debate went on, it became clear that Cow Green was an issue that cut right across party lines. As with Parliamentary business in the eighteenth and early nineteenth centuries, it was the politics of interest and of personal conviction that structured the dispute. Most of those who spoke in favour of the Bill were Labour Members, but they were not without support from the Conservative benches.

R. W. Elliott (Conservative, Newcastle-upon-Tyne North) emphasized the value of ICI to an area that faced the problems associated with the declining shipbuilding and coal-mining industries. MPs on both sides of the House, he claimed, had done their best to bring employment to the North-East, and ICI had been encouraged to develop on Teesside. He believed that if water were not made available quickly, and drought conditions occurred in the 1970s, the effect on the national trade figures and on employment in the area would be disastrous.

Ted Leadbitter (Labour, The Hartlepools) claimed that 'in this region the primary thing at this stage is employment' and later observed that 'it is important to stress the point that in my region we cannot evaluate beauty and the scientific interest of flora until we have the social conditions for all those who live there to enjoy it.' They ought to look very seriously into the issues raised by the objectors : but he thought that they had exaggerated their case. If the Bill was not approved, the House might well inflict serious economic loss on the area.

Fred Willey (Labour, Sunderland North), the Minister of Land and Natural Resources, said that he was personally in favour of the Cow Green site, and so was the Minister of Housing and Local Government and the Secretary of State for Education and Science. He had been advised by the Water Resources Board that any of the alternative sites would mean taking a grave risk, for a succession of three or four dry summers would seriously interfere with output and employment. He acknowledged that, if more time had been available, the Water Board might have been able to choose from a wider range of alternatives. But the matter was urgent, and 'very reluctantly' he had to recommend the House to support the Bill.

Other Members also drew attention to the economic consequences of rejecting the bill, among them Ernest Armstrong (Labour, NW Durham) and James Tinn (Labour, Cleveland). As the former put it, 'The determining factor for me is that if the Bill were defeated, industrial development on Teesside would be impeded and delayed'. The latter argued that ICI had taken a justifiable gamble in going ahead with their new installations before making sure of the water they needed. British technology had given us a lead in world markets, and a heavy responsibility would lie on the House if they squandered it. They ought not to neglect the scientific case, but a careful study of the Select Committee's Report made it clear that the effect of the reservoir on the local flora would be minimal. Another Member to speak in favour of the Bill was Timothy Kitson (Conservative, Richmond, Yorks.): Cow Green was his choice, largely because the most likely alternative was Middleton, and if Middleton were flooded the reservoir would have a very serious effect on the forty or fifty of his constituents who farmed in that area. But he, too, was concerned with the wider issue of employment on Teesside. 'When one remembers that the Hailsham Plan was largely responsible for encouraging ICI to extend its development programme on Teesside,' he said, 'and bearing in mind the high unemployment figures we had not many years ago in this area, we must try to do everything possible to continue industrial expansion on Teesside.'

At the end of the debate nearly 200 MPs went into the division lobbies. It was, of course, a free vote. Considering that the Bill had been approved by the Select Committee, and was known to have the support of the Government departments concerned, the result was perhaps closer than might have been expected. The blocking motion was rejected by 112 votes to eighty-two. In party terms, 100 of the 112 MPs in favour of the Bill were Labour Members and twelve were Conservatives. Of the eighty-two MPs supporting Kimball's motion (that is, opposing the Bill) forty-four were Conservatives, twenty-nine were Labour Members and nine were Liberals.

Labour support for the Bill came predominantly from Members representing industrial constituencies in the North, the Midlands and Scotland. The bulk of them were trade unionists, or connected in others ways with industry. The opposition was much more of a mixed bag. Of the forty-four Conservatives against the Bill, thirty-three represented constituencies south of a line from the Wash to the Severn. The twenty-nine Labour Members voting against the Bill were equally divided between northern and southern constituencies, and a fair proportion of them were younger

Members with an academic or professional background. Nine of the twelve Liberals in the House voted, and all nine voted against the Bill.

The motives of Members on both sides must be a matter for conjecture. Doubtless many who voted for the Bill, particularly among the Labour Members, simply reacted instinctively in favour of a proposal that seemed to safeguard men's jobs. Understandably enough, for some of them conservation and amenity, and indeed almost anything else, would always take second place when the emotive issue of unemployment came into the question. Others may have looked one move ahead and calculated that to reject Cow Green would be to endanger Middleton and the agricultural interest. Others again may simply have been prepared to take a lead from the Government departments involved, though presumably very few Members would take the trouble to be present for a free vote on a Private Bill unless they were themselves genuinely interested in the outcome and had reasonably firm convictions of their own. On the other side, among the Conservatives voting against the Bill there was probably much less of an emotive reaction on the unemployment question to set against the claims of conservation and amenity. Some Conservatives, perhaps, thought that, if the Government was for the Bill, then they ought to be against it. Some Members of both parties may have reckoned that important though ICI were to Teesside, in this instance industry could well afford to pay a little more for its water in the interests of civilized causes like conservation and amenity.

But to judge from the tone of the speeches, it was emotion and sentiment, rather than a cool and open-minded appraisal of the issues involved, that dictated the attitude of most MPs. Contrary to what James Tinn said in the debate, the Select Committee at no time produced a summary of their findings or their reasons for approving the Bill. Most Members must have relied most exclusively on simplified, abbreviated and *ex parte* versions of the arguments put before the Select Committee. If the conservationists (or *mutatis mutandis* the industrialists) seemed to have a good case, that was enough. Instinctively and spontaneously, they plumped for either employment or conservation, either industry or amenity. Yet the Cow Green case, like many other disputes of this kind, was never simply a question of this or that, all or nothing.

In essence, the dilemma was this. The plant communities and wild countryside above Cauldron Snout undoubtedly had a certain value, which could not be quantified in money terms. Although there were differences of opinion as to the importance of the area to be flooded, everyone agreed that the reservoir would to some extent detract from its value, both scenically and scientifically. This loss of value was, of course, just as unquantifiable as the value of the area left unimpaired. But if the *value* of what the reservoir would destroy at Cow Green could not be quantified, the *price* of preserving the area intact was calculable. An alternative site was feasible, and by general consent the next best alternative was at Middleton. The price of saving Cow Green was simply the difference in cost and risk between Cow Green and Middleton. This difference was £3·0–3·5 million for certain, a possible threat to men's jobs and to exports, and the loss of good agricultural land. The problem, mercifully, was not so much to put a value on what would be sacrificed at Cow Green as to decide whether an established, specific price was worth paying in order to avoid that sacrifice. In the end, a decision of this kind is bound to rest upon subjective evaluations. And since this was a value-judgement *par excellence*, who better to give a collective verdict than the elected representatives of the people ?

Yet not everyone would agree that decisions of this kind are best made in the division lobbies. Whether or not the rare flora on Widdybank Fell were worth the price of preserving them was not a question that could ever be satisfactorily answered on the basis of facts alone. Two honest men, both in possession of all the relevant information, could obviously have come to opposite conclusions. But faced with the question 'to buy or not to buy', a prospective purchaser, if he is to make a rational decision, must surely appreciate what precisely he is being asked to pay for, and he must also understand precisely how much he is being asked to pay. How many MPs who voted on the Cow Green Bill really had the time or the patience to find out exactly what plants grew on Cow Green, why they were so important, to what extent they would be affected by the proposed reservoir, and how much it would cost in terms of money, risks and other sacrifices to build the reservoir elsewhere and keep Cow Green as it was? Those MPs who spoke in the debate were presumably better informed than most of their colleagues. Some of them even claimed to have read all or most of the evidence. But even allowing that they were speaking to persuade rather than to inform, many of them appeared to have only the loosest grasp on the facts of the case. Anyone listening to the debate might have been excused for thinking that if the Cow Green reservoir were built, the conservation movement in the United Kingdom (and probably overseas too) would collapse in ruins ; alternatively, he might have concluded from the arguments on the other side that if the reservoir was not built, ICI would soon be on the verge of bankruptcy, and in no time mass unemployment would return to Teesside.

Parliament decides: the House of Lords

The Bill had now to go through the House of Lords. During the summer it had become apparent that the friends of Cow Green were still full of fight.

In August there had been a renewed appeal for public subscriptions to support the efforts of the Defence Committee, and on 1 September Dr Bradshaw read a paper to the British Association at Nottingham, roundly condemning the proposed reservoir. To coincide with the formal First Reading of the Bill in the Lords, on 20 October the petitioners organized a mass meeting at the Caxton Hall, London, and borne up on a wave of enthusiasm many of the objectors were talking confidently of defeating the Bill in the second chamber.

In the North-East there was alarm and exasperation at the petitioners' refusal to lie down. When the Bill had emerged successfully from the Commons, some members of the Water Board, in their relief, had jumped to the conclusion that all would now be plain sailing. Sir Charles Allison, for example, magnanimously declared that he regarded the vote in the House of Commons not as a political success, but as a 'real victory for common sense', and a triumph over prejudice. ICI, he said, could now go ahead with their plans, and everyone on Teesside would rejoice. By October, however, it was apparent that the triumph of common sense was far from assured, and Allison was again bitterly denouncing the selfishness of the Bill's opponents. Any delay in building the reservoir, he said, would hit Britain's chemical exports at a time when all sections of the community were being asked to make sacrifices because of the economic situation. 'The naturalists and botanists,' he said, 'should realize that while they may have very devoted interests in this matter, other people's interests are omnipotent.'

On 8 November 1966 the Bill came before the Lords for its Second Reading. In a debate lasting nearly five hours, the speakers against included Lord Molson, Lord Hurcomb, Lord Strang, Lord Methuen, Earl Waldegrave and Lord Ritchie-Calder: among those in favour were Lord Lindgren, Lord Hawke, Lord Ilford, the Earl of Swinton and Lord Blyton. By now there was little to be said that had not been said before, though the quality of debate was somewhat higher, and many of the speeches showed a better grasp of the problem than in the Commons. There was a strong current of opposition to the reservoir, and it is possible that, had the objectors forced a division, they might have been able to defeat the Bill there and then. However, it is the invariable practice in the Lords for the chairman of Committees to advise the House to give opposed Private Bills a Second Reading, so that the evidence for and against can be investigated in detail by a Select Committee. This advice is usually taken, on the grounds that it would be wrong for uninformed Members to obstruct a Bill before the House has had the opportunity of considering the Report of a Select Committee.[12] On the understanding that a special Instruction would be given to the Select Committee, the objectors agreed not to oppose the Second Reading, though they reserved the right to vote against the Bill when it came back to them, whatever the Select Committee's views.

The terms of this Instruction (moved by Lord Molson) were clearly designed to focus attention on what the objectors thought were the more vulnerable aspects of the promoters' case. The Select Committee were instructed to give special consideration to (i) the need to provide a supply of water that would meet the foreseeable requirements of Teesside for at least the next twenty years, and (ii) other sites for reservoirs, and other methods of supplying water to meet the needs of the more immediate future.

Lord Molson argued that if ICI were prepared to spend £100 000 of their shareholders' money on a crash programme of scientific research, that surely was conclusive proof that what was to be submerged at Cow Green was of great scientific value. The Cow Green reservoir, he said, was only a short-term expedient. Before a final decision was made, they should allow more time for the Water Resources Board to carry out a thorough review of all the alternatives, taking into account the water needs of Teesside over the next twenty years. As to the risk of drought, no one who had lived through the previous few summers could really feel that there was much danger of three or four dry summers in succession in the near future. The fact was that ICI would be paying only 1·2p per m³ for their water from Cow Green, as compared with the average price throughout the country of 3·3p per m³. The company ought to be prepared to pay a higher price in the interests of conservation and amenity.

Lord Hurcomb drew attention to the international repercussions of flooding Cow Green. Many of the leading botanists and ecologists in Europe were dismayed at the proposal. The short-sighted destruction of this unique area, he said, would seriously set back the world movement for the conservation of nature and natural resources. Earl Waldegrave thought that this was one of the few cases where conservation should take priority over industrial development. 'If we feel that there is no case here', he declared, 'then we should be honest about it and repeal conservation legislation and abandon the whole idea.'

On the other side, Lord Hawke pointed out that every man-made lake arouses intense opposition from some group, and this time it was the botanists. Some of them made great claims, though he had been told that their presence in the area was not particularly noticeable before the Cow Green scheme came to be talked about. 'I sometimes wonder,' he said, 'whether we are not in danger of becoming a little bemused by science. After all, what is science ? Science is knowledge, and knowledge is all very well ... but whether the national interest is served by that knowledge depends on whether it conduces to the health and happiness of the human race. Judged on that particular standard, I should have thought that some of the scientific case here looks a little thin.' And in a robust, no-nonsense speech, Viscount Slim observed that 'we earn our living, not by admiring, or even studying botanical specimens, but by keeping ahead of our competitors in the struggle for production and for new methods of production.'

From the Government front bench, Lord Kennet told the House that the Government's attitude was unchanged, and they still supported the Bill. The dispute, he said, was an irreconcilable conflict between two very strong cases. It had so far been marked by confusion, hasty words, and attempts on the part of both sides to discredit the professional competence of the other. The House of Lords, he suggested, was no place for ungentlemanly conduct of this kind. 'I hope that we shall be able to say la er', he added, 'that from the moment when the Teesdale Bill went before the Lords such unseemliness ceased, and the thing was thenceforth considered calmly and on its merits.'

As in the Commons, some of the peers who took part in the debate reacted to the Cow Green scheme in a predictable way. Theirs was almost a reflex action. This was a conflict between industry on the one hand and conservation and amenity on the other. Spontaneously and instinctively, and by reason of their background and interests, their hearts were on one side or the other. Peers like Lord Hurcomb and Lord Strang, who were associated with the conservationists or amenity world, were against the Bill, while others, like Lord Blyton and Viscount Slim, who were connected with industry, were for it. In the Lords, however, there were signs of a more thoughtful approach. To judge from their speeches, several peers with no known predisposition one way or the other, had adopted a more rational and open-minded attitude, asking themselves what really would be the cost to industry of not building Cow Green, and what really would be the cost to scientific research of going ahead with the reservoir. Speaking against the Bill, Lord Henley pointed out that if the reservoir were not built at Cow Green there was little likelihood of throwing thousands of men out of work; the worst that could happen was that ICI and one or two other companies would be put to more expense and some inconvenience. On the other side, the Earl of Swinton emphasized that the reservoir would affect only a very small area of scientific interest. But had it come to a vote, the chances are that most peers would have voted on the basis of principle and instinct, and not as a result of a careful assessment and comparison of the arguments on both sides.

Select Committees of the House of Lords usually consist of five peers. In view of the controversial nature of the Bill, and because of the widespread interest that it had aroused, two further peers were added on this occasion. Under the chairmanship of Lord Grenfell, the Committee was made up of the Lords Crook, Raglan, Clwyd, Croft, Granville-West and Boston. Lord Crook was a man of wide experience in central and local administration. He had taken an interest in the problem of water supply for many years, and had been chairman of the Select Committee that examined the Water Board's Private Bill authorizing the Balderhead reservoir in 1959. Lord Boston had also been a member of the Select Committee on Balderhead. Of the remainder, one was a farmer, but none of the others seemed to have had any particular connection with industry, water supply or the conservationist movement. The Select Committee sat for the first time on 22 November 1966. During the next two months they were to meet on nineteen days, and on 19 December they spent a rain-soaked day in Upper Teesdale, inspecting some of the possible sites.

When they appeared before the Committee, both sides rehearsed much the same arguments and produced many of the same witnesses as in the Commons. The Water Board's case was still based on the three propositions that they needed extra water, that they needed the water urgently (even more urgently now), and that there was no reasonable alternative to Cow Green. Having heard the botanists before the Select Committee of the House of Commons, ICI and the Water Board were even more convinced that they were exaggerating the scientific importance of Cow Green and the extent to which the value of Widdybank Fell would be diminished if a reservoir were built there. It was very easy, they said, for experts to make too much of the importance of their own speciality. This was exactly what these dedicated enthusiasts had done over Cow Green. In point of fact, they argued, Cow Green had scarcely been heard of until the reservoir was proposed at the end of 1964. In this connection, the ex-manager of the Cow Green mine was produced to testify that in the period from 1940 to 1954 he had never seen anyone scrutinizing the vegetation on Cow Green. He also mentioned that in his day heavy excavating equipment had been freely used on the site, and debris and earth had been strewn about quite indiscriminately on what he now learned was virtually hallowed ground.

And this time, the promoters were able to counter-attack the objectors with evidence from an independent scientist. Out of the blue, and to the surprise and delight of ICI, a young botany lecturer, Dr K. W. Giles of Birkbeck College, took his life in his hands and volunteered to testify in the Lords that the Cow Green site was nowhere near as important as had been alleged by some of the eminent academics. Apparently, Giles had been incensed by what he regarded as the exaggerated claims made on behalf of the plant communities on Widdybank Fell. 'I would say,' he told the Select Committee, 'that roughly 50 per cent of the botanists in this country are completely unconcerned about the fate of Cow Green. Inevitably, counsel for the objectors suggested that it was presumptuous, not to say impertinent, for a relatively inexperienced botanist to challenge the views of established authorities in their own field. Giles was unabashed. It was the content and quality of an argument that mattered, he replied, not the reputation and standing of the man who put it forward. He contended that the case for the petitioners had been at no time supported by valid scientific evidence directly and positively related to the area in question. To make extravagant claims, on the basis of weak evidence, he suggested, could only do harm to the public image of the science of botany, bringing the discipline into disrepute and at the same time damaging the cause of conservation.

Moreover, the promoters were now able to produce the results of their tests carried out on the site during the summer. These experiments, as the petitioners conceded, confirmed the Water Board's contention that the Cow Green site would not leak and established conclusively that extensive grouting would not be required. The petitioners had made great play with the damage that grouting would do on and around the site; whilst they were no doubt relieved to learn that it would not be necessary, at the same time this news did deprive them of one of their main arguments.

In its essentials, the Cow Green dispute was still a conflict of values. But the terms of reference given to the Select Committee had somewhat changed the character of the argument. In the Commons the onus had seemed to be on the objectors to demonstrate that in order to preserve the rare plants and rugged countryside above Cauldron Snout it was worth spending several million pounds of hard cash and worth endangering jobs in an area where unemployment was a serious problem. It was an unenviable task, though the petitioners had come close enough to success to encourage them to continue their fight. The special Instruction to the Select Committee of the House of Lords altered the situation. In the Lords the Water Board and I C I were on the defensive, for the onus was now upon them to show that Cow Green really was better than any of the alternatives, both in the short run and also considered as part of a long-term strategy for meeting the water requirements of Teesside.

Whilst Upper Cow Green was never formally abandoned by the objectors, their main effort from now onwards was to be devoted to showing that, from every point of view, Cow Green made far less sense than Middleton. Tactically, this shift of emphasis was very much to the advantage of the petitioners. Comparing the merits of two reservoir sites is a somewhat less metaphysical exercise than determining whether a particular price ought to be paid to preserve unusual assemblages of rare flora. If the objectors could once establish that on planning grounds there was a better case for Middleton than for Cow Green, then the more chancy question of values – and who could tell what value their Lordships might place on rare plants ? – might well fade into the background.[13]

From the petitioners' point of view it became increasingly important that the Select Committee should concentrate upon the comparative merits of Cow Green and Middleton as sources of water, for as the hearings continued the nature of the scientific value attributed by the botanists to Cow Green underwent a significant change. As the petitioners now acknowledged, it was the 'inspirational' value of this area that was really important : it was on Widdybank Fell that Pigott and hundreds of others had first been fired with enthusiasm for botanical studies. Cow Green ought to be preserved because sites like this were becoming more and more precious in an overcrowded Britain. There was nothing trivial or untenable about this argument. But in the Commons, it will be remembered, the botanists had claimed that results of great practical value might very easily come out of pure research on the rare flora at Cow Green.

The case for Middleton had already been set out in the House of Commons ; but in view of the special Instruction, the arguments for and against this site became even more important in the Lords. In brief, the petitioners maintained that the additional water from Cow Green would soon be quite inadequate, because the Water Board, as usual, were working on much too conservative an estimate of I C I's future needs. The reason for this, of course, was that industrial consumers were unwilling to commit themselves to guaranteeing loan charges for water they might never need. Within a few years of completing Cow Green, they said, the water men would be looking for a new source. Inevitably, they would then turn to Middleton ; and when Middleton was developed, Cow Green would be superfluous. Since it was bound to be flooded in the end, why not settle for Middleton at the beginning ? It was true that a number of Sites of Special Scientific Interest would be affected at Middleton. And it was unfortunate about the farmers. But scientifically Middleton was nowhere near as valuable as Cow Green, and many of the smallholdings there were not really economic. If the Government continued with its policy of encouraging amalgamations in the farming industry, some of these small farmers would, in any case, be leaving sooner or later.[14]

Admittedly, there was the difficulty over the later completion date at Middleton, for it certainly could not be ready before 1973. Between 1970 and 1973, the petitioners argued, Jeffcoate's borehole scheme would fill the gap. If the underground aquifers in the magnesian limestone and bunter sandstone were pumped for only limited periods in each year, as much as 121×10^3 m^3 a day could be abstracted in the dry months. This would be quite enough to tide the Water Board over until Middleton came into service.

On the other side, I CI and the Water Board were now to devote much of *their* effort to demonstrating that the 'Middleton plus borehole' scheme ought to be rejected. The Middleton site, they reminded the Committee, would cost about three times as much as Cow Green. It was opposed by the farmers, and it would cause a great deal of hardship and disturbance. Some of the people who lived and worked in this part of the valley were of an age which would make it difficult for them to earn a living elsewhere, and those who were tenant farmers would get very little compensation. If such a large site was developed in the late 1960s, its full yield would not be taken up until the late 1990s, a situation that would make the cost of water unnecessarily high in the meantime. Middleton, in other words, would provide far too much water much sooner than anyone needed it. So far as the critical gap between 1970 and 1973 was concerned, the Water Board – with the full support of the Water Resources Board – argued that it would be wrong to gamble on Jeffcoate's borehole scheme providing enough water by the early 1970s. Even Jeffcoate had conceded that the scheme *might* fail : if it did, and Middleton was not ready, the consequences could be disastrous.

Nor was it inevitable that after and in addition to Cow Green there would have to be a reservoir at Middleton or at some other site in Upper Teesdale. Looking ahead, a variety of possibilities might solve the problem of future needs. Whilst it would be wrong to rely on a borehole scheme to meet the requirements of the immediate future, the Water Board and their advisers were prepared to agree that in the years after 1974 it should be possible to abstract 68×10^3 m³ a day from underground sources. This would help meet the long-term need. Then again, with the passage of time, the Water Board would gain more experience in operating river-regulating reservoirs, and would be able to reduce wastage. There was the possibility of bringing water into the Tees Valley from a reservoir in the Tyne or Wear Valleys. By the 1980s, the much-discussed barrages across Morecombe Bay or the Solway Firth might have been built ; it might then be possible to carry water across the Pennines to the Tyne, the Wear and the Tees. By the 1980s, desalination might have become an economic possibility.

The proceedings came to an end on 23 January 1967, and the following morning the chairman of the Select Committee announced their recommendation. They recommended that the Bill should be approved. Because it was such an important Bill, and because of the special Instruction, on 6 February the Committee took the unusual step of publishing a Report explaining how and why they had reached their decision.

The Select Committee were entirely satisfied that the Bill's promoters had established their need for an addtional 158×10^3 m³ a day, most of which would be required by 1970. They were satisfied that the operations of ICI in the North-East would be severely prejudiced in the early 1970s if this extra water was not forthcoming. There was a considerable market for the fertilizers, nylon and petrochemicals that ICI would be producing, and if this market was not exploited, exports would suffer, and the national interest would be damaged. On economic grounds, therefore, the Committee were in no doubt that the water ought to be made available to the promoters at the earliest possible date.

Because of the water industry's method of financing capital works, because it was impossible to forecast the effect of the Government's regional policy, and as there was no telling what impact research would have on water consumption in the future, it was very difficult to predict accurately the future needs of industry. For these reasons, the Committee felt unable to make a reliable forecast of water requirements in the area for a period as far ahead as twenty years, which was what they had been asked to do.

They had also looked carefully at a number of alternative sites for the reservoir. Only two of the possible sites – Upper Cow Green and Middleton – could be regarded as genuine alternatives to Cow Green. Neither would provide the proven need for water in time, or at a cost at all comparable with Cow Green. Upper Cow Green could not be brought into service before 1974, four years after Cow Green, and it would cost £9 million, as against £2·0–2·5 million for Cow Green. The dam at Upper Cow Green would have to be twice as high and almost three times as long as at Cow Green, and consequently a reservoir there would constitute a far more serious intrusion into the local scenery than would the reservoir proposed in the Bill. Moreover, the Committee were satisfied that some of the botanical objections to Cow Green would also apply to Upper Cow Green. A reservoir at Middleton would provide twice as much water as Cow Green. But it could not begin to provide water until 1973, and it would cost £8·0–9·5 million.

It was true that in the late 1970s water supplies over and above the yield from Cow Green would be needed. But the Committee were prepared to accept assurances given by the Water Resources Board that these extra supplies would not necessarily have to come from the Tees Valley. Nor was it certain that they would have to be stored there. They did not believe that in the long run a reservoir at Middleton was inevitable ; and to plump for such a large reservoir there at this stage might well conflict with subsequent proposals from the Water Resources Board designed to meet the requirements of the North of England as a whole.

Middleton had other serious drawbacks. If the valley was flooded at this point, some thirty-nine agricultural holdings would be affected, twenty-seven farmhouses would be destroyed, about 4.0×10^6 m² of agricultural land would be inundated, and part of the village of Newbiggin would be submerged. The Committee had concluded that as between Cow Green and Middleton, even if everything else had been equal, they would not have been justified in recommending the destruction of houses, farmsteads and farmland at Middleton unless they had been satisfied that an extremely high degree of scientific and amenity disturbance would occur at Cow Green if the reservoir were constructed there instead. On the evidence, they did not feel that the disturbance to be anticipated was of that nature or magnitude.

The Committee noted, for example, that of the species of rare plants that would be submerged at Cow Green there was not one of scientific significance that did not exist elsewhere in Upper Teesdale. They appreciated that the petitioners were concerned over certain assemblages of plants, as distinct from individual specimens, and they accepted that a measure of damage was bound to occur if the Bill went through. But in view of the need for the scheme, and since individual specimens existed elsewhere and similar assemblages might also exist in Upper Teesdale, they were of the opinion that the damage should be accepted. The Committee had been impressed by evidence that of 1.2×10^6 m² of sugar limestone on Widdybank and Cronkley Fells only about 0.1×10^6 m² would be flooded. This, they felt, was not a sacrifice that could be reasonably resisted.

They had also considered the effect of the reservoir on the landscape and amenities of the area. As a result of their visit to Upper Teesdale, they had reached the conclusion that any man-made scheme would indeed intrude upon the character of the countryside. But (they suggested) a comparatively shallow reservoir of the type proposed for Cow Green might, in time, merge into the landscape.

The Committee had given long and careful thought to the possibility of using underground aquifers instead of building a reservoir. They agreed that a borehole scheme might make a substantial contribution to meeting future needs. But there was some uncertainty about the yield obtainable from these underground sources. The Director of the Water Resources Board had said that a borehole scheme large enough to provide the quantity of water required would not be a viable proposition for three or four years. In any case, a pilot scheme would be needed to show whether the technical difficulties could be overcome. There would be the problem of obtaining statutory powers from Parliament, and arrangements would have to be made with landowners about wayleaves and sites for the small buildings required. Taking everything into account, the Committee thought that it would be hazardous to rely on boreholes alone to provide the necessary quantity of water by 1970.

In short, the Committee felt that only a reservoir could provide the extra water that was needed, and they were satisfied that the least harmful site for such a reservoir was at Cow Green.

The Bill returned to the floor of the House for its Third Reading on 23 February 1967. Opening the three-hour debate, Lord Grenfell told the House that his Committee had been unanimous in their conclusion that Cow Green alone would meet the needs of the situation. In the light of all the evidence, no other decision had been possible, and he asked the Lords to give the Bill a Third Reading. Reluctantly, the conservationists accepted the committee's verdict. In a speech that clearly made a deep impression on the House, Lord Strang conceded that in the circumstances the Committee probably could not have come to any other conclusion. But the Cow Green controversy had wider implications. There was a lesson to be learned from this case, and they ought to be clear what the moral was. A body of presuppositions governed the development of modern society, he said. When conflicts like Cow Green occurred, these presuppositions served almost universally to resolve the conflict in one way rather than the other. What were these guiding principles? They had been spelt out by J. K. Galbraith in the last of his Reith Lectures for 1966. There he had outlined what he took to be the faith of modern industrial man, the goals and values which determine his conduct, to which everyone, including their Select Committee, was expected to give priority. These were: technology is always good: accordingly, firms must always expand; the consumption of goods is the principal source of happiness; idleness is wicked as an alternative to work; and, finally, nothing should interfere with the priority that we accord to technology, growth and increased consumption. Galbraith himself, as Lord Strang pointed out, did not subscribe to this view. Indeed, he had gone on to argue that through the state, society should assert the superior claims of aesthetic over economic goals, and particularly of environment over cost. If it did not, the industrial system would continue to have a monopoly of social purpose.

Unfortunately, he said, the record of successive British Governments was nothing to boast about. For twelve years, as chairman of the National Parks Commission, he had fought what was often a losing battle in defence of the countryside. They all knew about the Industrial Revolution and its effects on the environment, and everyone was properly horrified at the desecration of the countryside that had occurred in the days of *laissez-faire* industrialization. Rightly, they put the blame on the greedy capitalist. Now, in the new industrial revolution, were they not doing the same thing all over again? This time there was a difference, and the difference was that now it was the Government itself, along with industry and the trade unions, that was constantly giving precedence to the claims of development. Unless a halt was called somewhere, the dwindling countryside would continue to be eaten away, and the already damaged coastline would be even more desecrated.

Lord Hurcomb said that he had come to the conclusion that it would not be right to press his opposition further. With better planning and more foresight a less objectionable scheme might have been devised. As it was, under pressure of time, the House would have to take what was essentially a wrong decision. There was little use in setting up agencies to protect sites of scientific importance and to preserve the natural beauty of the countryside if these considerations were in normal departmental practice to be disregarded under pressure from developers of all kinds, advancing the familiar, but often unjustifiable, claim that their proposals alone were practicable, and urgently necessary on some ground of immediate economic advantage. Far too often, he said, the arguments for those interests and values that could not be quantified failed to make an impression on authority.

Right to the end, the underlying proclivities that all along had shaped attitudes to this particular case were still coming to the surface. Lord Nugent of Guildford declared: 'I would say to the noble Lord, Lord Strang, that I feel we are talking about the lives of men and women in this area, which have to be matched against the tremendously appealing considerations of amenity and landscape which turn our hearts over. This is not just a matter of pounds, shillings and pence: it concerns the jobs and the lives of the people who live there.' Those who set a higher value on conservation and amenity naturally took a more sceptical view of the amount of unemployment that would occur if the Cow Green reservoir were not built. As Lord Chorley put it, 'One can be so easily led away by these sentimental appeals of bread and butter for thousands of people.'

The last word came from Lord Kennet on the Government front bench. He summed up the Cow Green conflict as a 'head-on clash between the quantifiable and the unquantifiable; between industry, which is used to giving precise figures and calculating precise pay-offs, and on the other hand a fortuitous alliance of pure science and the preservation of natural beauty.' He went on: 'I think that whatever posterity comes to feel about the presence of the reservoir at Cow Green it may well remember the passage of this Bill through both Houses as the moment when the British Parliament accepted to the full its duty to examine, regardless of tedium and regardless of cost, the fundamental conflict of interests between one ponderable – industrial and economic progress – and two imponderables – pure research and the preservation of natural beauty.'

Now that all the evidence had been assembled and tested, what was the Government's view?[15] Lord Kennet's final analysis makes it clear that the Minister, presented with the same evidence as had been put before the two Select Committees, would have approved the Cow Green site, chiefly because the objectors would not have convinced him that the sacrifice of unquantifiable values justified the additional cost and risk entailed by any alternative scheme. What the botanists called Upper Teesdale, he said, covered about $28\cdot0 \times 10^6$ m^2. Within this area there were $1\cdot2 \times 10^6$ m^2 where the soil consisted of an outcrop of sugar limestone, mixed with peat. This smaller area was divided between Widdybank Fell and Cronkley Fell. The Cow Green reservoir would flood about $0\cdot1 \times 10^6$ m^2 of the $0\cdot7 \times 10^6$ m^2 of sugar limestone on Widdybank Fell. The rest would not be affected. In other words, altogether there would be a one-sixteenth reduction of the population of glacial relict flora. This was no doubt regrettable, said Lord Kennet; but seen in perspective it was a sacrifice that could hardly justify the very considerable cost necessary to avoid it.

There was no division at the end of the debate. On 22 March 1967 the Tees Valley and Cleveland Water Bill received the Royal Assent, and the fate of Cow Green was settled at last.

Notes

1. It was the commissioning of the river-regulating reservoir at Balderhead which had brought the Board's output up to 292×10^3 m^3. In arguing the case for Balderhead in 1959 the Water Board had assured Parliament that a yield of 292×10^3 m^3 would certainly be enough to meet their requirements until 1983. This estimate was to be falsified embarrassingly quickly as a result of the new developments at Billingham in 1963.

2. Which members of the Nature Conservancy Nicholson consulted was never publicly disclosed. Nor were the 'certain quarters' ever identified, though it was to be suggested that Nicholson was referring to members of the Botanical Society of the British Isles and the Botany Department of the University of Durham. Informal feelers from ICI to the Durham botanists produced results that were not so reassuring. Nevertheless, the company comforted itself with the reflection that it was, after all, the Conservancy which was the official voice of the scientists.

3. For the year 1971 there was no difference between the estimates of the Water Resources Board and the Tees Valley and Cleveland Water Board. But for 1981 the Water Resources Board estimated a deficiency of $94\cdot5 \times 10^3$ m^3 per day more than the Water Board. This discrepancy arose because the Water Board had made no allowance for increased demands by major industrial consumers beyond those to which these industrialists were committed under existing agreements, whereas the Water Resources Board had allowed for what they thought was a reasonable rate of growth in industrial demand up to the end of the century.

4. As the report put it, a decision to use Upper Cow Green or Middleton

would involve 'considerable extra costs in money, labour and materials which could otherwise be used elsewhere'. A phrase of this kind was a salutary reminder that the cost of anything is the alternative that is foregone in order to have it. If either of these other two reservoir sites were chosen, something else would not be done. But nobody could be sure what that something was. And even if anyone had known, there would still have been a value problem, for to express the additional costs of Upper Cow Green or Middleton in terms not of money but of the most likely alternative use foregone, would have settled nothing in the absence of general agreement about the value of these other purposes as compared with the value of what would have to be sacrificed if Cow Green were flooded.

5. In the early days of its existence, the National Parks Commission had been assured by the Ministry of Housing and Local Government that reports of this kind would be automatically attached as appendices to the Ministry's own submissions to Select Committees on Private Bills. By an oversight, and much to the annoyance of the Commission, on this occasion its memorandum was not put before the Select Committee of the House of Commons.

6. Under the 1965 Science and Technology Act, the newly created Natural Environment Research Council formally took over the functions of the Nature Conservancy, reconstituting the Conservancy as one of its constituent committees. In the interests of consistency and continuity the term 'Nature Conservancy' has sometimes been retained in the text when it refers specifically to this committee of the NERC.

7. At a later stage, when an argument developed as to whether a spokesman for the NERC should be called before the Select Committee to give evidence that favoured the petitioners' side of the case, the Department took the view that a Research Council had a public function independent of the Government and ought to be heard independently and publicly on matters involving that function. If the Department had had to give way at ministerial level, plainly they were still prepared to do what they could to help the interest they represented.

8. The Nature Conservancy divides National Nature Reserves and Sites of Special Scientific Interest into two categories. Sites in the first category are important, but often typical of many similar areas; if a sufficiently good case can be made out for an alternative use, they are considered expendable. In its second category, the Nature Conservancy includes areas that it considers unique and not negotiable under any circumstances. The Moor House Reserve was in the first category. Now that it knew more about what was to be found on Cow Green, the Conservancy placed this area in the second, sacrosanct category. The Water Board and ICI, however, argued that if they were to switch their attention to Upper Cow Green, they would probably encounter just as much opposition there. It was all very well for the petitioners to give assurances that they would not object to that site. But what was to prevent some new society springing up, asked counsel for the promoters. In his mind's eye, he said, he could already see the cars with their rear-window stickers urging men of good will everywhere to 'Save Upper Cow Green'.

9. This was a persuasive line of argument. But the petitioners at no time made it clear who was to be responsible for paying for Middleton, and for that part of its potential yield which nobody as yet needed. As an expert witness on water finance put it, 'The Minister has no power to require an industry to pay for more water than it says it wants.'

10. The North Riding and South Durham branch of the NFU were thrown into great consternation whenever there was any talk of building the reservoir at Middleton. It will be recalled that Middleton had been mentioned (though dismissed) in the Water Resources Board's Report of October 1965. Thereafter, the NFU became an ardent supporter of the Cow Green site. They also made it abundantly clear to the Select Committee that if ICI and the Water Board should be misguided enough to turn their attention to Middleton they would meet determined and bitter opposition from the farming interest.

11. Kimball was a farmer and represented an agricultural constituency. Most agriculturalists favoured Cow Green, if only because the most likely alternative seemed to be Middleton. But, like many Englishmen, he also succeeded in combining an enthusiasm for field sports with a keen interest in conservation and the preservation of the countryside. Kimball had been a member of the Select Committee that considered the Balderhead reservoir in 1959; he knew, therefore, how quickly ICI's earlier forecast had gone astray.

12. It is rare for the House of Lords to refuse a Private Bill, or any part of it, a Second Reading. However, on a celebrated occasion on 8 February 1962 a notable speech from the late Lord Birkett was largely responsible for persuading the Lords to reject the clauses in the Manchester Corporation Bill authorizing the abstraction of water from Ullswater and the building of a reservoir at Bannisdale.

13. Organizations that supported the petitioners' cause readily fell in with this strategy. In a Report to the Minister of Housing and Local Government on 18 October 1966 the National Parks Commission specifically advocated Middleton in preference to Cow Green, claiming that the recreational potential of the former would compensate for the loss of agricultural value.

14. In Teesdale itself, the very idea of flooding the valley at Middleton had generated a great deal of anger. On 25 November 1966 the Barnard Castle RDC wrote to the Water Board referring to rumours that were circulating to the effect that if Cow Green was not approved, the reservoir would have to go to Middleton. The RDC reaffirmed that they would strongly oppose the Middleton site. So far as the Water Board controlled the situation, the farmers had no cause to worry. Sir Charles Allison had apparently told the secretary of the local branch of the NFU that, so long as he was chairman of the Water Board, they would never attempt to build a reservoir at Middleton, whatever the outcome of the Cow Green proposals. Under no circumstances, he said, would he ever contemplate flooding the homes and farms of so many people. In so far as sentiment is always important, particularly when disputes are settled through the political process, the agricultural problem was a serious weakness in the petitioners' case for Middleton. Looked at objectively and dispassionately, no doubt some of the smallholdings on the site were

uneconomic. But laymen are not easily convinced that homes and livelihoods should be sacrificed in the interests of plants and botanists.

15. Had the Water Board proceeded by way of an Order under the Water Act of 1945, the Minister of Housing and Local Government would have given the final decision after both sides had put their case at a public local inquiry. It is one of the odder features of Private Bill procedure that Ministers make up their minds, and Government departments submit their Reports, *before* all the evidence has been collected and tested. Whilst Committees know that these Reports cannot be definitive, they are bound to carry a great deal of weight. It is true that representatives of the departments concerned listen to the Select Committee proceedings, and give their departments' considered view before counsel on both sides sum up. It is open to Ministers to say that as a result of what has come out of the Committee's hearings they have changed their minds. But unless startlingly fresh and important evidence has come to light the odds must be very much against such a change of heart, particularly if several departments have already spent a good deal of time in reaching an agreed governmental view.

6 Anglesey: aluminium and oil

Richard West and Paul Foot*

Aluminium

The Labour government of 1966–70 was kind to the Rio Tinto-Zinc Corporation Limited (RTZ). Anthony Wedgwood Benn, the Minister of Technology, backed the opening of a uranium mine in South West Africa, a territory held illegally by a cruel and racist regime. The Prime Minister himself, Harold Wilson, opened a new plant at the Bristol smelter which was soon to dismiss 900 men and be sold to the Australians. It was again Wilson who encouraged RTZ to build an immense, polluting, and possibly superfluous aluminium smelter in Anglesey – subsidized by a 40 per cent grant out of the taxpayer's pocket. Since the completion of this smelter, which was justified on the grounds that it would bring employment to Anglesey, the unemployment rate on the island has risen to new heights.

Early in 1967, when Britain faced the financial crisis that led to devaluation, the Government decided that Britain must have her own large-scale aluminium industry. For half a century, Britain had depended almost entirely on imports from countries like Canada and Norway with good hydro-electric resources, since power accounts for at least 15 per cent of aluminium production costs. It was calculated that Britain, by processing the powdery white alumina (aluminium oxide) instead of importing the aluminium bars, would save as much as £50 million a year on her balance of payments. It was planned to provide the power for these British aluminium plants by building nuclear power stations subsidized by the Government. When the Norwegians, then our partners in EFTA, complained of unfair competition, Anthony Crosland (President of the Board of Trade) assured them: 'I firmly believe that our proposals do not carry a risk of any reduction in Norwegian imports to Britain, but will in fact allow an increase.'

According to the *Financial Times*, the initiative for the British aluminium plan 'came from the mining group Rio Tinto-Zinc, which was interested in an ambitious package involving building and fuelling a nuclear power station linked to a smelter'. The alumina supply for the smelter was to come largely from Comalco, the Australian company owned jointly by RTZ and Kaiser. At this time most of Comalco's bauxite from its Weipa reserves went to its own alumina refinery at Gladstone, also in northern

---

*In this chapter, the sections on Aluminium and Oil by the sea shore were written completely by Richard West and the section on Oil in Parliament was written completely by Paul Foot.

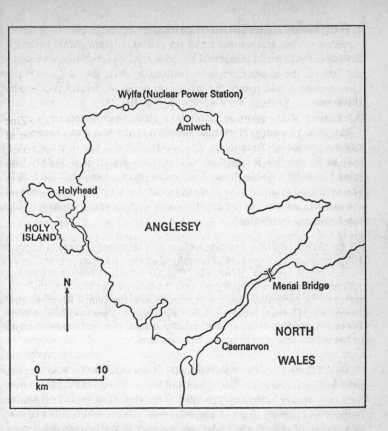

Queensland. The alumina was then sent to Comalco's aluminium smelter at Bell Bay in Tasmania. But the Weipa bauxite reserves were so huge and Gladstone had so big a capacity, that RTZ and Kaiser wanted a new smelter in Britain. The cost of freighting alumina from Australia to Britain would be only a tiny item in the cost of the aluminium.

The RTZ plan was hailed by *The Times* as 'one of the most imaginative and enlightened industrial projects of the new technological age'. Its sister paper the *Sunday Times* was less enthusiastic: 'What the Government could have had was a nice clean-cut deal for an aluminium smelter at Holyhead that would have cost the taxpayer heavily and earned a handsome profit for RTZ.' At one stage it was suggested that RTZ should buy a half share in the £100 million nuclear power station at Wylfa, also in Anglesey – and then collect 45 per cent of the purchase price as an investment grant from the Board of Trade. Unfortunately for RTZ, the other four big manufacturers of aluminium resented this preference for a relative newcomer. They too wanted to set up new aluminium plants backed by investment grants and subsidized electricity. All the contenders wanted to act fast on the assumption, later justified by fact, that a Conservative Government would reduce the investment grants. As a result, not one but three smelter projects were approved – a 100 000 t plant for British Aluminium at Invergordon; a 60 000 t plant, to be increased later, for Alcan at Lynemouth, Northumberland; and the one that concerns this chapter, Anglesey Aluminium Ltd, at Holyhead. The Anglesey plant was to be run by RTZ, their old partners Kaiser and British Insulated Callender's Cables, one of the major aluminium users. Both RTZ and British Aluminium have intimated since that they would not have built the smelters without the benefit of Government grants. Even at the time, the *Economist* complained:

... for the rest of British industry, looking with increasing concern at its power bill, there must be alarm at the philosophy of an electricity supply system created for, industrially speaking, 'giants only'. True, the DEA [Department of Economic Affairs] has said 'in considering projects the Government will have the fullest regard to the competitive position of other firms in the United Kingdom which by their size of location would not have these special contracts available to them'. But more than this will be needed if orthodox industrial power consumers are not to feel second-class citizens paying first-class fares.

An RTZ director, Pat Robinson, said afterwards that because his company had been first in the field it had had 'the pick of all the available sites' for a new smelter in Britain. The town of Holyhead has a good deep-water harbour and railway depot. A nuclear power station, which could be used as a source of power, was under construction at Wylfa, only a few miles away. Since Anglesey has a chronic unemployment problem, the Labour Government had offered a 40 per cent development grant to companies bringing work there. In theory, though not always in practice, the unemployed form a pool of eager, available man-power. With Wylfa power station nearing completion, the construction force could move to Holyhead to work on the site of the smelter.

It has been reported that RTZ made detailed plans for the Holyhead smelter as early as 1964. 'Long before the smelter projects became widely publicized through the Government announcements we were already planning a major development,' said Robinson in 1968. In the autumn of 1966, RTZ had started to buy land round Penrhos on the north-east side of Holyhead island. On 3 March 1967, the *Holyhead and Anglesey Mail* published a reader's letter referring to the 'possible development near Holyhead' of 'the biggest aluminium factory in the world'. Later that month the same newspaper published a bunch of letters under the heading of 'Holyhead and the Aluminium Rumour'. One correspondent complained that

the land that is going to be used for this proposed factory is rich farming land and not so long ago the local authority turned down a request to build a holiday camp on the same site; a request for permission to site some caravans nearby was also turned down by the Welsh Office, yet this filthy, stinking factory (and believe me it will stink) is being pressed for, with no thought of people who have recently built houses nearby which will no doubt lose their value now. Penrhos Beach will become the outfall of the effluents killing all the fish and wild life in the vicinity.

RTZ Services Ltd issued a soothing statement: 'The project may or may not come to fruition . . . it is merely one of a number we are studying'. But public argument over the smelter was already fierce.

The main supporters of RTZ were certain councillors and officials of Anglesey County Council, and the District Councils of Holyhead and Valley (the towns on either side of the site). They believed that the smelter would not only bring money and jobs but might attract other industry to the area. *The Times*, as ever friendly to RTZ, reported that the islanders believed themselves near to 'an economic miracle'. In the eyes of the local authorities, 'the Rio Tinto men are the most welcome invaders ever to cross the Menai Straits'. The company had an important supporter in Cledwyn Hughes, the Secretary of State for Wales, who was MP for Anglesey, lived in Holyhead, and had long campaigned for its economic development. The Transport and General Workers Union, which is powerful in Holyhead, favoured the smelter. The district secretary, Idwal Edwards, predicted objections but called on the union to use all its endeavours to ensure that these were put aside. The regional organizer, Tom Jones, described the fight to secure the RTZ plant as 'a front line battle in which no effort would be spared'. Perhaps TGWU officials felt that the new jobs would be useful in bargaining with the railway and dock authorities who are the main employers in Holyhead. But undoubtedly they had much support from working-class people, as well as from land agents, builders, shop-keepers and publicans. One Anglesey local patriot, W. O. Slade of Llangefni, welcomed the smelter as recompense for an ancient injury to the island. He wrote to the *Holyhead and Anglesey Mail*:

Anglesey's copper mines were once world-famous and enjoyed the privilege of dictating the world copper price. . . . The Rio Tinto mines in Spain put a stop to all this. They sold cheap copper, and the Anglesey mines could not compete. Parys mines might be an eye-sore to some – to me it's a landmark. I do not know if there is any connection between Rio Tinto mines and the smelters. If there is they have a debt to the island which might be still an economic bastion but for the cheap Spanish copper.

Rio Tinto was indeed responsible for the collapse of the Parys mine, whose production of copper fell from 2813 t in 1872 (the year before the opening of the Rio Tinto mine) to 180 t only seven years later.

The opposition to RTZ, voiced vehemently in the local press, came from farmers, conservationists, and people with homes near the proposed smelter. The National Farmers Union (NFU) and the Farmers Union of Wales (FUW) were perturbed by the proposal to take good arable land for the smelter and for the pylons to bring it power. The farmers were still more perturbed by the possible danger of fluoride effluent. Delegates went to Germany and Switzerland to study the effect of aluminium smelters on local livestock. Professors of botany, zoology and marine biology were consulted and gave their predictions. This possible threat to the atmosphere was the chief concern of those living near the proposed site. Their fears were increased by an article in the *Holyhead and Anglesey Mail* by an Anglesey engineer, Arthur Arnold. Headed 'A land-based Torrey-Canyon' – a reference to the tanker that spilled oil off the Cornish coast – the article quoted Gabor and Galbraith to rouse the people of Anglesey from their apathy. Arnold scoffed at the RTZ argument that if the chimney-stack were high there would not be harmful fluoride concentrations:

Another way of saying this would be: 'There would not be high concentration, but it will certainly be spread out.' The higher the stack, the more probable it will be that prevailing winds will drive effluent towards Llanddeusant and possibly the new drinking water reservoir in mid-county. . . . What are property owners in the vicinity to do, and what of Trearddur Bay, which is only 1½ miles [2·4 km] away? I would be pleased to contribute to a collection for the erection of a house on Peibio shore for the Prime Minister's use, or even the Welsh Secretary's.

Perhaps unknown to the writer, the Welsh Secretary did actually own a house near the proposed site of the smelter. Most opponents of RTZ conceded that Anglesey needed employment but thought it should come in tourism and light industry. One protestor urged the Government to make Holyhead a container port for overseas goods: 'We have non-tidal berthing, railway to hand, and it would make clean use of our splendid harbour.' An Anglesey Residents' Association was formed in the summer of 1967. Most of its members were local Welsh, but supporters of RTZ claimed with some justification that its most vocal leaders were middle-class English people who came to the island only for holidays or retirement.

On 4 October 1967, RTZ applied to Anglesey County Council for a site on Holyhead measuring $3 \cdot 0 \times 10^6$ m², of which $1 \cdot 9 \times 10^6$ m² would be for industrial purposes and $1 \cdot 1 \times 10^6$ m² for an 'Amenity Area'. On 20 October, a group of RTZ executives came to Valley to meet Valley and Holyhead councillors. They brought a scenic model of the site and a pamphlet 'Aluminium project for Anglesey', stating that the plant would provide jobs for about 800 people of whom about 200 would be specialists and administrators. Priority would be given to local people in the recruitment of staff. It was emphasized that 'there will be no fumes, smell or pollution', although there might be 'a plume of water vapour occasionally visible at the top of the ventilation stack'. The newspaper report of the meeting included one new, even sensational piece of information:

There was mention of room on the site to increase the output of the reduction plant from a first stage of 120 000 t a year to 300 000 t. . . . What is more, RTZ plan to import the alumina raw material for the first stage reduction plant, but ultimately they may build another plant to convert crude bauxite into aluminium.

This was news indeed! And it did not escape the attention of one Holyhead resident, N. Ceen, who wrote to the local newspaper next week:

It has been interesting to follow the way in which public opinion has been so conditioned that even the outrageous demands of Rio Tinto-Zinc's final (phase 2) plan has aroused applause rather than protest. The published production target for phase 2 is 300 000 t of aluminium per annum to be extracted from bauxite – not the clean white powder originally described. It is well to note that in order to reach that target, 520 000 t of mud waste would be produced, that 340 million cubic feet [$9·6 \times 10^6$ m³] of corrosive fluoride gas would be liberated at the anodes and 6700 million cubic feet [$189·5 \times 10^6$ m³] of poisonous carbon monoxide and carbon dioxide would be similarly released. . . Many promises have been made but not one legal guarantee has been given to ensure the purity of our air and the cleanliness of our water supply, our beaches and the sea.

The protest by Ceen against RTZ's 'phase 2' plan became so embarrassing that the Company wrote to Anglesey County Council to say it had 'no plan or intention to establish such a plant'. However, the same letter contained a rather ambiguous reference to the 'phase 2' plan. 'We have no intention of raising the matter again and would certainly not wish to do so as long as it was apparent that such a plant would not be welcomed by the people of Anglesey.'

RTZ played down its 'phase 2' plan because it had not yet won over the island to 'phase 1'. The NFU had dropped its objection to the plan in return for generous compensation, but the FUW turned down the offer and provided a list of 428 objecting island farmers. At least half Anglesey County Council, as well as the officers of its Planning Department, were sceptical of the benefits of a smelter. In an effort to overcome these doubts, RTZ took three councillors and five officials on a free trip to West Virginia to see a smelter run by its partner Kaiser. The party comprised the Chairman, Clerk, Medical Officer of Health, and the Planning Officer of Anglesey County Council; the Chairman and Clerk of Valley Council; and David Lloyd Hughes, the Clerk to Holyhead Council (and also the brother of Cledwyn Hughes, MP and former Cabinet minister). The Valley Council Clerk, Trebor Jones, said how much he was looking forward to the trip – 'one like this comes once in a lifetime' – provoking some waspish comments from the public.

The Chairman and Clerk of Anglesey County Council produced a favourable joint report on Ravenswood, West Virginia. The smelter had stopped a drift away from the area and had turned a village of 1100 people into a well-planned, attractive, town of five times the size. Without exception, everyone interviewed by the delegates welcomed the establishment of the industry, and local farmers reported no sickness of bones or teeth in their herds. Two churches were now packed on Sundays where one had sufficed before. But the report had to admit 'that the impact on visual amenity of the Penrhos project would be much greater than that of the reduction plant at Ravenswood.' One should not doubt the honesty of the evidence in the report, yet it seems odd that these officers of the local authority should have confined their research to a foreign smelter chosen by one of the applicants, run by another, on a trip paid for by both.

The Anglesey Medical Officer of Health had reservations about the Ravenswood smelter. He went to some pains to stress that he did *not* see a bauxite plant in Virginia, yet he included in his report a photograph of 'a modern Bauxite plant – for which planning approval is not sought at this time but which development is not discounted in the brochure submitted by RTZ'. In other words, he was pointing out that the Ravenswood Plant offered no evidence of the effects should RTZ introduce 'phase 2'. Moreover, he was uneasy about the fluoride emission at Ravenswood. One of the Kaiser senior executives at Ravenswood had told the MOH that 'if he were building a plant for the Government and not for a private concern, he would insist on the activated alumina treatment in baghouses together with a tall stack – the stack being a safety valve in case of baghouse breakdown'. The MOH noted that the level of fluoride emission at Ravenswood was 16·5 per cent above what it had been when the plant started. The technologists were ignorant of the cause, which could not be attributed to increased production of aluminium.

On 14 November 1967, Anglesey County Council met to debate RTZ's application to build a smelter on Holyhead. One white-haired old man gave an impassioned speech in Welsh, to the bewilderment of the RTZ executives who had been asked to the meeting. Other councillors asked, in English, if it was right for Anglesey to sell its birthright for a mess of pottage. As a result the council decided to seek expert advice from university sources before voting in one month's time. When this decision was taken, the Clerk to the ACC threw down his pen in an angry gesture. He was an eager advocate of the RTZ plan, and during the next month he summoned, individually, every member of the Council for a persuasive talk on the need for a smelter. However, university professors who had been called in by the Council warned of the dangers of atmospheric pollution unless RTZ took the most stringent preventative measures. When the smelter came up once more in debate on 14 December, the Planning Committee of Anglesey County Council tied 10:10 on whether to grant the RTZ application. The Chairman used his casting vote in favour of RTZ but later withdrew his decision. The full council meeting that afternoon was overwhelmingly favourable to the application, but opposition from farmers and other groups was still so strong that the Clerk and Chairman decided to ask the Secretary of State for Wales for a public inquiry.

The public inquiry opened at Holyhead on 9 January 1968. The opposition to RTZ came from the Anglesey Residents' Association, the two farmers' unions, and the Council for the Protection of Rural Wales. Early on in the proceedings, the National Farmers Union withdrew its opposition in return for compensation. The Counsel for RTZ, Keith Goodfellow QC, appealed to national as well as to local patriotism by arguing that the plant was important to Britain. Two scientists employed by Kaiser were brought from the United States to deny 'that there would be any noise, smell or air pollution from the proposed plant'. A barrister for Anglesey County Council condemned the 'so-called Anglesey Residents' Association', and claimed support for the plant from the overwhelming majority of the people of the island. The planning consultants for RTZ advanced the curious notion that the smelter chimney would somehow improve the landscape.

The lucid report by County Planning Officer, N. Squire Johnson, presented in November 1967, gave a summary of the arguments for and against the smelter. The possible disadvantages he envisaged included the ugliness of overhead power lines that might be erected to serve the smelter and the possible introduction of a bauxite plant and other heavy industry, as well as the other dangers which have already been discussed. But the subject that was to dominate the three-week inquiry was the danger of fluoride emission from the smelter chimney. In his report, the County Planning Officer referred to the claim in the RTZ pamphlet that 'a well-designed modern aluminium plant does not emit smells or fumes, which could cause harm'. But he remarked that

the experience which Anglesey residents have had in connection with similar installations has not been too happy. The OCTEL plant at Amlwch, which the planning authority were assured would not cause any nuisance, under certain weather conditions is anything but pleasant, and the Ferodo factory built outside Portdinorwic is a source of the most unpleasant smells for many periods during the year. There is no doubt that the RTZ Company were being as honest as they can when they say that the plant would not have any smell or fumes which could cause harm, but similar assurances have been given before, and under certain conditions smells and fumes have been emitted. There is also the possibility of something going wrong with a plant of this complexity.

Similar warnings were given by the Medical Officer of Health. After enumerating the hazards of a smelter like the one at Ravenswood, the MOH declared: 'I am confident that if *all* modern methods of treatment of such gaseous effluents are incorporated in modern plants (i.e. activated alumina baghouses and tall stacks) using modern techniques of production that this hazard to agriculture can be eliminated.' The Ministry of Health and the Alkali Inspectorate of the Ministry of Housing and Local Government had confirmed that 'no health hazard to humans or farm animals can be expected.' The MOH went on to report:

The Alkali Inspectorate, I understand, have from the outset been consulted by RTZ's chemical engineering consultants about pollution problems and their proposals for solving them. Mr Ireland, the Chief Alkali Inspector, said that they have found the company most cooperative in the control of its air pollution at other sites. I understand from one of the company's Medical Officers that it is their intention, should approval for building be given, that an industrial medical service to look after the health of the workers be set up and that monitoring of levels of noxious substances within and without the plant be made operational immediately and I hope beforehand.

However, the MOH pointed out that the aluminium industry included four different kinds of production: the mining of bauxite and its conversion to alumina; the electrolytic reduction of alumina to aluminium; alloying or fabrication; and the harnessing of byproducts from the above products. He concluded his report with this important warning:

Since each of these processes present different and important aesthetic, planning, social and health considerations, I think it essential that we obtain assurances from the company as to their intentions regarding the future development of their interests in Holyhead should this scheme receive approval by the necessary Authorities, before the County Council gives its blessing to this proposed factory – if we do not, we could well be caught in an avalanche with no return to the status quo.

At the inquiry, RTZ offered oral assurances but no legal guarantees about future plans for the Holyhead works, including the hypothetical 'phase 2' treatment of bauxite. Even more important, RTZ gave no legally binding guarantees on the level of fluoride emission from the aluminium smelter. When the inquiry opened, Anglesey County Council stipulated that the fluorine content of the gases emitted from the pot rooms should not exceed 162 kg per day [360 lbs per day] with fluorine concentration not exceeding 0·5 mg m⁻³ and that the fluorine content of the gases from the stack should not exceed 148 kg per day with fluorine concentration not exceeding 2·5 mg m⁻³. The Council also proposed that the low-level emission of gases from the pot rooms should be scrubbed. The company rejected this proposal as 'impracticable'. RTZ insisted that the works would need to emit only 128 kg per day of fluorine at 0·44 mg m⁻³ from the pot rooms, and only 121 kg per day of fluorine at 2·2 mg m⁻³ from the stack. When RTZ gave this estimate of emissions well below the maximum set by the County Council, the listeners at the inquiry did not trouble to press RTZ for legal guarantees. They were still more reassured when a letter was read from the Alkali Inspectorate expressing profound satisfaction with the measures RTZ had prepared to control the effluents. It was felt that the problem of air pollution could now be left to the Alkali Inspectorate. The inquiry petered out, and the Inspector recommended the smelter. As regards air pollution:

Leaving aside fluorine, he [the Inspector] is satisfied that dispersed emissions would have no adverse effects either upon human health or upon the environment at large. As regards fluoride emissions, he accepts the calculated estimates of the company as representing a reasonable assessment of what might ultimately eventuate, but nevertheless considers it right to have regard to an uncertainty factor of 2, in order to provide for imponderables, especially the achieved levels of pot-room containment and the vagaries of dispersion in ever-changing meteorological conditions. On the basis of the company's estimates, or even applying the uncertainty factor of 2, the Inspector concludes that there are no reasonable grounds for expecting any hazard to human health, either within or beyond the limits of the site, or for assuming that the general environment would be significantly affected.

When the smelter was built and went into production, the levels of pollution soon exceeded those that RTZ had predicted. With the permission of the Alkali Inspectorate, total emissions were up 54·7 per cent above the stated level, while emissions of fluoride from the main stack were three times greater than the amount that Anglesey County Council had laid down as tolerable. It was officially explained that since the inquiry, RTZ had designed a different kind of smelter. Originally there were to have been two stacks – one of about 90 m and one (for the anode plant) of about 38 m. But in practice all emissions (except some from the potroom louvres) went through a single stack of about 122 m. There were also reports that the fluoride extraction plant was giving trouble and had broken down twice. Duncan Dewdney, Chairman of Anglesey Aluminium Ltd and Executive Director of RTZ, was asked what he would do if the company could not contain pollution at the new level of 86 per cent as against the previous 95 per cent. According to *The Ecologist* magazine,

He replied that the company would have to spend more on scrubbing equipment. Why then, he was asked, were the company not prepared to install equipment that would maintain a scrubbing efficiency of 95 per cent as promised, particularly since the smelter had been constructed under its budgeted cost. It appears that the company has no intention of either installing this equipment or of going back to the original figures.

It is important to bear in mind that air pollution from factories can normally be prevented if sufficient money is spent. At any rate, that is the view of F. E. Ireland, the Chief Alkali Inspector, who said in a lecture in Manchester in November 1970:

If money were unlimited, there would be very few if any problems of air pollution control which could not be solved fairly quickly. We have the technical knowledge to absorb gases, arrest grit, dust and fumes, and prevent smoke formation. The only reason why we still permit the escape of these pollutants is because economics are an important part of the word 'practicable'. Most of our problems are cheque book rather than technical, and attitudes which take little account of the economics of scarce resources, on which there are so many claims, can so easily blur the importance of the right choice of priorities.

This lecture was given on 10 November. On 3 November Inspector Ireland had replied to a letter from Mrs M. Biggs of Trearddur Bay, Holyhead, who had complained of the air pollution from Anglesey Aluminium. He wrote in this letter:

We do not accept that the estimates submitted by the Company at the public inquiry were binding in any way. They were given in all good faith as typical of what emissions were expected in order to meet our targets, *on which the figures were based* [italics added]. They represented our preliminary estimate of what might be achieved on the evidence of known technology. The important point of the inquiry, in relation to air pollution, was that the company should meet the requirements of the Alkali Inspectorate. When we got down to details of design and in the light of practical tests carried out in the USA on full-scale plant, it soon became obvious that we had to change our original thoughts on prevention and dispersion in order to keep the project viable. . . . Industry cannot be handicapped by rigid rules based on estimates.

To which one can only reply 'Why not?' The point of the public inquiry was not, as Ireland seems to believe to help RTZ to make money out of its smelter, but to safeguard the interests of the people of Anglesey. In the same letter, Ireland rebukes Mrs Biggs:

The important point, which you seem to miss, is that it is the effect of the emissions at ground-level which matters most and not the mass emission of pollutants. In this, our requirements have not changed and the environment is safeguarded just as much under the new conditions as under the old, perhaps even with a minor improvement.

Another important point which Ireland seems to miss is that the *mass* emission of pollutants is just as harmful when they are widely scattered as when they descend on a patch round the factory.

Nevertheless there is evidence of pollution close to the plant. Since the prevailing wind in Holyhead comes from the south-west, the area most affected is along the shore to the north. The $1 \cdot 1 \times 10^6 \, m^2$ tract of company land set aside as a so-called 'Amenity Area' is skirted by what the company calls 'a nature trail'. A pamphlet, put out by RTZ, reads 'Welcome to Penrhos Nature Trail. The path you are about to follow is a new one laid down by Anglesey Aluminium Ltd and forms the course of a nature trail established by the Company in response to European Conservation Year. Also laid down by Anglesey Aluminium Ltd is a fine film of dust which, as I saw in autumn 1971, turned blackberries pale white.

One of the people living near Anglesey Aluminium's 'Nature Trail' is Douglas Bond of 2 Brunyglos, who told me:

We don't grow anything in the garden now. It would turn strange colours and we wouldn't feel like eating it. If you take the dog for a walk he comes back all black... We got used to the vibration. We didn't mind it so much as the flying dust. There's a drain going out from the works to the sea. It's supposed to be only surface water but they throw in oil and things... There used to be a fieldful of mushrooms and cows but not now. Nobody from the firm has been here to see if we're all right.

His wife wiped a rag on the washing line and showed me the streak of dirt. 'Last week it was terrible,' she went on. 'But when it blows from the north we have a washing-day like nobody's business – bedspreads and all... You get a sulphury taste in the mouth... All the pheasants and birds have disappeared.' Among those who lived at Penrhos, near to the smelter, was Cledwyn Hughes, the MP and Cabinet Minister. He has since moved to Trearddur Bay on the other side of Holyhead Island.

The main argument put forward for the establishment of a smelter was the extra jobs it would bring to Anglesey. Certainly by late 1971 there were some 800 people employed by Anglesey Aluminium. Many of these were local people. For example, the Clerk of Holyhead Urban District Council, David Lloyd Hughes (the brother of Cledwyn Hughes MP), announced in November 1968 that he was going to become the Administrative Manager to Anglesey Aluminium Ltd. He took with him as his assistant the former Assistant Clerk of the Council, Miss D. M. Williams, who had also collaborated with Hughes on a book entitled *Holyhead: The Story of a Port*. Even former critics of the company later took employment with it. On the other hand, some former friends of the company afterwards turned into opponents. One of the foremost is Tom Jones, the Transport and General Workers' Union leader, who had fought a 'front-line battle' for the smelter, only to see it declared a 'one-union shop' for the Electrical and Plumbing Trades Union. Jones described this decision as a 'stab in the back'.

Before the smelter, unemployment in Anglesey averaged 7 or 8 per cent, although it had risen as high as 12·5 per cent. During the period of construction when there were ample labouring jobs, unemployment fell to 4·8 per cent. As the construction work tailed off, unemployment increased to 11·6 per cent in October 1971. The area manager for the Department of Employment, R. K. Lewis, predicted that unemployment was bound to go over 12 per cent in the winter. In the Holyhead region alone there were 446 men and 84 women unemployed. The Deputy Planning Officer for Anglesey, Mr Powell, said that industrial projects on the island caused a new problem when the construction died away :

A chap comes over from Ireland, say, and he gets married and his children are doing their O-levels and he doesn't feel like moving again. It's the same with our own young men. They would have left the island but they stayed for the construction work and when that dies away it's too late for them to move. Unemployment used to be round 6 to 8 per cent but now it's over 10 per cent which is completely unacceptable.

This experience of new projects helps to explain why the County Planning Department fought the plan (approved by its Council) to build an oil terminal for Shell on the north of the island.

The smelter has so far been discussed in relation only to Anglesey and the little district of Holyhead. The arguments about jobs or beauty, although important, could be described as parochial. One should also take a look at the smelter in terms of its national, even international meaning. As we heard, RTZ might not have built a smelter in Britain without a substantial Government grant. The Government of the time defended such grants by the necessity to strengthen Britain's balance of payments. Whether such measures were necessary I leave to the economists. One can only point out that shortly after the Anglesey smelter had been approved, Labour Chancellor Roy Jenkins revealed to an astonished country that, due to an accounting error, Britain's reported deficit over the last few years had in fact been a substantial surplus. Yet for the sake of our balance of payments, Britain had spent colossal sums on private-enterprise industries – such as Rolls-Royce, the Concorde project and Upper Clyde Shipbuilders – which now appear to have been economically unprofitable.

Britain's decision to build three new aluminium smelters has since been deplored by important men in the industry. Delegates to a meeting of the Organization of European Aluminium Smelters (held in London in September 1971) were told by Stewart Spector, chief analyst of Oppenheimer & Co, that production would have to be kept in check if the excess world capacity were to be brought into balance. He said that programmes to introduce new smelters in 1972 'most definitely will have to be postponed, cancelled or kept idle upon completion'. He said that to obtain a 9 per cent return on investment capital on a new smelter a primary ingot price of 68 cents per kilo was needed against today's market price level of 53 cents per kilo.

At the same meeting, Krome George, the president of Aluminium Co. of America (the world's largest producer of aluminium), blamed British policy for adding new capacity to the world market. He told the delegates :

Here in the United Kingdom a major primary aluminium industry has been created literally overnight, based I must say in all candour, on Government construction grants of up to 40 per cent and on Government-subsidized [electric] power. It has disturbed well-established market relations – particularly in Norway and Canada and through Canada to the United States – and for what purpose ? I assume some Government planning objective was achieved; but our industry has been damaged simply because excess capacity was created which would not have been created if normal economic and financial restraints had been allowed to operate. As a result many private investors in the aluminium industry around the world stand to suffer financially in one way or the other.

It should be said in fairness here that if the Anglesey smelter was a mistake, the blame rests *not* with RTZ but with the politicians, in Anglesey and in London, who encouraged its construction. RTZ is not responsible to the British Government or to the people of Anglesey. It is responsible to its shareholders in Britain and abroad. And here one must stop to consider, briefly, the effect of the Anglesey smelter on Comalco.

Comalco's Weipa deposit provides the bauxite for its alumina plant at Gladstone, also in Queensland. Much of this alumina is now shipped for smelting to Holyhead. It will be recalled that the Weipa deposit was let by the Queensland Government to Comalco for a peppercorn rent. Furthermore, the processing of bauxite to alumina is not a very profitable operation. The profitable part of the operation, smelting aluminium from alumina, is done in Tasmania, Holyhead, or other smelters abroad. Those Australians who purchased Comalco shares in the famous floatation of 1970 might ponder two questions :

Did RTZ, in 1967, consider building a new smelter in Queensland ? In the past this would have been unthinkable, since Queensland lacks the hydro-electric resources on which smelting used to depend. But by 1967, RTZ was looking to nuclear power as a substitute and indeed had offered to build a nuclear power station to fuel its Anglesey smelter. The Australian Government at about this time was expressing the wish to build an Australian nuclear power industry. The uranium was available – from

RTZ's own Mary Kathleen mine, which had been closed when RTZ switched the flow of production from Australia to its Canadian subsidiaries.

The second question leads on from the first. With the opening of the Anglesey Aluminium works, RTZ (with its partners Kaiser) now operates smelters in both the UK and Australia. It can control the flow of aluminium according to demand, just as it also controls much of the flow of uranium on three continents (and perhaps soon on a fourth). This international control puts Comalco into the same position as Mary Kathleen Uranium. As the Australian subsidiary of a foreign company, it is vulnerable to a depression in the price of aluminium. If RTZ, a British company which has received a 40 per cent construction grant to build a smelter in Britain, had to reduce production either in Anglesey or in Tasmania, which would it choose? It is a question that might well be asked by Comalco shareholders.

Oil in Parliament

Shell is the second biggest company in Britain, with a turnover larger than that of ICI and Unilever combined. Its recent proposal to build a single-buoy mooring oil terminal in the sea off the west coast of Anglesey in Wales met with passionate and widespread opposition. But Parliament passed the Bill. How did it happen?

The 'single-buoy mooring' (SBM) is one of the results of the increasing size of oil tankers, spurred on by competition between the world's oil companies and the long hauls which the ships have to make, particularly to Japan. There are now 350 tankers in the world of more than 100 000 t, and 240 of these are of more than 166 000 t. There are several tankers being built of more than 300 000 t, and a tanker of a million t – a huge floating island – is a distinct possibility. These monsters are too big for the established unloading stations in rivers like the Mersey and the Humber, which are closely policed and protected against collision and pollution. The single-buoy mooring provides a method by which tankers can unload while still at sea. They tie up at anchored buoys, and pump their oil through the buoy, through pipelines on, or under, the seabed, into tanks on the seashore and then to the refinery. Shell have built sixteen such SBMs all over the world. Almost all of them are in the Far East or in Africa where there are few or no facilities for unloading oil in safely-policed river ports, and where the authorities are often notorious for their carelessness about pollution. Shell's most recently built SBM, for instance, is in Durban, South Africa, where the government's generosity to large foreign companies is legendary.

The proposal to build a single-buoy terminal – the first in Britain – off the coast of Anglesey, North Wales, was from the outset likely to meet with more opposition than Shell had met anywhere else in the world. To start with, there are excellent opportunities for off-loading oil in the Mersey. Secondly, there was the possibility of polluting one of the few areas within easy reach of industrial Lancashire and the Midlands where the beaches are not polluted. Thirdly, there was the discovery of oil in large quantities in the North Sea, on the other side of Britain, which will result in a drop in demand for oil imported from Britain's west coast.

The proposal came originally, in 1970, from the port authority on the Mersey – the Mersey Docks and Harbour Board. It was persuaded that the oil companies would need somewhere outside the Mersey to off-load their oil. A Parliamentary Bill was drawn up by the Board for building a single-buoy mooring off Anglesey and eight enormous storage tanks on the island. In the latter half of 1970, however, there was intense activity by spokesmen for Shell in an effort to obtain an even more influential sponsor. As Prufrock of the *Sunday Times* put it on 5 July 1971: 'Shell's PROs criss-crossed Anglesey meeting people, showing films, explaining, cajoling, dampening talk of pollution.'

By February 1971, the Mersey Docks and Harbour Board had dropped its sponsorship of the Bill, which was promptly taken up by Anglesey County Council. The County Council had been offered part of the proceeds of the oil terminal, which, it was accurately calculated, would result in an annual revenue to the Council of about £170 000, rising to £200 000 by 1990. The enthusiastic support which Shell has had for its project from the Anglesey County Council was not founded, then or since, on independent or exhaustive investigation. The Anglesey Planning Officer, Mr Squire Johnson, conducted an inquiry into the effects on Anglesey of the SBM. His report to the Planning Committee and the special Single-Buoy Terminal Committee was unfavourable. It concluded that, on balance, the SBM would do more harm than good to the island, and recommended against the project. Mr Johnson's recommendations were not accepted by the Planning Committee or the Single-Buoy Terminal Committee.

The concern shown by the County Council to discover the true facts about the terminal was demonstrated by council chairman, Councillor G. A. Williams, when he answered questions from a House of Commons Committee in June 1972:

Q You were told no doubt by Shell what the risks were at an SBM?
A Yes.
Q You did not consult any other independent person, an engineer, for example, about the risks of spillage at an SBM?
A No.
Q Would I be right in saying that your conclusions in relation to SBMs, and

the risk of spillage there, are based largely on what you have been told by Shell?

A They are based to a substantial extent, yes, but, if I can say, there are seafaring men on the County Council. They know people who are closely connected with the sea, and they know what it is all about, and that is how one came to this conclusion.

Q When you were told by Shell about SBMs you did not, for example, ask them about figures at SBMs in other parts of the world, did you?

A Not to the extent that the table which has been put in has done so, no.

Q Did you ask at all?

A We were told that there were no instances of sea pollution at that time.

The County Council, therefore, agreed to sponsor the Bill without consulting a single independent witness about the dangers to the island from such a development, and on the basis of an assurance from Ṣhell that there had been 'no instance of pollution' in any of Shell's SBMs anywhere in the world.

The Bill duly went before the House of Lords where it was read a second time on 9 June 1971. The main speaker for the Bill was the Earl of Lauderdale, formerly Patrick Maitland, Conservative MP for Lanark from 1951 to 1959, who said he had 100 shares in Shell Transport. Most of the Lords who spoke on the Second Reading opposed the Bill, which was sent to a Select Committee of five peers: Viscount Hood, former Deputy Under-Secretary of State at the Foreign Office, Viscount Hall, former Chairman of the Post office, Lord Moyne of the Guinness family, Lord Crawshaw, a former Conservative MP, and Lord Royle, a former Labour MP.

The Committee examined representatives of Shell and of the objectors to the Bill, a motley collection of Anglesey residents, conservationists and naturalists, for six days in June and July 1971. The first spokesman for Shell was Mr John Drummond, who was described as an 'executive' of Shell International Petroleum company. He based the case for the SBM on the 'national interest' in the supply of more oil to Shell's refinery at Stanlow. By 1973, he said, demand at Stanlow would rise to 17 million t a year, and 'this would steadily rise during the next two decades, so that by 1985 we would be on about 25 million t and by 1990 30 million t'. Mr Drummond was also adamant that there was no threat of pollution of any kind from the SBM. Asked about pollution at other Shell SBMs, he assured their Lordships:

There was no pollution incident on any occasion. In fact, there has never been a pollution incident since the buoys first went into service 10 years ago. . . I think there was a recorded spillage incident in 1970 only. . . It was a small one of 15 t at Port Dixon in Malaysia and was in fact the first spillage there had been there, although that buoy had been in operation for six years; and it was cleaned up immediately without a pollution incident.

All this was certain, because, Mr Drummond said, Shell kept a 'triple check' on oil spillages at SBMs, and regarded spillage incidents 'with great concern'.

A few hours later, the House of Lords Committee heard Captain Alexander Dickson, a director of Shell International Marine, testify that Mr Drummond's report had been wrong. There had, he said, been at least one other oil spillage at a Shell SBM, in Durban, but he could not be sure how many there had been in total. Mr Blunt, counsel for the objectors, then asked Captain Dickson:

Q Would Shell be prepared to disclose their records in relation to these single buoy moorings?
A Oh, yes indeed.

Mr Blunt then asked their Lordships to order Shell to disclose their records. 'My Lords,' he said, 'it is most unsatisfactory that no one should have the opportunity to inquire into Shell's say-so.' Mr Kenneth Jupp, QC, counsel for the promoters, then rose to cool down the atmosphere. 'My Lords,' he said, 'it is very simple. If those instructing my learned friend will speak to those instructing me, we are certainly prepared to let them see any records of spillages, and records are kept of spillages.'

The following day – 1 July 1971 – Shell did not come up with the records. Mr Jupp however was able to improve on the information of his witness the previous day: 'I have now handed to my learned friend,' he told their Lordships, 'the record of three – and there are only three – incidents of spillage which have come to light in the period 1966–70 at all these terminals in the world. There are only three incidents of spillage and two have been mentioned to the Committee already . . . '

Chairman Are you happy about this, Mr Blunt?
Mr Blunt Yes, subject to the fact that my friend has not yet said that my clients can go and see the records if they want to.
Chairman I thought he had.
Mr Jupp My Lord, yes. We will conduct them to the Shell building, and they can look at these things themselves if they are so minded.
Mr Blunt I am much obliged. Even if this cannot happen until after this inquiry before your Lordships has ended, we can go and see them then, and have the opportunity of being satisfied.

By the end of the hearing four days later, the objectors still had not seen the records, and the House of Lords Committee, still under the impression that there were 'only three' incidents of spillage at Shell SBMs, voted by three votes to two to allow the Bill to go forward. The dissenters were Lords Moyne and Crawshaw. Unfortunately for Shell, however, their counsel had given a specific pledge to the objectors that the records of spillage would be made available. All through the next four months, the lawyers for the objectors harried Shell for the records, without success. Instead of allowing access to the records, however, Shell wrote to the House of Lords Committee admitting that the information of their witnesses about oil spillages had been completely inaccurate. The House of Lords Committee was duly reconvened on 8 December 1971 to hear 'further evidence tendered by the promoters'.

Mr Jupp started the proceedings by apologizing for having given the wrong information the previous June and July. 'Inquiries,' he said, had been made and had revealed 'many more spillage incidents than the witnesses had any conception of'. This was due, he said, to the fact that their [Shell's] 'world-wide organization is very decentralized'. Mr Jupp made no mention of the fact that the two previous Shell witnesses, Mr Drummond and Mr Dickson, had both stated emphatically that the information was all at the disposal of Shell, and that spillages were very closely checked. Mr Jupp did not call Mr Drummond, who had said there was only one spillage at all Shell's SBMs, or Captain Dickson, who had said that there were only two, or even himself, who had said that there were only three. Instead he produced a chart which showed that there had been 150 spillages of oil at Shell's SBMs, some of them disastrous. At some SBMs, the spillages had got worse with time. At Kawasaki in Japan, for instance, there had been four spillages in 1969, ten in 1970 and ten in 1971. In January 1970, a massive spillage of 29·5 t took place at the SBM at Port Dickson, Malaysia, causing an oil slick 1800×150 m. The worst evidence came from the most modern SBM at Durban. In fifteen months, there had been twenty-seven spillages, in which 57 t of oil had been spilt into the sea.

No one was called to say whether or not this new information from Shell was accurate. The only Shell witness was Captain Adam Macdonald, the Marine Superintendent of Shell and BP South African refineries. The unfortunate Captain Macdonald laboured under the cross-examination of the objectors' counsel, Mr Harold Marnham QC. He admitted that the full records of spillages were not made available, despite previous promises. 'We simply have to assume,' said Mr Marnham, 'rightly or wrongly, that these tables are accurate extracts from the records that are kept ?'

A Yes.
Q You do not know if they are accurate or not, except in the case of Durban ?
A I know the company's policy is one of honesty.

It never seems to have occurred to the House of Lords Committee to insist that the records be made available so that Shell's evidence could be tested. Accepting the company's word, three of the five peers (Lords Hood, Hall and Royle) voted once again to allow the Bill to go forward. After some opposition in the House of Lords Third Reading debate, in which the Bill was carried by forty-six votes to twenty-four, the Bill went on to its next obstacle – the House of Commons. There the Bill had a formidable supporter in Mr Cledwyn Hughes, Labour MP for Anglesey, and former Secretary of State for Wales. Mr Hughes introduced the Second Reading without mentioning that Shell had misinformed the House of Lords Committee, and still refused to allow access to their records. He spoke movingly about unemployment in his constituency, and suggested that the single-buoy terminal would bring 100 jobs to Anglesey.

There was little dissent. Two Conservative MPs disliked the Bill because of the damage it would do to the environment. Two Labour MPs, Mr Gordon Oakes (Widnes) and Mr Will Edwards (Merioneth) spoke firmly in approval of Cledwyn Hughes and Shell. Mr Eric Ogden, a former miner who sits for Liverpool, West Derby, was worried about unemployment in his constituency. He said: 'I want assurance . . . that the establishment of the buoy will not mean reduction of traffic coming into the Mersey.'

Unopposed at the Second Reading, the Bill went to another Select Committee of four MPs – two Tories, Mr Frank Taylor (Moss Side) and Mr Wilf Proudfoot (Brighouse and Spenborough) and two Labour, Mr James Bennett (Glasgow, Bridgeton) and Mr R. Parry (Liverpool, Exchange). For seven days in June 1972, the four men listened closely to evidence which was much more detailed than in the House of Lords. Once again, Shell changed their witnesses, calling Mr A. J. Carter, the manager of Shell's UK Manufacturing, Planning and Economics Division, and Captain P. M. Overschie, Marine Superintendent of Shell International Petroleum, London, who confirmed that Shell would not permit the objectors to the Bill – or for that matter Members of Parliament – to look at their records of oil spillages.

During the Commons Committee sittings, the following facts were established beyond doubt:

1 The total number of permanent jobs brought to Anglesey from the SBM project could not exceed thirty-five.

2 The total net annual revenue from Shell to Anglesey could not exceed £150 000 – a sum equivalent to a 3 per cent reduction in the island's revenue from tourism.

3 The port of Liverpool and the Mersey was not at all congested – as was argued, for instance, by Captain Overschie – and was almost entirely safe from collision or spillage. A Mersey Docks and Harbour Board spokesman told the inquiry that the Board would lose about £1·3 million in revenue each year if the buoy was built. Current revenue is £3·0 million a year.

4 Shell's SBMs throughout the world were constantly liable to oil spillage, and the spillage from the Durban SBM had caused a furore in the South African Parliament. A Mr Raw, MP for Durban Point, had publicly challenged the Minister responsible: 'If he (the Minister) would like to come and swim on Durban's Addington Beach and then go home and try to scrape the oil off his feet, he would find a week later he would still be scraping the oil off his feet.'

5 Spillages of similar size at Anglesey, a number of experts told the MPs, would have a catastrophic effect on the island's beaches and on the rich and rare marine and bird life in the area.

These facts emerged in the course of relentless cross-examination by Mr David Blunt, the counsel for the objectors. The objectors, by this time, had organized themselves into a much more powerful body than the loose collection of bird-lovers and Bangor University students who had started the campaign. All the interested preservationist societies, prominently the Council for the Protection of Rural Wales, scientists, marine biologists, tourist associations, residents' associations and Welsh Nationalists had linked together into a single organization – the Anglesey Defence Action Group (ANDAG). From the outset, ANDAG was weakened by opposition to its objectives from representatives who would normally come to their aid. The County Council was against them, and so was their MP. In spite of these difficulties, however, the new organization, refurbished with money voluntarily collected from sympathizers, set about presenting a far more substantial case against the Bill than had been possible in the Lords. Above all, their research had been focused with devastating effect on Shell's central argument for the buoy: the alleged rise in demand for oil imported from Britain's west coast.

The objectors called Professor Odell, Professor of Economic Geography at the Netherland School of Economics. Professor Odell pointed out that the finds of oil in the North Sea, and the forecasts of further finds which had exceeded all expectations, had completely changed the forecasts for oil supply to Britain. Odell estimated that the demand for oil at Shell's refinery at Stanlow, Cheshire, would increase from 12·5 million t in 1972 to 25 million t in 1982. On the basis of even the minimum forecasts for oil finds in the North Sea, Odell reckoned that at least 10 million of the extra 12·5 million t needed would be piped to Stanlow across Britain from the North Sea. The other 2·5 million t could come 'quite easily and safely' from the Mersey, whose oil loading facilities were underused. Odell's evidence was dynamite, which exploded the core of Shell's argument. If demand for imported oil was not to increase, why build a mighty terminal to off-load extra oil which would not be needed ?

In their defence, Shell called Professor Colin Robinson, Economics Lecturer at the University of Surrey. He told the Committee that in his view the forecasts for North Sea gas had been overestimated, and that the forecasts for North Sea oil had 'probably' been overestimated. 'The likely pattern,' he thought, 'would be that oil imports would rise for a few years, and then, later in the 1970s, would conceivably fall.' This was some good to Shell's case, but not much. The case for the terminal rested on the supposition that demand for oil imports would rise in the late 1970s and 1980s – which Professor Robinson had denied.

Shorn of the argument about the *quantity* of imported oil needed, Shell's lawyers shifted their ground, and argued that the *quality* of the oil needed at Stanlow meant an increased demand for imported oil. Mr Blunt, for the objectors, listened carefully as Mr A. J. Carter explained this new argument, and then asked for the figures to prove it. Mr Carter did not have the figures. 'I had assumed,' said Mr Blunt, 'that Shell would have this information because this is the sort of information you need if you are making projections as to consumption and supply.'

Mr Carter Of course, but I do not have it with me.
Mr Jupp (*for the promoters*) We have certainly got it. It is wrong to say we have not got it. We cannot produce the figures out of a drawer like that.

Mr Carter was then excused from the witness stand while Shell looked out the figures. Six days later – 13 June 1972 – Mr Carter returned to the Committee with his figures. Mr Blunt studied them for some time before realizing they were not the ones he wanted. He asked Carter:

Q It [the document produced] does not enable me to see what share in the market the Stanlow Refinery has in each of these sectors of the products spectrum.
A That is true. I am afraid, Sir, you are asking questions which are very important in our commercial activities, and I am afraid that I must resist giving any information.

Mr Frank Taylor and his colleagues made no comment about this refusal on the grounds of commercial secrecy to produce the figures which were needed to substantiate Shell's claims for their mammoth project. Not one word of criticism was directed at the company by any of the MPs.

In his closing speech to the Committee, Mr Blunt said:

Sir, it is not Shell who should decide what is in the national interest; it is for Parliament to decide. If they wish Parliament or any other body to make a decision as to this, then they must prove it; they must lead evidence and tender themselves or their witnesses for cross-examination. They have not done this. It follows, if you give them their powers, you will be affording to a rich and powerful cartel a privileged position. In my submission, it is constitutionally wrong to do so, and you should accordingly reject the bill on this ground as a matter of principle.

The MPs were not impressed. Unanimously, they handed the rich and powerful cartel its 'privileged position' and the Bill came back for Third Reading with the Committee's recommendation to accept.

For the Bill to pass the House of Commons, it had to get its Third Reading by the end of the Parliamentary session – in this case on 28 October. Time was found on 18 October, and Mr Cledwyn Hughes moved the Third Reading with some lyrical passages about the Shell Oil Company. He and his supporters were hoping that there would be no real opposition, but Mr Gerald Kaufman, Labour MP for Manchester, Ardwick, had been shocked by the evidence before the Committee. He started a long and powerful speech against the SBM which lasted until the time came 'for closure'. Mr Hughes anxiously moved 'that the question be now put', but this was opposed, and Mr Hughes could not find the 100 MPs necessary to force the closure. Discussion of the Bill, therefore, was postponed, and most observers felt that the Bill had been killed. There was great pressure on Parliamentary time in those last few days of the session, and in the ordinary course of events the Third Reading of a delayed private Bill would not have been given priority. Suddenly, miraculously, the Government found the necessary time, and the debate was resumed on 24 October.

In spite of the 'neutrality' towards the Bill claimed by Mr Peter Emery, Parliamentary Under-Secretary for Trade and Industry, Gerald Kaufman is convinced that the Bill was saved by the Government's business management. Among the speakers in the resumed debate was a new champion of Shell, Mr Eric Ogden, Labour MP for Liverpool, West Derby, who had in the Second Reading debate demanded an assurance that the Liverpool docks would not lose employment and revenue as a result of the single-buoy terminal project. That assurance had not been forthcoming. Lieutenant Commander Leonard Hill, port manager of the Mersey Docks and Harbour Board, had told the House of Commons Committee that the new terminal would take work away from the Mersey to the value of £1·3 million. The Mersey stages, he told the Committee, were 'only about 50 per cent occupied at the moment.'

Mr Ogden was not worried. He told the House of Commons that he had visited South Africa during the summer recess, and that Shell had arranged for him to see their SBM at Durban. Everything there, Mr Ogden said, had been fine :

I want to put on record my appreciation of the help I have had [from Shell] as a member from Merseyside, but everyone knows that I am a sponsored member of the National Union of Mineworkers. I am not ashamed of my union knowing this, knowing that I talk to the Shell Oil Company. If the coal miners of this country are to learn more about fuel policy, we have to know what our competitors are doing.

Mr Ogden dismissed the suggestion that £1·3 million would be lost to the Mersey as a result of Shell's operations. 'The £1·3 million,' he said, 'is a balance. The figures are false. The Mersey Docks and Harbour Board does not object to the Bill, and I doubt whether it accepts those figures.' Mr Ogden forgot to notice that the Mersey Docks and Harbour Board had given those figures to the House of Commons Committee.

When the speeches were over, a small group of Labour MPs went out of the chamber to vote against the Bill. They had assumed that Mr Kaufman and the conservationist Tory MPs who had spoken against the Bill had organized a division against it. No tellers arrived, and they returned to the chamber to hear the Speaker declaring the Third Reading carried without a division. Mr Kaufman explains : 'There were so few of us against the Bill – no more than a dozen – that it seemed more derisory to have a vote than not to do so. We'd put our protest on record with our speeches, and that was what counted.' Thus Shell got their Bill through the House of Commons without a single vote being recorded against it.

Everything that has happened since the Bill passed the House of Commons has strengthened the case for the objectors to the Anglesey terminal. The oil finds in the North Sea have exceeded the wildest expectations of the original forecasters. The prognosis of Professor Odell about the possible supply from the North Sea has been proved an understatement; almost half as much oil again as the amount predicted by Odell has already been found. The decisions of the oil producing countries to raise their prices three times during the last three months of 1973 and the first three of 1974 have led to a sharp increase in the activity around North Sea oil; and the centre of gravity for the British oil companies and the industry dependent on it has shifted from the west coast to the east coast. At the same time, what little evidence has emerged about spillages from single-buoy moorings in other parts of the world indicates that spillages are continuing. The rate of spillage at the Durban oil terminal *doubled* from 1972 to 1973.

Undeterred, however, Shell has pressed ahead with the construction of the single-buoy terminal at Anglesey. After divers had inspected the sea bed, the company announced that it could not possibly carry out the pledge of its supporters in Parliament (notably Lord Lauderdale) to bury the pipeline from island to buoy underneath the sea bed. Some of the pipeline, said Shell, would rest *on* the sea bed, thus presenting further risk of damage and spillage. There was some mild criticism of this decision in the *Sunday Times*, but none in Parliament.

The single-buoy terminal, if and when it is constructed, will serve as a minor convenience for the Shell Oil Company's tanker movements. It will serve no indispensable function, since the declining volume of imported oil can easily be dealt with by existing loading facilities. The cost of construction is unlikely to be less than £60 million. The Government – that is, the taxpayer – will be contributing at least £10 million of this in various forms of grant and depreciation allowance. If spillages occur from loading the buoy, even at half the Durban rate, they will effectively destroy one of the finest, and last remaining, unspoilt stretches of coastline available to holidaymakers in the north-west. It will wipe out whole colonies of rare birds featured prominently in Shell's expensively-produced wildlife literature. Moreover, the buoy will increase the danger of collision in Liverpool Bay. And it will filch at least a quarter of the total revenue from oil in the Mersey docks. The small financial gain to Anglesey will be wiped out by a proportionate decrease in tourism in the island, and the number of jobs created will be thirty-five – at a cost to the taxpayer of about £300 000 each.

This monstrous project was subjected to the full scrutiny of modern Parliamentary democracy. It passed through a local planning inquiry – at which Shell's counsel was Sir Elwyn Jones, Attorney General in the 1966–1970 Labour Government; numerous debates in the local authority; three readings and six days of Select Committee in the House of Lords; three readings and seven days of Select Committee in the House of Commons. Before Parliament, the highest court in the land, Shell first of all gave wrong information about spillage figures, then refused to produce their spillage figures, then changed their case to forecasts about different types of oil, then refused to produce the forecasts on which the changed case was based. In the course of the proceedings, Mr C. I. Jones, who appeared before the House of Lords Committee as a representative of the Department of Trade and Industry (Petroleum Division) said : 'Our basic policy on oil supply is to leave it to private industry to devise the means and methods of supplying the customer.'

Lord Crawshaw Have you given thought to the position of how to bring it into the country or anything like that?
     A No. Again, I think that is something that is best left to private industry.

Later on, Mr Jones embellished his point: 'We leave the siting of refineries or terminals to the industry; and we leave it to them also to push it through the various procedures'.

'Pushing it through the various procedures' can be a tedious business, but at least the outcome is never in doubt.

Oil by the sea shore

The approval of plans for a Shell oil terminal at Amlwch, on the northern coast of Anglesey, shows once again that British big business, in its task of destroying the country for the sake of financial profit, has no more obsequious ally than the British Labour Party. The Wilson government (1966–1970), the Welsh Labour MPs and the Labour members (although called independents) of Anglesey local authorities, have managed to turn this once beautiful island, the Mother of Wales, into a heavy industrial region, criss-crossed by power pylons, tainted by flouride fumes and soon, almost certainly, to be lapped by petroleum spillage. The Labour politicians both at Westminster and on Anglesey have justified this industrialization on two counts: it was in the national interest and it would bring employment locally. In fact it has effected an actual rise in the unemployment rate. It has been in the interest not of the nation but of those private-enterprise corporations which seized the humbly offered gifts.

Some time in the mid-1960s, Shell decided that Amlwch (pronounced roughly *amloch*) was the finest site in Europe for a super-tanker terminal, where the oil could be piped ashore from the ships to a 'farm' of up to sixteen storage tanks, each twice the size of Conway Castle, from which it would pass through an overland pipeline to Shell's refinery on Merseyside. The sea drops to a great depth just off Amlwch, which means that tankers of 200 000 t or more would be able to off-load at a single-buoy mooring, a device which, so Shell claims, has enabled them to land oil safely all over the world, in all weather conditions. The other attraction of Amlwch for Shell was the high level of unemployment in Anglesey. This offered, in theory, a pool of available workers for the construction of the terminal; it could be and has been used as an argument against conservationists; finally it was used to win support and even the possibility of a grant from the government in Westminster.

Anglesey people have never been loth to despoil their island for money. The hills above Amlwch are scarred and blotched by spoil from the Parys mines which until 100 years ago provided much of Europe's copper ore. Even closer to Amlwch, Shell has joined in opening an Octel factory, whose fumes and ugliness prevented the town being classified as an area of outstanding natural beauty, so leaving it open to still further uglification by Shell. The nuclear power station at Wylfa provides virtually no jobs for local people but has defaced the northern half of the island with two lines of tall pylons. In 1967 Rio Tinto-Zinc and two partners obtained a 40 per cent grant from the Wilson government to erect an aluminium smelter on Holy Island, just west of Anglesey. This plan was eagerly backed by the Clerk to Anglesey County Council, most of the Labour council and by the Transport and General Workers' Union. When local residents raised fears of pollution, RTZ flew a party of local civil servants and politicians to see a smelter in West Virginia, at the same time giving assurances that fluoride emissions would not rise above an acceptable level. Since the opening of the smelter, fluoride emissions have risen to three times that level, while unemployment has risen to new record heights. According to the *Daily Telegraph* (5 June 1972):

The present unemployment rate in Anglesey is 9·1 per cent, of which probably 95 per cent or more are Welsh people. At the time of the smelter's construction from 1969 to 1971, the labour force was estimated at about 50 per cent local and 50 per cent non-Welsh. The May 1972 unemployment average was 3·8 per cent for England and Wales with the Welsh region average 5 per cent. So the Anglesey figure isn't excused on grounds of high unemployment generally. Comparable figures are 7·7 per cent for Wales as a whole in May 1969 falling to 5·6 per cent (3·8 per cent) in May 1970 and rising to 9·5 per cent (4·5 per cent) in May 1971.

The *Daily Telegraph* used this case to debunk the assumption of 'capital projects bringing employment to regions of high unemployment'.

This RTZ experience may explain why even Anglesey County Council was wary at first of Shell. The Planning Officer, who had warned of the possible dangers of the aluminium smelter, came down firmly against the oil terminal in an exhaustive and balanced report. Even the Clerk of the Anglesey County Council, Idris Davies, who had used his enormous influence in favour of RTZ, was at first luke-warm about Shell. In July 1969, according to the then Councillor William Grove-White, one of three who tabled a protest against the terminal,

Idris Davies persuaded me not to put it to a vote, to postpone it until there was more information. He assured me that he hated the idea of a terminal. And later he said publicly that Shell would have a hard sell as there were no serious employment possibilities.

The supporters of the Anglesey Marine Terminal Bill (a private Bill sponsored by the county council) sounded more resigned than enthusiastic. This was apparent at the public inquiry held in Amlwch in October and November last year [1971]. The main argument for the terminal put forward by the county council was: 'It is almost inevitable that it will go through because of national interest.' The same fatalistic argument was employed by Councillor Alun Williams, the main spokesman for the Terminal Bill both in Parliament and Anglesey. When he was asked at the inquiry: 'Why did you say it is clear that the project will come?' Mr Williams replied: 'The fact that it was already in the door before we knew anything about it.'

The inquiry was an unequal contest. The counsel for Shell was Sir Elwyn Jones MP, a former Labour Attorney General and one of the more expensive QCs in the country. The objectors to the terminal, as in most such public inquiries, were amateurs with little legal or technical knowledge. Few could afford more than a day or two off work to question the company and its defendants. Several of them were English rather than Welsh – a fact that did not go unnoticed by Shell and its public relations advocates. Yet even these unskilled objectors raised questions that were not and could not be answered by Councillor Alun Williams and other advocates of the terminal. Why, after the experience of RTZ, would Shell not give assurances on oath about oil pollution? What guarantee had the council received that Shell, or some other company, will not build a refinery next to the terminal? Above all, why had Anglesey County Council persistently refused to accept or even hear the advice of its Planning Officer?

Nevertheless, the Terminal Bill passed its Third Reading in the House of Lords in February 1972 in spite of considerable opposition. Lord Goodman said it was improper 'that all considerations should be overridden for sixty jobs', which was the number Shell then promised for Amlwch. Now they promise a mere thirty-five. Lord Moyne protested that Shell was acting as judge in its own cause, which should be studied by independent experts. After a vote of forty-six for, twenty-four opposed, the Bill went on to the Commons, where it was given an easier ride. Anglesey's own MP, Mr Cledwyn Hughes, who had once championed the RTZ smelter (and later moved house, thereby getting out of range of its stench), claimed that the terminal would reduce the risk of oil pollution, create up to ninety permanent jobs in the area, give the county council an income of up to £200 000 a year and give Britain the best facilities for receiving monster super-tankers in Europe. He was given support by Mr Goronwy Roberts (Caernarvon) and Mr Elystan Morgan (Cardigan). But it is interesting to observe that, by this stage in the argument most advocates of the terminal had forgotten the earlier argument that it was in the national interest to provide Britain with oil.

By 1972 even the dimmest Welsh Labour MPs had begun to grasp that the desperate urgency for oil had been reduced by the prodigious new finds of petroleum in the North Sea. From being merely an oil-comsuming nation, Britain was fast becoming a major producer. When Shell tankers moor off Amlwch to unload their crude oil for the Mersey refinery, other Shell tankers and foreign tankers as well will be moored off the east coast to take abroad British crude oil piped to the shore from the depths of the North Sea. For these oil 'farms' can be used both ways – either ship to shore, or shore to ship. Oddly enough, those local authorities on the east coast of Britain who had asked if there was pollution danger in this transference of oil have been told by the oil men that there is far *less* danger transferring from land to ship than vice versa. Conversely, there is more danger transferring from ship to land – as at Amlwch.

One of the strengths of Shell is the natural ignorance of the public about the oil industry's workings. Anglesey first learned of the Amlwch terminal when someone noticed a reference in a Shell house magazine. In February this year [1972] an Amlwch woman, Mrs Grace Marshall, who had been staying with her family in Australia, returned home by ship, stopping at Durban, South Africa, in March. Here Mrs. Marshall took her small daughter to North Beach only to find that this much-advertised playground of Southern Africa (whites only) was covered with lumps of jellied oil. She also learned that Durban people blamed this pollution on Shell's SBM, which had come into operation more than a year before. When Mrs Marshall got home to discover Shell's plan for a local SBM she warned all who would listen of what had happened at Durban. 'Although I am not up on the technical matters of the proposals,' Mrs Marshall told the *North Wales Chronicle*: 'I know from experience that one does not realize the value of things like beaches and historic buildings until one is deprived of them.'

Opponents of the Amlwch terminal got in touch with a Durban conservationist group, who sent a bundle of newspaper cuttings as evidence of the havoc wrought by Shell's SBM. The *Natal Mercury* had written (10 April 1972):

A major row is expected over the latest spillage at the Reunion single-buoy mooring – at least five tons of oil which burst from an under-sea hose early yesterday. The spillage – one of the most serious of about thirty since the system went into use eighteen months ago – occurred while the tanker Vestan was discharging 90 000 tons of crude oil. After discharging about 60 000 tons without incident the tanker stopped pumping to take on ballast. When pumping resumed the hose burst... The main cause of spillages has been mechnical failure although human error has also resulted in oil escaping into the sea.

The rival Durban *Daily News* had an eloquent headline a few days later: 'Oil leak saga drags on'. In Parliament at Cape Town, Durban MPs asked the government often, angrily and in vain if it can stop the pollution and force the oil companies to compensate the sufferers. For example W. V. Raw, opposing a refund of customs duty to Shell and BP, uttered this challenge:

I want to tell the hon. the Deputy Minister who wants to give Rands 41 977 back in customs duty, that if he would like to come and swim on Durban's Addington beach and then go home and try to scrape the oil off his feet, he would find that a week later he would still be scraping oil off his feet.

Another Durban member, D. E. Mitchell, grew so enraged at this point that he told the Minister of Sport and Recreation: 'Run away and play with your yo-yo, man', but cooled down later to explain that detergent could not remedy the pollution, as the Minister of Transport had suggested :

I repeat that the putting of detergents on the oil slicks does not dispose of the oil. Two kinds of chemical reactions take place in so far as that oil is concerned. In respect of the one reaction, it may well be that there is a greater danger now to the marine life in that ocean than there would be from any other source whatever. Secondly, the reaction as far as the oil is concerned which allows it, as I have said, to come ashore not as a liquid but in great big semi-liquid, semi-solid blobs which disperse through the sand and which can go down as far as eighteen inches to two feet [roughly 45–60 cm]. Therefore to talk about sweeping it up, as has been suggested in some quarters, is a lot of nonsense.

Armed with this information, the main opponents of Shell on Anglesey Council obtained a special meeting for 6 July 1972 to discuss an amendment delaying the oil terminal Bill. A rumour was started and published in the *Guardian* that Shell had offered to fly objectors to Durban to see for themselves. Shell denied this. The resolution was signed by fourteen members, or nine more than the five who had voted against the oil terminal in the past. Besides the pollution question, Anglesey opponents of the terminal pointed out that the expected revenue would be far less than predicted, that only thirty-five jobs would be created, and that since the advent of North Sea oil the import was no longer of such keen 'national interest'. Voicing these arguments on the day of the debate, the *North Wales Chronicle* deplored Anglesey County Council's 'extraordinary role of advocate for a giant international commercial concern whose profit-seeking activities could bring tragedy to a beautiful county'.

The debate on 6 July was a rum affair. The main speaker for the Bill was Councillor Alun Williams. He talked of 'national interest . . . the cardinal principle you cannot get away from these days.' He reminded the council that they had already voted overwhelmingly for the promotion of this Bill, which had passed through the Houses of Lords and Commons. 'It well behoves the Anglesey County Council,' he claimed, 'to pay due deference to the decisions of the Houses of Parliament.'* 'You will not be concerned with what goes on in South Africa,' he declared, but went on to say that Durban did not have the advantage of two Acts of Parliament. 'The municipal authority in Durban is powerless and that is what this is all about,' he said. He ended his main peroration with an emotional outburst in Welsh, which I fear I missed as the press are not provided with the translation headphones available to the English councillors.

* In fact, the Bill did not have its third reading in the Commons until October 1972, over three months later [PJS].

Although four of the five main opponents were Plaid Cymru supporters, three of them spoke in English and with commendable coolness. No such reason inspired their Labour opponents. For example, Alderman Robert Roberts declared: 'You say you want to wait until you've gone to Africa. I'm sure there's many of us here will join in a whip round to have you go to Africa on a single ticket.' Another Labour ancient, Councillor Manley Williams, said that Durban beach had always suffered from oil pollution: 'An ex-naval man told me . . . "We were bathing in Durban. It seems that there was a great spillage. We came out of the water looking almost like the inhabitants of South Africa. We were almost arrested because we were black" ' (laughter). An Irish councillor in a terrible temper yelled: 'It's vandalism and the unemployed, that's where the pollution is,' then stormed out of the chamber, although returning in time to vote for Shell. One councillor's voice succeeded in breaking as he appealed: 'I ask you on behalf of the unemployed of Anglesey. Don't let us forget them.'

When Shell first applied for the site, their defenders in Anglesey argued that they were bound to succeed. The project would come, Alun Williams had said, because it was 'already in the door before we knew anything about it'. The same people last week argued that even at this late stage any delay might stop the project, which now appeared to them as positively desirable. In contrast to the debate on RTZ, when councillors and officials were flown to the United States to see a smelter, it was not thought necessary or desirable to fly people to Durban to see the effect of an SBM. 'Any deferment kills the Bill,' declared one councillor. 'What do they want – a nice trip down to South Africa, or to kill the Bill?'

Outsiders may be puzzled by this Labour deference to big business. But Councillor Mrs Enid Morgan, the Welsh Nationalist who had led the protesters, knows her fellow councillors well. 'There are people here,' she told me, 'who would welcome a heroin factory if it gave people jobs.'

Note on further reading

There appear to be very few books dealing in detail with the issues raised by physical-resource exploitation at a local level. In addition to the studies of Oxfordshire ironstone and the Cow Green reservoir (reproduced in this book as Chapters 2 and 5), Roy Gregory's *The Price of Amenity* (Macmillan, 1971) includes case histories of the proposed power station at Holme Pierrepont (Nottingham), the fight against natural gas installations at Bacton (Norfolk) and the affair of the Abingdon (Berkshire) gasholder. This excellent, if expensive and perhaps not faultless, book apparently represents the only serious interest the academic world has taken in the grass roots politics of physical resources – a curious, though not entirely unexpected, state of affairs.

In a more 'popular' vein, though none the worse for that, Jeremy Bugler's *Polluting Britain* (Penguin, 1972) reports 'on the lack of effective control of industrial air pollution; on the industrial pollution of our rivers and estuaries; on the contamination of our coastal waters by industry and by municipal corporations; on industrial workers whose hearing is damaged by the noise in which they are forced to work; on land made derelict by companies; and on the new areas that industrialists have their eyes on'. These topics indicate a bias towards the problems of pollution rather than resources as such; but as Bugler himself points out, there is an increasing overlap between the two. What makes Bugler's book particularly important, however, is that it names names and assigns blame, which is a welcome relief from the certain-company-not-a-thousand-miles-from-here school of writing and investigation. Moreover, in this book and elsewhere Bugler has perhaps done more than anyone to expose the absurdities of the Alkali Inspectorate.

Of the hundreds of books dealing with the more general aspects of pollution and 'the environment' I will say little except to mention and recommend John Barr's *Derelict Britain* (Penguin, 1969), an early light too often unrecognized in the blaze that followed. But to return to physical resources, a book of outstanding importance is Richard West's *River of Tears* (Earth Island, 1972), an absorbing account of the ways in which the Rio Tinto-Zinc Corporation and its associated and once-associated companies exploit resources of many kinds in South Africa, South West Africa, Rhodesia, Lesotho and, of course, Britain (Bristol, Anglesey and Merioneth).

All in all, this is numerically a pretty meagre collection of books, even allowing for omissions; and yet the fact that attempts were made to prevent or delay publication of three of the four volumes listed here is in itself sufficient indication of their importance. One cannot but conclude that there would be some merit in having more people investigate the details of what happened last year and fewer speculate inconclusively and vaguely on what may or may not occur in some future century.

PJS

Acknowledgements

Permission to reproduce material in this book is acknowledged to the following sources:

Chapter 2, 'Oxfordshire ironstone', and Chapter 5, 'The Cow Green reservoir'. both by Roy Gregory, which appeared in *The Price of Amenity* published by Macmillan.

Chapter 6 part 1, 'Aluminium', by Richard West which previously appeared in *River of Tears* published by Earth Island Ltd., and part 3, 'Shell by The Sea Shore' also by Richard West which appeared as an article in the *New Statesman*. Both parts are reprinted by permission of A. D. Peters and Company.

Chapter 6 part 2, 'Oil in Parliament', by Paul Foot which previously appeared as an article in *The Sunday Times*.

Index